GORBACHEV:
MANDATE FOR PEACE

GORBACHEV:
MANDATE FOR PEACE

Mikhail S. Gorbachev

PaperJacks LTD.

TORONTO   NEW YORK

PaperJacks

GORBACHEV:
MANDATE FOR PEACE

PaperJacks LTD.

330 STEELCASE RD. E., MARKHAM, ONT. L3R 2M1
210 FIFTH AVE., NEW YORK, N.Y. 10010

Richardson & Steirman edition of *A Time for Peace* published 1985
Richardson & Steirman edition of *The Coming Century of Peace* published 1986
Richardson & Steirman edition of *Toward a Better World* published 1987

PaperJacks combined edition published December 1987

CDN. ISBN 0-7701-0839-3
US. ISBN 0-7701-0836-9
Printed in the USA

TABLE OF CONTENTS

BOOK ONE

A TIME FOR PEACE

1

MIKHAIL GORBACHEV

AT THE March 12, 1985 Plenary Meeting of the Central Committee of the Communist Party held in Moscow, Mikhail Sergeyevich Gorbachev was elected General Secretary of the Central Committee of the Communist Party of the Soviet Union. He was entrusted with the highest post in the political leadership of the country in which nearly 277,000,000 people of more than 100 nationalities live side by side.

In many respects, Mikhail Gorbachev's life is typical of an entire generation of Soviet Communists who make up the nucleus of the Party.

Mikhail Gorbachev was born on March 2, 1931 in the village of Privolnoye in the Stavropol territory, a vast region north of the Caucasus mountains. The area is famous for its grain harvest, for its sheep breeding, power-engineering specialists, chemists, scholars, and doctors. The people of the Stavropol region are an industrious and tenacious people, who for centuries have grown grain and grazed their flocks under difficult, often harsh conditions; but they later built canals, developed industries, and founded cites and health resorts on the arid steppe.

Mikhail Gorbachev's parents came from peasant stock who earned their living by the sweat of their brows. His grandfather, a hard-working and respected man, was the founder and chairman of a collective farm. His father, Sergei Andreyevich, was an agricultural machine operator who had fought at the front in the Great Patriotic War. He was a modest man, deeply respected for his skills and knowledge of economic matters, and his wisdom and even-handedness in Party affairs.

Mikhail Gorbachev's mother, Maria Panteleyevna, is industrious and well respected. She is seventy-four years old and still lives in the Stavropol region, from which she refuses to be separated.

Mikhail Gorbachev's natural gifts and inquiring mind, his self-discipline and energy, and his love of the land stood out even in childhood. At fourteen, he had already learned to handle a grain combine during the long hours of the strenuous harvest.

When he was eighteen, he was awarded one of the most esteemed Soviet awards: the Order of the Red Banner of Labor.

After finishing secondary school, where he was awarded a Silver Medal of Graduation, he enrolled in the Department of Law at Moscow State University and he received his law degree in 1955. Twelve years after graduation he attended a second institute of higher education — an agricultural institute — and became a specialist in agricultural economics. His many-sided education and continual striving for knowledge are at the root of his approaches to the solution of life's problems.

Early in his youth, Mikhail Gorbachev, the son of a communist and an active member of the Young Communist League, showed a deep-seated interest in sociopolitical matters. He was able to captivate people with his brilliance and to interest them. He was not embarrassed to learn from friends, to adopt better ideas, and to support new ones. His originality of thought and his charm attracted people to him. At twenty-one he joined the ranks of the CPSU, and by the time he was thirty, he was elected for the first time as a delegate to a Party Congress — the highest governing body of the CPSU.

After graduating from Moscow University, he returned to the Stavropol territory, where he participated actively in developing the youth movement and was elected to executive posts in the Young Communist League. From March 1962 Mikhail Gorbachev was engaged in party work. Over the years, he was promoted consistently to key party posts: First Secretary of a City Party Committee; Second Secretary of a Territorial Committee, and from April 1970, First Secretary of one of the Party's most authoritative organizations: that of the Stavropol Territory. In March 1971, at the 24th Congress, Mikhail Gorbachev was elected a member of the CPSU Central Committee.

Gorbachev gained experience in the Stavropol territory. It was a highly developed and diversified economy, and he grew there as a citizen and political leader. He had a profound grasp of the problems of agriculture and industry, science and education, health care, and social welfare. During these years, major programs were initiated in the Stavropol territory for developing mechanical engineering, the chemical industry, the construction of resorts, canal building, the expansion of irrigation. New developments in farming and animal husbandry were also introduced.

In solving complex tasks of production, Mikhail Grobachev devoted much of his attention to working people, aware of their needs and concerns, and organized and stimulated the labor process. He was always in the thick of every operation. He spent time with people in factories, shops, farms, and research laboratories. These were the places where he worked, not in his private office or in lecture halls. It was here that he developed his knowledge of people and a deeper knowledge of life.

His fields of interest are very wide. Mikhail Gorbachev is interested in literature and theater. He studies new works in political economy, philosophy, law, and art with intense concentration. He travels around the Soviet Union and visits foreign countries frequently.

In 1978 the Plenary Meeting of the Central Committee elected Gorbachev Secretary of the Central Committee. Two years later, he was elected a member of the Politburo. For the last fifteen years, voters have entrusted him with the mandate of people's deputy to the highest body of power. Since 1985 he has been a member of the Presidium of the Supreme Soviet of the USSR, a permanent body of state power.

In his work in the highest bodies of party and government, the creative side of Mikhail Gorbachev's character—as a communist, politician and organizer—revealed itself most fully. His style and method of his work are reminiscent of the style and method bequeathed to party leaders by Lenin: collective leadership, and ability to analyze a situation profoundly, to know people's views, to learn from the past, to pursue a charted course, to unite people, and to live in their interests.

Because of work, his devotion to duty, his conviction, his ability to convince others, his consistency of action and fighting spirit, his skill in grasping the essence of issues; and his rejection of meaningless routine; his democracy and humane sympathy, Mikhail Gorbachev has won the highest award in the Soviet society:

the confidence and respect of the Party and the people.

Soviet society and its economy have always been characterized by dynamism. The rate of industrial growth in the USSR in the postwar years was twice as great as that of developed capitalist countries. Since the beginning of the 1970s, however, the country experienced difficulties in economic development. Radical changes in the economic situation were not taken adequately into account. The persistence necessary to reorganize structural policies, the forms and methods of administration, and the very psychology of economic activity was not present. The Party and the people were confronted with the task of surmounting these negative tendencies in order to sharply change the state of affairs for the better.

In the April 1985 Plenary Meeting of the CPSU Central Committee, Mikhail Gorbachev delivered a report on the new tasks of the party and the people. The provisions of the report, the interest and discussion they provoked, and the decisions of the Plenary Meeting marked a turning point in the development of our country. Soviet society has entered a period of qualitative changes in its economic and social life.

In implementing the course set by the April Plenary Meeting, the Central Committee and the Soviet government have worked out large scale measures for a wide range of issues that will affect the restructuring of the national economy. The General Secretary of the Central Committee has conducted a series of business meetings with party and economic leaders, directors of enterprises, scientists and specialists. In keeping with good party tradition, he consulted with rank-and-file workers, with those who directly produce material benefits. His meetings with Muscovites and Leningraders, his trips to the Ukraine and Belorussia, the oil workers of Siberia, and the grain growers of the Virgin Lands in Kazakhstan had an enormous social impact, aiding the active implementation of the course worked out by the party.

The Central Committee sees the situation in the following way: the national economy must be brought in the shortest possible time to the most advanced scientific and technological positions, the highest world level in productivity. We must learn properly to use all the advantages and possibilities that socialism gives us, in order to obtain substantially greater results with fewer expenditures. To achieve this goal, we must free ourselves from economic methods that have exhausted their usefulness, and to succeed in breaking through to qualitative heights in science and technology, and on this basis make our country more powerful and wealthier materially and culturally. This is the main task facing Soviet society at the moment.

It has been stated justifiably that foreign policy is an extension of domestic policy. In Soviet politics this relationship is organic and indissoluble. The Soviet Union strives for broad and multi-sided cooperation with all the governments of the world, particularly socialist countries. Our principle is equal and beneficial relations, assistance in developing natural resources, and strengthening friendship among peoples.

What changes in the world would the Soviet Union consider beneficial to it? First of all—an end to the arms race—the elimination of the threat of nuclear war. Every ruble it spends on defense it would rather spend on peaceful needs, on raising the well-being of working people. Obviously, the United States and other capitalist countries can also find better uses for the money currently being spent on the manufacture of arms. It is important to take into account the problems faced by developing countries. The Soviet Union's point of departure for insisting on an end to the arm's race is the fact that it is immoral to throw away hundreds of billions of dollars on the creation of the means to annihilate human beings when hundreds of millions of people are hungry, deprived on life's essentials.

It is precisely from this standpoint that Mikhail Gorbachev's announced the suspension of all Soviet atomic explosions on August 6, 1985. The suspension will remain in effect until January 1, 1986, or beyond that date if the USA also refrains from conducting nuclear tests. The USSR has called on the USA to resume negotiations for a total ban on nuclear tests. The Soviet leader believes that the total ban on nuclear tests would stop the arms race as its most dangerous point—the development of qualitatively new weapons—and would be a serious contribution to preserving and strengthening the policy of nonproliferation of nuclear weapons.

Great attention is paid in the USSR to Soviet-American relations. The state of these relations is vitally important for mankind, and has an enormous influence on the international situation as a whole.

It is the deep-seated conviction of the General Secretary of the CPSU Central Committee that confrontation is not an inherent defect in the relations between the USSR and the USA. Instead it is an anomaly, a condition that is lacking in all logic. Differences in social systems provide absolutely no reasons for bad relations, let alone for inspiring enemity. In its dealing with all states, the USSR pursues a policy of peaceful coexistence. In this way, each of the social systems can prove which is the better by the strength of its example and not by the strength of its arms. The General Secretary emphasizes that this is the credo of the USSR.

Peace is the most important goal of the Communist Party and the Soviet State. This is demonstrated by Mikhail Gorbachev's announcement, in the name of Soviet leadership and people, that it will never originate war in the Soviet Union and the Soviet State will never start a war.

In his public appearances, Mikhail Gorbachev has repeatedly expressed his concern about burning conflicts in various parts of the world. In his view, sites of tension in Asia, Africa, and Latin America could be eliminated and peace restored if every member of the Security Council undertook the responsibility of honoring the principles of noninterference, not using of force, and noninvolvement of the countries on these continents in military blocs.

The Soviet Union's position on this issue has been formulated precisely and clearly: we are opposed to policies of threats and violence, to violations of human rights—especially such sacred ones as the right to life and work. We are opposed to having liberated and developing countries become a source that enriches monopolies, or be used for establishing military bases as springboards for aggression. We state openly and clearly: the Soviet Union is on the side of those who struggled for peace, national independence, and social justice.

Since the Great October Revolution, the first day of its birth—the land of the Soviets has advocated a world without wars and weapons, a world of social justice. The Communist Party and the

Soviet government have consistently and purposefully subordinated their policy to this ideal, and it is to this ideal that Mikhail Gorbachev has dedicated his life and his energy.

Mikhail Gorbachev's wife, Raisa Gorbacheva, is a graduate of the Department of Philosophy of Moscow State University. She is a candidate of philosophical sciences and is a senior lecturer. Their daughter, Irina, is a physician, a candidate of medical sciences. Her husband, Anatoli, is a surgeon. The Gorbachev's granddaughter, Ksenia, is six years old.

2

THE EXTRAORDINARY
PLENARY MEETING

IN THE foreign-policy sphere, our course is clear and consistent. It is the course of peace and progress.

A basic principle of our Party and state is to preserve and strengthen in every way the fraternal friendship with our closest friends and allies — the countries of the great socialist community. We will do everything in our power to expand cooperation with socialist states, to enhance the role and influence of socialism in world affairs. We would like to see a considerable improvement of relations with the People's Republic of China and believe that, given reciprocity, such improvement is quite possible.

The Soviet Union has always supported the struggle of the peoples for liberation from colonial oppression. Today our sympathy is with the countries of Asia, Africa, and Latin America, which are following the road of consolidating their independence and social rejuvenation. For us they are friends and partners in the struggle for a durable peace, for better and just relations between nations.

As to relations with capitalist states, we will firmly follow the Leninist course of peace and peaceful coexistence. The Soviet Union will always respond to goodwill with goodwill, to trust with trust. But everyone should know that we shall never relinquish the interests of our Motherland and those of our allies.

We value the successes of détente achieved in the 1970s and are ready to take part in carrying on the process of establishing peaceful, mutually beneficial cooperation between nations on the principles of equality, mutual respect, and noninterference in internal affairs. New steps along these lines would be appropriate in marking the fortieth anniversary of the great victory over Hitler's fascism and Japanese militarism.

Never before has so terrible a threat hung over mankind as now. The only reasonable way out of the existing situation is the reaching of an agreement by the opposing forces on the immediate termination of the arms race; the nuclear arms race on earth and the prevention of an arms race in space. We need an agreement on an honest and equitable basis without attempts at "outplaying" the other side and dictating terms to it. We need an agreement which would help all to advance toward the cherished goal: the complete elimination and prohibition of nuclear weapons for all time, toward the complete removal of the threat of nuclear war. This is our firm conviction.

Negotiations between the soviet Union and the United States will open in Geneva tomorrow. The approach of the Soviet Uniion to these negotiations is well known. I shall reaffirm only this: we do not strive for unilateral advantages, for military superiority over the United states, over NATO countries; we want a termination, not a continuation of the arms race and therefore propose a freeze of nuclear arsenals and an end to further deployment of missiles; we want a real and substantial reduction of the arms stockpiles — not the development of ever-new weapons systems in space or on earth.

We would like our partners in the Geneva negotiations to understand the Soviet Union's position and reciprocate. Then agreement will be possible, and the peoples of the world would heave a sigh of relief.

3

A MEETING ON DISARMAMENT

O<small>N</small> MARCH 22 Mikhail Gorba-
chev, General Secretary of the CPSU Central Committee, met in the
Kremlin with members of the Advisory Council of the Socialist
International on Disarmament.

Kalevi Sorsa, Vice-President of the Socialist International and
Chairman of the Advisory Council on Disarmament, congratulated
Mikhail Gorbachev on his election as General Secretary of the
CPSU Central Committee. Sorsa told about the activities of the
council for limitation and discontinuation of the arms race. The
parties in the Socialist International are concerned about the situation in the world, especially the incessant arms buildup. The Advisory Council of the socialist International opposes, in particular, the
militarization of outer space. The hope was expressed that the
Soviet Union and the United States would make every effort to curb
the arms race and to end it altogether. Sorsa said that the Soviet
Union and the United States would make every effort to curb the
arms race and to end it altogether. Sorsa said that the Socialist and
Social-Democratic Parties in the Socialist International would work
toward that goal. Noting that the limitation of the arms race was a
problem that affected not only the Soviet Union and the United
States, but the whole of mankind, he said that small countries and
neutral and nonaligned states also could and should contribute to the
cause.

Mikhail Gorbachev stressed that the foreign policy of the
CPSU and the Soviet state remained unchanged, as the March 1985
Plenary Meeting of the CPSU Central Committee had confirmed.
The Soviet Union would follow unswervingly a course of peace and
progress.

It was noted during the meeting that an alarming situation had
arisen in the world. The threat of nuclear war continues to grow.
The arms race, if not curbed now, could enter a qualitatively new
phase in which uncontrollable processes would begin. The situation
is complicated further by deliberate actions to undermine international trust and to step up confrontation in every sphere. Threats of

armed force and open intervention in the affairs of independent states are resorted to merely because the realities of today's world do not suit certain people.

The peace-loving public of the entire world calls for an end to the dangerous arms race and removal of the threat of war. Great hopes in this respect are pinned on the new Soviet-American talks started recently in Geneva.

It is of primary significance that the objective of the talks, as set down in the joint Soviet-American statement, will be the working out of effective accords aimed at preventing an arms race in outer space and ending the one on earth, at limiting and reducing nuclear armaments, and strengthening strategic stability. In the final analysis, the sides agreed, the talks are intended to bring about the elimination of all nuclear weapons everywhere.

Progress in the Geneva talks and their fruitfulness, Mikhail Gorbachev stressed, depend on whether both sides will abide strictly by all parts of their agreement on the subject and aims of the talks. The Soviet Union will do everything in its power to fulfill this agreement and will judge the intentions of the American side by its actions. It is essential that each side should show goodwill and readiness for reasonable compromises, and most important of all, that the principles of equality and equal security should be observed strictly.

We are resolutely against the talks being turned into a kind of cover for continued escalation of the arms race, said Mikhail Gorbachev. That is why the Soviet Union proposes a freeze on the sides' nuclear arsenals and an end to the further deployment of missiles. Among other things we are convinced that an end to the deployment of new U.S. missiles in Europe with a simultaneous end to the implementation of soviet countermeasures would help resolve substantially the entire range of issues under discussion in Geneva.

The efforts of the most diverse public and political forces of our time are directed toward preventing nuclear war. Such is the aim of the major peace initiatives put forward by the Soviet Union and other countries of the socialist community. These initiatives are in accord with the UN resolutions that reflect the views of the world community. The public and leaders of many countries have been speaking out unequivocally for a return to détente, an end to the arms race, and the development of political dialogue and cooperation between states. The antiwar movement, which has become a major sociopolitical force in many countries, advocates that goal emphatically. The awareness is spreading that in a nuclear age the security of states cannot be based on force or threat of force. Security is possible only when it is security for all. All this strengthens the conviction that, given the necessary efforts, there can be a change in the situation, and improvement in the international climate.

We know about the activities of the Advisory Council of the Socialist International on Disarmament and appreciate its efforts to promote constructive dialogue and negotiations, Mikhail Gorbachev said. The parties of the Socialist International, considering their political leverage and influence, can help improve the international situation in many ways and bring about an end to the arms race, and increase their contribution to saving mankind from nuclear catastrophe. The international situation urgently demands energetic and effective efforts by the working-class and democratic movement in the struggle against the threat of war. The CPSU, of its part, is prepared to cooperate vigorously with all peace-loving public forces, including the parties in the Socialist International. This is our firm and invariable course, and we will continue to pursue it consistently.

4

A PRAVDA
INTERVIEW
WITH
MIKHAIL GORBACHEV

*Q*UESTION: Pravda is getting many letters from readers at home and abroad on international affairs. How would you describe the present international situation?

Answer: I can understand the heightened interest of the people in international affairs. Broad masses of the people on all continents want to exert a definite influence on the future of our world.

This is not surprising. The world is full of complex problems — political, economic, and social. Two opposite social systems — socialism and capitalism — exist. This is a fact. Dozens of new states with their different histories, traditions and interests are active in the international arena. This, too, is a fact.

In building international relations in today's world, we cannot avoid taking this into account. We must not ignore the interests of other states or, what is more, try to deny them their right to choose their own path of development. In a broad sense, this is the policy of peaceful coexistence under which each of the systems will prove which is better by force of example and not by strength of arms.

Another conclusion, just as pertinent, is that it is necessary to stop the arms race. The international situation has reached the point where one has to ask: what other path lies ahead? Is it not high time for those who determine the policies of stages to stop and think so as to avoid taking decisions that might push the world towards a nuclear holocaust?

There is an acute need for international cooperation in establishing a dialogue and searching for realistic solutions that would ease tension in the world and help block the avenues of the arms race.

All countries, large and small, should take part in this goal. Understandably, a special role here belongs to the nuclear powers, and first of all, to the Soviet Union and the United States of America.

Our country has always pursued and will continue to pursue a vigorous and constructive foreign policy aimed at consolidating peace. This was confirmed at the recent Plenary Meeting of the

CPSU Central Committee at which the foreign-policy principles of the Soviet state were outlined.

Question: Much of the world depends on the state of Soviet-American relations. Do you think there are possibilities for their changing for the better.

Answer: Relations between the Soviet Union and the United States are an exceptionally important factor in international politics. But we are far from looking at the world through the prism of those relations alone. We understand what role other countries have to play in international affairs and take this into consideration when evaluating the general situation in the world.

Are there any changes for the better in Soviet-American relations at the moment? There is no simple answer to this question. There is some ground for hope, but a great deal, that gives cause for alarm.

New Soviet-American talks on nuclear and space arms have begun in Geneva. This is a positive note. We defined the subject and aims of the talks jointly with the United States and, to put it briefly, defined them as follows: not to start an arms race in space, and stop the arms race on Earth and proceed toward a radical reduction in nuclear arms, so as ultimately to do away with them altogether.

Now we have to carry out what we have agreed upon. The talks are important. I am saying this first of all because the direction for the further development of Soviet-American relations and for world development as a whole is now being decided. The choice is either an arms race in all spheres and the growing threat of war, or the strengthening of universal security and a more enduring peace for all.

There are some changes for the better in other areas of Soviet-American relations, but they are very small. On the whole, relations remain tense.

Washington relies on strength and makes no secret of it. And it is counting on gaining superiority in strength that would lead to the subordination of the rest of the world to America. For it, diplomacy and talks are subordinated literally to missiles and bombers. It is a fact that new strategic arms programs are being pushed through Congress by the same people who are conducting the talks in

Geneva on behalf of the United States.

Everybody has heard a great deal about the "Star Wars" plans announced by the United States administration. The terminology appears to be taken from science fiction, but it is used to hide a real and serious danger to our planet. I would describe as fantastic the arguments that are used to serve as a basis for the militarization of space. They talk about defense but prepare for attack. They advertise a space shield but are forging a space sword. They promise to liquidate nuclear armaments but in practice build up these armaments and improve them. They promise the world stability, but in reality are working to disrupt the military equilibrium.

Since people intuitively sense the danger of the "Star Wars" plans, the authors of these plans want to make them believe that they amount to nothing more than harmless research, which, moreover, promises technological benefits. By dangling this bait, they want to turn their allies into accomplices in this dangerous venture.

It is even asserted that by creating space weapons it is possible to do away with nuclear arms. This is a trick to deceive people. Just as the emergence of nuclear weapons did not eliminate the conventional types of arms and only brought about the accelerated race in both nuclear and conventional arms, the creation of space weapons can have only one result: the arms race will become even more intensive and will embrace new spheres.

I have singled out those aspects which especially complicate Soviet-American relations, sometimes bringing them to the verge of acute tension. But it appears that there are people in the United States who regard such a state of affairs as normal and view confrontation as almost natural.

We do not think so. Confrontation is not an innate defect in our relations; it is an anomaly. It is not inevitable that it should be maintained. We consider an improvement in Soviet-American relations not only extremely necessary, but also possible. But, of course, reciprocity is required.

Question: There is a great deal of interest in the possibility of your meeting with the President of the United States. What are the prospects for a meeting?

Answer: The question of such a meeting has been touched upon in my correspondence with President Reagan, I can say that a positive attitude to such a meeting has been expressed on both sides. The time and place of this meeting will be fixed later.

On a broader plane, our correspondence touched upon the search for joint ways of improving relations between the Soviet Union and the United States and imparting a more stable and constructive character to them. I am convinced that a serious impetus should be given to the development of Soviet-American relations at a high political level. We propose to the government of the United States that these matters should be conducted in such a way that all our peoples and other nations would see that the policies of the Soviet Union and the United States are oriented not toward hostility and confrontation, but toward a search for mutual understanding and toward peaceful development.

Question: From what you have said, it follows that work is needed in a wide range of fields. But still, what do you regard as the main lever for achieving a radical change for the better?

Answer: Intensive joint efforts. And, indeed, efforts in a wide range of fields. A mutual understanding of the need to facilitate the settlement of conflict situations in the world would have a beneficial influence on our relations and an international relations as a whole. A great deal can be done to mutual advantages through this development of bilateral ties between the Soviet-Union and the United States.

But still, what you called the main lever lies in the sphere of security. In what way exactly can we make a start here?

If one has come to the negotiating table to discuss reductions in arms, one should at least refrain from building them up. That is why we propose that the Soviet Union and the United States introduce, for the entire duration of the talks, a moratorium on the development (including research), testing, and deployment of attack space weapons and a freeze on their strategic offensive arms. At the same time, the deployment of American medium-range missiles in Europe should be terminated and, correspondingly, the buildup of our countermeasures.

American leaders are declaring that they are for radical reductions in armaments. If that is so, it would be logical first to put a brake on the arms race and then to proceed immediately to arms reductions.

We are for honest dialogue. We are prepared to demonstrate our goodwill again. And, as of today—and I would like to emphasize this—the Soviet Union is introducing a moratorium on the deployment of its medium-range missiles and suspending other countermeasures in Europe. The moratorium will last until November of this year. The decision we shall make after that will depend on whether the United States follows our example: whether it will stop the deployment of its medium-range missiles in Europe.

To sum up, the opportunities for improving Soviet-American relations, for improving the international situation, in general, do exist. These opportunities should not be missed. They should be translated into definite policies and practical measures.

5

CONVERSATION WITH REPRESENTATIVE THOMAS O'NEILL

*O*N APRIL 10, General Secretary of the CPSU Central Committee Mikhail Gorbachev received Speaker of the House of Representatives of the U.S. Congress Thomas O'Neill, who headed a delegation from the House of Representatives on a visit of the Soviet Union at the invitation of the Supreme Soviet of the Soviet Union. Mikhail Gorbachev and Thomas O'Neill held a conversation in the Kremlin attended by Chairman of the Soviet of the Union of the USSR Supreme Soviet L. N. Tolkunov and members of the U.S. House of Representatives Robert Michael, Dan Rostenkowski, and Silvio Conte, and U.S. Ambassader to the Soviet Union Arthur Hartman.

Welcoming the American congressman, Mikhail Gorbaschev expressed satisfaction that the authoritative delegation from the House of Representatives held an active political dialogue with their colleagues from the USSR Supreme Soviet, which both sides assess as positive. We know the role played by Congress in America's political life, he said, and we attach great importance to developing contacts along the parliamentary line as one of the elements of invigorating Soviet-American relations.

The times are such now that people shaping policy in the two countries should definitely converse with one another. The world situation is disquieting, even dangerous, and there is a kind of ice age in relations between the Soviet Union and the United States (at least, this was so until very recently.)

Mikhail Gorbachev emphasized that the Soviet leadership sincerely wishes that Soviet-American relations return to normalcy. We do not think that behind present tensions in these relations is some fatal clash of national interests. On the contrary, our peoples can gain much from the development of broad and fruitful cooperation, to say nothing of the fact that they are united by the dominating common interest of ensuring security and preserving the very life of our peoples. The difference in the social systems, in the ideology of our countries is no cause for curtailing relations, much less for kindling hatred.

Life shows that Soviet-American mutually beneficial cooperation is quite possible. A number of fundamental documents signed by both sides in 1972 and 1973 laid the groundwork for fruitful cooperation in various fields. This cooperation also contributed to the extension of détente in international relations as a whole, in particular to the success of the European Conference in Helsinki. In 1972 the leaders of the Soviet Union and the United States put their signatures to a document saying that peaceful coexistence between our two countries is the only sensible alternative in this nuclear age.

This implies, of course, the recognition of the right of every people to arrange its life as it sees fit, without interference in its internal affairs, without attempts to shape other countries according to one's own fashion or to impose one's will on other people.

A genuine improvement in relations between the Soviet Union and the United States, Mikhail Gorbechev stressed, requires political will by the leaders of both countries. On the Soviet side, such a will exists. If it is displayed by the American side as well, then many fundamental issues currently separating our countries will gradually begin to be solved.

Mikhail Gorbachev dwelt in detail on matters of ensuring the security of the people of both countries, of preventing nuclear war and, in particular, on the Soviet-American talks in Geneva.

The Soviet Union, he said, agreed to the new talks with the United States, guided by a sense of profound responsibility to its people, to other peoples for the cause of peace on earth. We are satisfied that the United States accepted our proposal for talks. We agreed to them in order to conduct them honestly and seriously, seeking to agree on tangible real results, on very large reductions in strategic nuclear weapons and medium-range weapons. But it is possible to attain these objectives only if the American side gives up its provocative designs of extending the arms race into outer space, where it wants to secure the possibility of making a first nuclear strike with impunity under the cover of "defensive" weapons. That is why the solution of the issues relating to ending the nuclear arms race on earth and preventing it in outer space is a single problem that must be resolved in its entirety, as agreed upon by the Soviet Union and the United States in January of this year.

It is difficult to understand how one can tally statements by the United States on the intention to reach agreement on nuclear weapons reduction with the feverish everyday actions to build up these weapons, Mikhail Gorbachev said. Claims made by the U.S. administration and propaganda that the Soviet Union enjoys a certain superiority in various types of nuclear weapons are an utter distortion of the fact. Mikhail Gorbachev cited facts and figures to show that, in reality, there is parity; a rough balance between the Soviet Union and the NATO countries in all of these weapons. That is precisely why, wishing to fulfill the hopes of peoples, to reach now the first specific results at the talks in Geneva and ensure their further success, the Soviet Union has proposed a most natural and sensible solution: in the first place, to put an end to a further buildup of the nuclear arsenals on earth, to halt preparations for the creation of weapons for deployment in outer space, and on this basis, under the conditions of mutual trust thus strengthened, immediately to begin preparing agreements to reduce the accumulated weapons stocks. To prove its sincerity and goodwill even more convincingly, the Soviet Union has declared that it is unilaterally halting further deployment of its medium-range missiles and suspending the implementation of other countermeasures in Europe until November of this year.

It might seem that, given intention to reach agreement, these proposals and actions by the Soviet Union, which have been evaluated the world over as an important and constructive goodwill gesture, would be grasped. Yet the U.S. administration has displayed absolutely incomprehensible haste, expressing a negative attitude immediately and describing our actions as "propaganda." Under these conditions, how can we not doubt the sincerity of the intention of the United States at the Geneva talks?

The Soviet Union strives sincerely for the attainment of concrete accords in Geneva and wants Soviet-American relations to return to the channel of normal mutually advantageous cooperation and mutual respect, Mikhail Gorbachev said. He asked the congressmen to convey this to the Congress and administraton of the United States.

Speaker O'Neill and the other American congressmen declared

themselves in favor of an improvement in relations between the United States and the Soviet Union and for success at the talks in Geneva. They expressed great satisfaction with the meeting, describing it as frank and useful.

6

PLENARY MEETING
OF THE
CENTRAL COMMITTEE

COMRADES, we are on the eve of the fortieth anniversary of the great victory over fascism. Remembering the huge price paid for the victory by the Soviet people and other peoples of the anti-Hitler coalition, recalling again and again the tragedy which befell mankind, the Communist Party and the Soviet Government consider the main task of their foreign policy to be the prevention of such a tragedy ever occurring again, especially the prevention of a nuclear catastrophe.

The Soviet Union and our Party have been and will forever remain faithful to the sacred memory of the immortal feat of the peoples who routed fascism.

The Soviet Union declares once again that it will pursue steadfastly the Leninist policy of peace and peaceful coexistence which is determined by our social system, morals, and world outlook. We are in favor of stable, correct and, if you like, civilized interstate relations based on a genuine respect for international law. But it must be crystal clear that international relations can be channeled toward normal cooperation only if the imperialists abandon their attempts to solve the historical argument between the two social systems by military means.

The united community of socialist states, its economic and defensive right and its unity of action in the international arena are an invincible force in the struggle for mankind's peaceful future. The attainment of military-strategic balance with the states of the aggressive NATO bloc is a historic achievement of the fraternal countries of socialism. This parity must be preserved by all means for the sake of peace, as it reliably checks the aggressive appetites of imperialism.

As before, we will spare no efforts in providing the Soviet armed forces with everything necessary for the defense of our country and its allies, to ensure that no one will take us by surprise.

Today mankind has an enormous potential for peace, as well as experience and sufficient historical and social outlook to understand where the policy of aggression can lead. This understanding is more and more firmly uniting the peace forces, stepping up the antiwar and antinuclear movements and mobilizing ever-new progressive and democratic forces for the struggle against the threat of war. It is no surprise that Washington's egotistic militarist policy provokes ever-growing criticism and resistance in many countries. Communist and workers' parties, trade unions, and other mass public organizations are making a great contribution to the common struggle for peace.

No nation wants war. In this fact lie enormous reserves and possibilities for the implementation of the policy of peace and progress. Everything must be done to prevent the forces of militerism and aggression from gaining the upper hand in international relations.

We are convinced that a world war can be averted. However, history has shown that the struggle for peace and universal security is no easy matter; it requires continuous efforts.Through the fault of imperialism, the international situation remains tense and dangerous. Mankind faces a choice: either to exacerbate tensions and confrontations or to search constructively for mutually acceptable agreements which would stop the material preparations for a nuclear conflict.

It must be stated in no uncertain terms that the responsibility for the present situation rests primarily with the ruling circles of the United States. They continue to advocate the arms race and sabotage disarmament. The world public is well aware of this posture. New types of weapons of mass destruction are being developed on their initiative. Today we are witnessing attempts to spread the arms race to outer space. Hundreds of U.S. military bases scattered around the globe are also destabilizing the world situation.

The United States claims openly that it has a "right" to interfere everywhere. It ignores and often openly tramples underfoot the interests of other countries and peoples, the traditions of international relations and current treaties and agreements, it constantly creates seats of conflict and military danger, making the situation in different areas of the world tense. Today the United States is threatening the heroic people of Nicaragua with military reprisals in an attempt to deny them their freedom and sovereignty, as was the case in Grenada. Solidarity with the forces of progress and democracy, with these countries and peoples which, in the face of the reactionary onslaught, are upholding their freedom and independence, is a matter of principle to us. In this respect our course remains as clear-cut as always.

We do not have to possess some special political insight to see how in recent years imperialism has stepped up its subversive activities and how it coordinates its actions against the socialist states. This covers all spheres: political economic, ideological, and military. Documents of the fraternal parties have stressed repeatedly that imperialism is attempting to stage acts of social revenge on the widest front possible, including the socialist community, the countries liberated from colonial oppression, the national-liberation movements, and the working people in the capitalist countries.

The economic expansion of the United States is growing in scope and intensity. The manipulation of interest rates, the plundering activities of the multinationals, the political restrictions in trade and boycotts and sanctions of all kinds are creating a climate of tension and mistrust in international economic relations, destabilizing the world economy and trade and undermining their legal base. The exploitation of recently liberated countries is growing while the process of their economic decolonization is being blocked. By concentrating the growing mass of financial and material resources of other countries in its hands, the United States directly or indirectly places them at the service of its giant military program.

Under these conditions, there is a growing interest around the world in the idea of working out and implementing measures to normalize international economic relations and ensure economic security of states.

The complexity of the international situation and the acute nature of prevailing tensions obligates us to continue to give top priority to matters of foreign policy.

The overall improvement and enrichment of cooperation, the development of comprehensive contacts with the fraternal socialist countries, the ensuring of their close cooperation in the political, economic, ideological, defense, and other fields, the concern that the national and international interests of the participants in the great community should be combined organically—all these tasks are becoming increasingly important.

The implementation of the decisions of the economic summit conference of the CMEA member countries held last June is now on the agenda for joint work by the fraternal countries. This goal is demanded persistently by both the community's common interests and the requirements of the socioeconomic development of each state, as well as by the specific features of the international situation.

The exchange of views which we had in the middle of March with the leaders of the parties and the state which are members of the Warsaw Treaty, enables us to declare confidently that we are unanimous in our conviction that while NATO exists, the Warsaw Treaty Organization must continue to play an important role in defending the positions of socialism in Europe and the world, serving as a reliable instrument in the prevention of nuclear war and the strengthening of international security.

The Soviet Union will purposefully and persistently consolidate mutual contacts and develop cooperation with other socialist countries, including the People's Republic of China. Our position on this matter is well known and remains in force.

We favor further expansion of comprehensive cooperation with the countries of Asia, Africa, and Latin America. The CPSU and the Soviet state invariably support the right of all nations to determine, according to their choice, their present socioeconomic system and to build their future without any outside interference. Trying to deny nations this sovereign right is hopeless and is doomed to failure.

We invariably advocate the development of normal, equal relations with capitalist countries. All controversial issues and conflict situations should be resolved through political means—this is our firm conviction.

The Politburo believes that the international documents of the détente period, including the Helsinki Final Act, have lost none of their importance. They exemplify the way international relations can be built if nations are guided by the principles of equality and equal security, by the realities in the world, if they do not seek any advantages, but mutually acceptable decisions and agreements. In connection with the tenth anniversary of the Conference on Security and Cooperation in Europe, it would be useful if, on behalf of the countries which signed the Final Act, the will to overcome dangerous tension and develop peaceful cooperation and constructive foundations in international life were once again to be expressed in Halsinki.

The Soviet Union is advocating fruitful and all-around economic, scientific and technological cooperation built on the principles of mutual benefit and excluding any sort of discrimination; it is prepared to continue to expand and develop trade relations, to develop new forms of economic relations based on the mutual interest of the sides in the joint mastering of research, engineering and technological innovations, the design and construction of enterprises and in the exploitation of raw material resources.

When posing the question in this manner, it is necessary to analyze the state of our foreign economic relations, to take a closer look at them while taking account of the future. There are favorable opportunities in this field despite international tensions. The approach to mutually advantageous economic relations and foreign trade must be extensive, large-scale, and projected into the future.

We are in favor of extensive, versatile, and mutually beneficial cooperation with the West European countries, with Japan, and with other capitalist countries.

It is common knowledge that we are ready to improve relations with the United States, as well, for mutual benefit and without attempts to impinge on the legitimate rights and interests of one another. There is no fatal inevitability of confrontation between the two countries. If we grasp both the favorable and the unfavorable experiences accumulated in the history of Soviet-American relations, the history—both recent and not-so-recent—then it must be said that the most reasonable thing to do is to seek for the ways that lead to the improvement of relations and to build the bridge of cooperation from both sides.

However, the first stage in the Geneva talks which has already been completed, gives us every reason to state that Washington is pursuing a policy of not reaching an agreement with the Soviet

Union. This conclusion can be seen if only from the fact that the United States refuses, in general, to discuss the nonproliferation of the arms race to outer space simultaneously with the discussion of limiting and reducing nuclear weapons. Thus it violates the agreement reached in January on the relationship between the three aspects: averting the arms race in space, the reduction of strategic nuclear arms, and the reduction of medium-range nuclear weapons in Europe.

The question arises: what is the explanation for such a position? The explanation is that certain circles in the United States still want to achieve a dominant position in the world, especially in the military field. We have often drawn the attention of the U.S. side to the fact that these ambitious plans lack any chance of success. The Soviet Union, its friends and allies and, in fact, all other states which adhere to the positions of peace and peaceful cooperation do not recognize the right of any state or group of states to attain supremacy and to impose their will on other countries and nations.

The Soviet Union has never set a similar goal for itself.

We would like to express the hope that the United States' present position will be corrected. This would provide the opportunity for achieving mutually acceptable agreements. The readiness for this exists on our side.

Evidence of this willingness is the Soviet Union's proposal for both sides to introduce, for the entire period in which the talks are held, a moratorium on the development of space weapons and a freeze on strategic nuclear arsenals. Continuing this line, the Soviet Union has declared unilaterally a moratorium on the deployment of medium-range missiles and the buildup of other countermeasures in Europe. The whole world has looked upon this decision as an important and constructive step which would facilitate the success of the talks.

Our recent moratorium is not the only step in this direction. In 1982 the Soviet Union pledged unilaterally not to be the first to use nuclear weapons. In 1983 it declared unilaterally a moratorium on being the first to place antisatellite weapons in outer space. The U.S. government did not reply to either of these initiatives with even a single gesture of goodwill. On the contrary, Washington tries to put the activities of the Soviet Union, which are aimed at reducing the danger of war and achieving accords, in a false light, to generate mistrust in them. In other words, everything is being done to avoid positive steps in reply.

People cannot but be surprised at the haste with which the U.S. Administration gives its standard and usual no in reply to our proposals. This is clear evidence of the United States' reluctance to work for reasonable results. I will say one thing: the arms race and talks on disarmament are incompatible — this is clear to anyone who does not resort to hypocrisy and does not pursue the goal of deceiving public opinion. The Soviet Union will not support such a course and those who are now embarking on political games and not serious politics should be aware of this. We would not like a repitition of the sad experience of the preceding talks.

For its part, the Soviet Union will be persistently working in Geneva for reaching practical and mutually acceptable agreements which would make it possible not only to put an end to the arms race but to achieve progress in disarmament. Today as never before we need the political will for the sake of peace on Earth, for the sake of a better tomorrow.

*   *   *

These, comrades, are our tasks and the main trends in our domestic and foreign policies. They will of course be discussed in detail at this Plenary Meeting which is to determine the nature of the pre-Congress work of the entire Party, of each of its organizations.

We must hold the Plenary Meeting in a way which would allow us to sum it up in Lenin's own words:

"We know our tasks today much more clearly, concretely and thoroughly than we did yesterday; we are not afraid of pointing openly to our mistakes in order to rectify them. We shall now devote all the Party's efforts to improving its organization, to enriching the quality and content of its work, to creating closer contact with the masses, and to working out increasingly correct and accurate working-class tactics and strategy."

The Party and the Soviet people expect from us comprehensive, well-thought-out and responsible decisions and it can be said in all confidence that they will be supported by the Communists, by all the people. This support will find its expression in their social awareness, their activity and their work.

7

FROM THE
SPEECH AT
THE PETROVSKY FACTORY

THE SOVIET PEOPLE know well the enormous efforts made by our Party and government to uphold peace, to save the Earth from a nuclear catastrophe. In his day, Lenin expressed the principled position of the socialist state clearly, saying: "We promise the workers and peasants to do all we can for peace...this we shall do.,"

Many years have passed since then. Our people have lived through hard years, through the bloodiest wars. Our state was becoming stronger and mightier with every passing year. Today we are a great world power which is ready to repel any aggressor. But today we promise workers and farmers to do more than ever before for peace. And we shall do this.

We live in tense times. You can see this. The life and death of hundreds of millions of people, the destiny of all mankind depends on whether the instigators of war will be stopped.

In present conditions, as we deal with the problems of strengthening international peace, we should, in the first place, consolidate the positions of socialist countries in the world arena, contribute to all-around cooperation between them. We are working toward this. I mean the expansion of economic cooperation and the economic integration of the member countries of the Council for Mutual Economic Assistance. Well-organized specialization and production cooperation, and vigorous interaction in developing science and technology make our whole community, and every member, stronger economically and stronger in the defense capability. They bring to naught the policy of economic pressure which is now being actively pursued by the West toward socialist countries.

The extension of the Warsaw Treaty this April—the political and defense basis of our fraternal alliance—for the next twenty years is an important event. This extension enables us to be still more active in our joint struggle for peace. On the whole, it should be pointed out, comrades, that the relations between the socialist-community countries are becoming closer and deeper, and contacts between their political leaders more fruitful. This is a great achievement. We shall spare no effort to encourage this process.

I have already had an opportunity to speak about our relations with the People's Republic of China. I think that time has shown both sides that neither China nor the Soviet Union benefit from estrangement and even less from unfriendliness and suspicion, and that good-neighborly cooperation is possible and desirable. For our part, we are going to work vigorously so that the negative period in Soviet-Chinese relations, which gave rise to many artificial problems, should be overcome fully. I am sure that eventually this will be achieved.

The current world situation is characterized by the ever-growing role in the international arena of countries which have recently freed themselves from colonial or semicolonial dependence and have embarked on the road of independent development. Much in world development will depend on the destiny of these countries and of how more developed states will build relations with them.

This question is absolutely clear for the Soviet Union. We regard the peoples who have liberated themselves from colonialism as our friends and equal partners in the struggle for peace and progress support their striving to consolidate their sovereignty fully, and defend their freedom and independence. Within the framework of equal cooperation, we are doing all we can to assist them in establishing advanced national economies of their own.

In a word, we are and will be doing everything to expand and deepen our equal and friendly cooperation with newly free countries. This expanded relationship has also been the goal of our recent meetings and talks with the leaders of such countries as India, Syria, and Nicaragua. We regard an alliance of the forces of social progress and national liberation as a guarantee of mankind's better future.

The imperialist countries are pursuing policies that are different in principle. For ages they have been exploiting labor in the colonies, plundering their natural resources, and keeping their peoples in poverty. These days, too, attempts are being made to tie those peoples to the capitalist system, using economic and military means, threats and intimidation, handouts and bribes. Many of these countries are caught in the noose of foreign debt, which is being drawn ever tighter. The newly free states are being told which policies to pursue at home. People who disagree or disobey are overthrown and assassinated. This is the common practice of the "free world" states, which are pursuing colonialist policies.

Aggressive capitalist forces are unwilling to recognize in practice the right of all states to sovereignty, independence, and the free determination of the ways of their development. These forces attempt to impose their mill on these countries and try to recarve and change the modern world in their own way at all costs. This is the major source of danger for nations at present, the biggest threat to universal peace.

The greatest problem today is that of ending the arms race, which has swept the world, and of reducing existing stockpiles. In principle, we need no nuclear or other weapons to build normal relations with the capitalist world if it renounces its aggressive plans toward the Soviet Union and other socialist countries.

We are prepared to compete with capitalism exclusively in peaceful creative activities. Therefore we are for the development of political dialogue and interaction with capitalist states, for the large-scale development of mutually beneficial trade, economic, scientific, technical and cultural relations, and are ready to develop such relations on a stable long-term basis. But these relations must be honest and genuinely mutually advantageous, without any discrimination. Attempts to use trade as a tool for interfering in our domestic affairs are futile. We do not need such trade. We can do without it.

We are ready for talks not only on ending the arms race, but on the greatest possible arms reductions, up to general and complete disarmament. As you know, our talks with the United States are currently under way in Geneva. Their goal, as the Soviet leadership sees it, is to stop the arms race on earth, and prevent it in outer space. We have agreed to hold the talks because we want such goals to be achieved in practice. But, by all appearances, this is the very thing the U.S. administration and the military-industrial complex which it serves do not want. They do not seem to be willing to achieve serious agreements. They continue implementing a huge program for the accelerated development of ever-new weapons of mass destruction in the hope to achieve superiority over the socialist countries and to dictate their own will to these states.

Not only have the Americans failed to put forward any serious proposals in Geneva for slowing down the arms race but, on the contrary, they have been taking steps to make it impossible. I refer to the so-called "Star Wars" program, to create space-based strike weapons. Claims about its "defensive" character are tales for naïve people. Their idea is to try to paralyze the strategic arms of the Soviet Union and to get a chance to carry out a nuclear strike against our country with impunity.

That is the essence of the matter which we cannot but take into account. The Soviet Union, should it be faced with a real threat from space, would find an effective way to counter it — let no one doubt that. I say it quite definitely. So far one thing is clear: the American space militarization program is a solid wall barring the way to appropriate accords in Geneva.

By its militaristic policy, the U.S. administration is making itself heavily responsible before humanity. Let me add that should it resolve to take up a more sensible stand, there would be a prospect for a mutually acceptable agreement on far-reaching, really deep cuts in nuclear-arms stockpiles by both sides. There would be a way to scrap these weapons altogether and remove the threat of nuclear war, which is what all the peoples of the earth are dreaming about.

But if our partners at the Geneva talks should stick to their stalling tactics at the meetings of the delegations, to dodging the solutions they have assembled for while speeding up their military programs — in space, on earth, and at sea — we would naturally have to reappraise the whole situation. We just cannot let the talks be used again for pulling the wool over people's eyes and covering up military preparations with the object of securing U.S. strategic superiority and world domination. I am sure our opposition to these designs will be supported by the real forces of peace all over the world, and we are supported by the Soviet people.

The Party's Central Committee notes with great satisfaction that our peace-oriented foreign policy has the full understanding and approval of the Soviet people. The main point is that not only do the Soviet people approve of it, but they are backing it up with what they do, with their work. The more effective this work is, the richer and stronger our country is, the greater will be its contribution to world peace and the progress of humanity.

8

OUTER SPACE
FOR
PEACE ALONE!

A REPLY to the Union of Concerned Scientists*

July 5, 1985

Dear Mr. Kendall,

I have received the message sent by you on behalf of the Union of Concerned Scientists calling for a ban on space weapons. I want to say that I deeply respect the opinion of prominent scientists who are more keenly aware than many others of what dangerous consequences for mankind the spreading of the arms race to outer space and the conversion of space into an arena of military rivalry could have.

The Union of Concerned Scientists has every grounds to demand that a clear and irrevocable political decision be made which would prevent militarization of outer space and leave it free for peaceful cooperation. This issue indeed requires a bold approach. The standards of yesterday, and narrow, moreover illusory, notions, of one-sided benefits and advantages are not applicable here. What is needed now as never before is a farsighted policy based on understanding of the realities and the dangers which we shall inevitably encounter tomorrow, if today those who can and must make the only correct decision evade the responsibility that rests with them.

On behalf of the Soviet leadership I want to make it quite clear that the Soviet Union will not be the first to step into space and weapons. We shall make every effort to convince other countries, and above all the United States of America, not to take such a fatal step which would inevitably increase the threat of nuclear war and spark off an uncontrolled arms raced in all areas.

Proceeding from this goal, the Soviet Union, as you evidently know, has submitted a radical proposal to the United Nations—a draft treaty on the prohibition of the use of force in space with regard to earth. If the United States joined the vast majority of states that have supported this initiative, the issue of space weapons could be closed once and for all.

At the Soviet-American talks on nuclear and space arms in Geneva, we are trying to reach agreement on a full ban on the development, testing and deployment of space-based strike systems. Such a ban would make it possible to preserve space for peaceful development, research, and scientific discoveries, and moreover, to start the process of sharply reducing and ultimately scrapping nuclear weapons.

We have also repeatedly taken unilateral steps intended to set a good example to the United States. For two years now the moratorium introduced by the Soviet Union on the placement of antisatellite weapons in outer space has been operative, and it will continue to remain in force as long as other states do likewise. Lying on the table in Washington is our proposal that both sides terminate completely all work on the development of new anti-satellite systems and that such systems as the Soviet Union and the United States already possess (including those still undergoing tests) be eliminated. The actions of the American side in the near future will show which decision the U.S. Administration will prefer.

Strategic stability and trust would clearly be strengthened if the United States agreed together with the Soviet Union to reaffirm in binding form its commitment to the provisions of the Treaty on the Limitation of Anti-Ballistic Missile Systems, a treaty of unlimited duration. The Soviet Union is not developing strike space weapons or a large-scale ABM system. Nor is it laying the foundation for such a system. It abides strictly by its obligations under the treaty as a whole and in its particular aspects, and observes unswervingly the spirit and the letter of that highly important document. We invite the American leaders to join us in this goal and to renounce plans for space militarization now in the making, plans that would inevitably lead to the negation of that document, which is the key link in the entire process of nuclear arms limitation.

The Soviet Union proceeds from the premise that the practical fulfillment of the task of preventing an arms race in space and terminating it on earth is possible, given the political will and a sincere desire by both sides to work towards this historic goal. The Soviet Union has that desire and that will.

I wish the Union of Concerned Scientists and all its members success in the noble work it is doing for the good of peace and progress.

Yours respectfully,

Mikhail Gorbachev

Note: The Union of Concerned Scientists was awarded the Nobel Peace Prize for 1985.

9

STATEMENT
ON THE
ARMS RACE
JULY 29, 1985

THE CONTINUING nuclear armaments race is fraught with an immense threat to the future of world civilization. It is leading to higher tensions in the international arena and a greater war danger, diverting enormous intellectual and material resources away from constructive purposes.

From the very beginning of the nuclear age, the Soviet Union has fought consistently and vigorously to end the accumulation of nuclear weapons, to curb military rivalry, to strengthen trust and peaceful cooperation among nations. The whole of the activity of the Soviet Union conducted on a vast scale within the United Nations framework and at multilateral and bilateral talks on the limitation and reduction of armaments is projected toward this goal. The Soviet Union is not seeking military superiority—it favors maintaining the balance of military forces at the lowest possible level.

It is our conviction that ending all tests of nuclear weapons would be a major contribution to the strengthening of strategic stability and peace on earth. It is no secret that new, ever-more perilous kinds and types of weapons of mass annihilation are developed and perfected in the course of such tests.

In the interest of creating favorable conditions for an international treaty on a complete and universal ban on nuclear weapons tests, the Soviet Union has proposed repeatedly that the nuclear states agree to a moratorium on all nuclear blasts, starting from an agreed date. Regrettably, it has not yet been possible to take this important step.

Seeking to facilitate the termination of the dangerous competition in building up nuclear arsenals, and wishing to set a good example, the Soviet Union has decided to stop unilaterally any nuclear explosions, starting from August 6 this year. We call on the government of the United States to stop its nuclear explosions, starting from this date which is observed worldwide as the day of the Hiroshima tragedy. Our moratorium shall be operative until

January 1, 1986. It will remain in effect, however, as long as the United States, on its part, refrains from conducting nuclear explosions.

Undoubtedly, a mutual moratorium by the Soviet Union and the United States on all nuclear blasts would be a good example for other states possessing nuclear weapons.

The Soviet Union expects the United States to give a positive response to this initiative and to stop its nuclear explosions.

This move would be in accordance with the aspirations and hopes of all nations.

10

REPLIES
TO QUESTIONS
PUT BY TASS*

QUESTION: How would you evaluate the reaction of the world to the new Soviet initiative: the introduction of a moratorium on nuclear explosions?

Answer: If one is to speak of the sentiments of the public at large, there would appear to be every reason to say that the new initiative of the Soviet Union, which has discontinued all nuclear explosions unilaterally and called upon the United States to follow suit, has been received with approval in the world. In many countries, including the United States, prominent statesmen, political, and public figures have been declaring support for the idea of a moratorium on nuclear-weapons tests and urging other nuclear powers to follow the Soviet Union's example. We have proposed a concrete, tangible measure. People see in it a hope for slowing down and then halting the nuclear arms race.

I know that our initiative is not to everyone's liking. Those in the West who have inked their policy with further escalation of the arms race and who derive considerable profits from it do not want an end to nuclear tests. They oppose the moratorium because they do not want the nuclear-arms production lines to come to a standstill. They cling to unattainable illusions of gaining military superiority one way or another. At the same time they are spreading falsehoods about the Soviet Union's policies, including those in connection with the moratorium on nuclear explosions that we have announced.

The moratorium was an honest and open move on our part. We introduced steps to stop the buildup and further improvement of nuclear arms. We had no intention at all of placing the U.S. leadership in a difficult position. The President of the United States was notified in advance of our move by a letter in which we suggested that the American side take the same step. We would like the U.S. leadership to respond positively to this call of ours.

---

* Published in *Pravda* on August 14, 1985.

Unfortunately, public pronouncements by officials in Washington on the moratorium issue create the impression that there they are now preoccupied mostly with finding the most adroit way of evading such a response. I shall not be mistaken if I say that the world expects a different attitude.

Question: President Reagan has said the other day that the United States could not afford a moratorium on nuclear tests because it has to complete its nuclear programs. At the same time, he asserted that the Soviet Union had completed an intensive series of nuclear explosions and could afford a respite. Is that so?

Answer: The decision to discontinue nuclear explosions unilaterally was made by the Soviet leadership after thorough study from every angle. It was not all easy to take such a step. To introduce a unilateral moratorium, we had to interrupt the test program and leave it unfinished.

In the current year before the moratorium, nearly the same number of nuclear explosions were carried out in the Soviet Union as in the United States. But if one speaks of all the nuclear tests that have been carried out to date, their number was much greater in the United States than in the Soviet Union. And the White House knows it.

But in taking the decision on a unilateral moratorium, the Soviet Union was guided not by arithmetic, but by political considerations of principle, by a desire to help end the nuclear arms race and to urge the United States and the other countries possessing nuclear weapons to take such a step. Our goal is complete and general termination of nuclear weapon tests, and not some respite between explosions.

The opinion has been voiced that the introduction of a moratorium on nuclear explosions is allegedly not in the interests of the United States. But a moratorium is an important step toward ending further perfection of lethal nuclear weapons. Besides, the longer the period without tests, the more rapid will be the process of "aging" of the stockpiled weapons. And, finally, a moratorium creates more favorable conditions for agreement on the termination of nuclear tests and for making headway toward scrapping nuclear weapons altogether.

The question arises: what does not accord with the interests of the United States, of the American people? This course does not suit only those who count on power politics, who devise plans to create ever-new types of nuclear weapons on earth and who have set themselves the aim of launching an arms race in outer space. But what has this to do with the genuine interests of strengthen peace and international security, a desire for which has been professed repeatedly by Washington?

Attempts are being made to explain the unwillingness to end nuclear tests by the assertion that the United States "lags behind" in nuclear arms. But this is merely a pretext. At one time there was talk about a "lag" in bombers, and later on it was missiles. However, every time that was a deliberate deception which was subsequently admitted in Washington. In other words, talk about a "lag" begins whenever there is a striving to achieve military superiority and when there is no real desire to settle arms-limitation issues. It is precisely on these matters that decisions should be taken by the political leadership—and not on the basis of diverse myths about the "Soviet threat," but proceeding from the actual situation and the genuine security interests of one's country and the interests of international security.

Question: How do you visualize the issue of verification in the context of the proposal to end nuclear explosions?

Answer: The scientific and technical possibilities existing in this country, the United States, and other countries give sufficient grounds for confidence that a nuclear explosion—even of a low yield—will be detected and will become known. Those who say the contrary know that it is not so.

Of course, unilateral steps to end nuclear explosions cannot resolve altogether the problem of a complete and general cessation of nuclear-weapons tests. For this problem to be solved once and for all, an international agreement is needed. Apart from the relevant commitments, it would also contain an appropriate system of verification measures—both national and international. In short, we are for verification of the ending of nuclear explosions, but we are against cessation of tests being substituted by their continuation in the presence of observers.

It will be recalled that the problem of the complete and general termination of nuclear weapon tests is by no means new. Several year ago it was examined in detail in tripartite talks between the Soviet Union, the United States, and Britain. At that time, verification was also discussed in great detail. In many respects, the sides came close to mutual understanding. But the United States broke off the talks because the limitations being worked out hindered the Pentagon's plans.

We have proposed repeatedly to the United States that the talks be resumed. And today, as well, we are calling on it to do this: to achieve complete cessation of nuclear-weapons tests. The holding of such talks and the achievement of results at them would be much easier in conditions when the Soviet Union and the United States would not be conducting nuclear tests. However, the United States does not want to return to the negotiating table. And this means that the United States does not want either an end to nuclear test or a reliable system of verification. That is the only conclusion that can be done.

It is said sometimes that the question of ending nuclear-weapons tests should be considered at the Geneva Conference on Disarmament. Very well, we are prepared to discuss it there, too. But, in Geneva, the United States and other Western countries have been sabotaging the conduct of such talks for a long time. Therefore, the point is not where to consider the cessation of nuclear-weapons tests. What is important is to consider this problem seriously and without delay, with a view, to the forthcoming Soviet-American meeting.

Question: Is it possible, nonetheless, in your opinion, to expect a positive solution to the question of nuclear tests?

Answer: I think it is. Although the present attitude of the United States to our proposal does not inspire optimism, one would not like to lose hope. The reason is this: too great a responsibility rests on the Soviet Union and the United States for them to evade the solution of major security matters.

What we suggest is a real possibility to stop the further buildup of nuclear arsenals and to tackle in earnest the task of reducing and ultimately eliminating them.

11

REVIEWING THE TREATY ON THE NON-PROLIFERATION OF NUCLEAR WEAPONS AUGUST 27, 1985

I GREET THE representatives of the states, participants to the Treaty on the Non-Proliferation of Nuclear Weapons, who have gathered in Geneva at a conference to review how that most important international agreement has worked.

The Non-Proliferation Treaty, drawn up by the collective efforts of many states, has demonstrated in practice its viability. Not a single state has acquired nuclear weapons since the treaty's conclusion. It is the broadest arms-control accord in terms of the number of parties to it An international order on nonproliferation has emerged on its oasis and become an effective instrument for peace.

Another important result of the Non-Proliferation Treaty is that it has provided favorable conditions for broad international cooperation in the use of atomic energy for peaceful purposes, which, in its turn, is so necessary for the solution of the problem of supplying energy to mankind and other major economic problems of concern to all peoples. The International Atomic Energy Agency has done a good service in the practical accomplishment of these tasks.

The Soviet Union stands resolutely for further expansion and development of such cooperation. It is important that atomic energy should really become an asset of the whole of mankind and serve only the purposes of peace and construction.

In keeping with its commitments under the treaty, the Soviet Union has been doing and will continue to do everything within its power not only to prevent the proliferation of nuclear weapons, but to halt and reverse the nuclear-arms race.

The Soviet Union has more than once taken unilateral steps, setting examples for others and thus contributing to the drafting of agreement son limiting and halting the nuclear-arms race. The Soviet Union has assumed a commitment not to be the first to use nuclear weapons. If those nuclear powers that have not yet done so had followed suit, it would have been equivalent, on the whole, to a general ban on the use of nuclear weapons.

Fresh evidence of our desire to ease the way to winding down the nuclear arms race is the proclamation by the Soviet Union of a moratorium on all nuclear explosions. It is beyond doubt that a mutual Soviet-American moratorium on nuclear explosions could provide favorable conditions for an international treaty on the complete and universal prohibition of nuclear weapons tests and contribute to a fuller implementation of the provisions of the Treaty on the Non-Proliferation of Nuclear Weapons.

The problem of curbing the nuclear arms race in the nuclear and space age is inseparable from the task of preventing the militarization of outer space. If outer space is put to the service of war, the nuclear threat will be dramatically escalated. But if outer space is kept peaceful and kept out of the sphere of military rivalry, an impulse could be given to the solution of the entire range of questions regarding the limitation and reduction of nuclear-arms arsenals. Simultaneously, broad possibilities would be opened for comprehensive international cooperation in various fields of human activity, both on earth and in outer space. It is for these reasons that at the 40th UN General Assembly the Soviet Union introduces for discussion definite proposals on international cooperation in the peaceful exploration of outer space under conditions of its nonmilitarization.

In short, we stand for energetic work in curbing the arms race in every area. Measures to prevent the spread of nuclear weapons clearly continue to play an important role.

I wish the participants in the conference success in their efforts to strengthen further the Treaty on the Non-Proliferation of Nuclear Weapons.

12

**TO
MRS. JAYNE SMITH**

AUGUST 28, 1985

Dear Mrs. Jayne Smith,

Please accept my deep condolences on the tragic death of your daughter Samantha and husband Arthur.

Everyone in the Soviet Union who knew Samantha Smith will remember forever the image of the American girl who, like millions of Soviet young men and women, dreamt about peace, and about friendship between the peoples of the United States and the Soviet Union.

Respectfully,

M. Gorbachev

13

MEETING WITH
U.S. SENATORS
SEPTEMBER 3, 1985

MIKHAIL Gorbachev, General Secretary of the CPSU Central Committee, a Member of the Presidium of the Supreme Soviet of the Soviet Union, received U.S. Senate Democratic leader Robert Byrd, President Pro Tempore of the Senate Strom Thurmond, and Senators Claiborne Pell, Sam Nunn, Dennis DeConcini, Paul Sarbanes, John Warner, and George Mitchell in the Kremlin on September 3. The senators are staying in the Soviet Union at the invitation of the Parlimentary Group of the Soviet Union.

During the meeting, Mikhail Gorbachev appraised the present state of Soviet-American relations and the international situation as a whole.

The Soviet Union, he said, stands sincerely for returning Soviet-American relations into the channel of normal, correct, and mutually advantageous cooperation, for getting a constructive dialogue going between our countries, for establishing at least a minimum of mutual trust and respect for each other's legitimate interests.

He pointed out that the main task today is to put an end to the arms race, to ensure a turn toward peaceful development and mutually advantageous cooperation. The decisive factor in Soviet-American relations is the state of affairs in the sphere of security. That is why the search for agreements on really major, central problems should be carried on in this sphere. Primarily, these are the problems concerning space and nuclear arms that are being discussed at the Geneva negotiations, as well as measures of military détente and the building up of trust in the broadest sense.

The Soviet people's intensive creative life, the far-reaching plans of our peaceful construction effort all determine the peaceable character of the Soviet Union's foreign policy.

He drew the U.S. senators' attention to the important peace initiatives that the Soviet Union has put forward recently, including the moratorium imposed by the Soviet side on nuclear explosions and the appeal to the United States to follow suit, as well as the proposal made by the Soviet Union at the United Nations on international cooperation in the peaceful exploration of outer space in conditions of its nonmilitarization. The implementation of these proposals would contribute to a radical resolution of the long-standing problems of space and nuclear armaments, strengthen mutual trust and military détente, and be a good incentive for practical advancement toward the ultimate goal: the elimination of all nuclear weapons everywhere, the strengthening of international security, and universal peace.

These initiatives have met with worldwide approval. Many people see in them real hope for ending, at last, the nuclear-arms race, for keeping outer space free from weapons. prominent scientists and public figures, among them americans, call for a response to these courageous Soviet initiatives. Such voices can also be heard in the U.S. Congress, which could certainly make a big contribution to the resolution of the problems existing between our two countries.

The Soviet Union and the United States, Mikhail Gorbachev pointed out, are the greatest military powers and will, to all appearances, remain such. Neither of the sides will resign itself to the other's gaining a lasting or decisive superiority. One cannot help drawing a conclusion from this fact: no test of strength should be held, matters should not be brought to a dangerous confrontation.

The positions of our two countries on a number of issues do not coincide, which is predetermined by the major differences between our two systems. But however deep these differences may be, they should not and cannot obstruct the main goal: our responsibility for averting the nuclear threat, for preserving peace.

Mikhail Gorbachev noted the importance of developing contacts between the USSR Supreme Soviet and the U.S. Congress, stressing that these contacts should serve the interests of peace and help normalize relations between the two countries.

Touching upon the Soviet-American summit, which the sides have agreed upon, Mikhail Gorbachev emphasized that the Soviet side was going to that meeting with sincere goodwill and with a desire to do everything possible to strengthen peace. It is necessary that the meeting should satisfy not only the peoples of our countries, but the peoples of the whole world. If the American side also displays goodwill, the meeting can produce positive results.

Senator Robert Byrd and the other U.S. senators expressed their thanks for a clear presentation of the Soviet position and noted the usefulness of the talk with Mikhail Gorbachev and the need for extending dialogue, improving the atmosphere in relations between the two countries, and developing mutually beneficial contacts in different fields. They called for the success of the forthcoming summit. At the same time, the American side repeated the arguments which, in large measure, amount to a justification of the U.S. administration's course in whipping up the arms race, even in space.

Mikhail Gorbachev emphasized, in this context, the need for a responsible and serious approach by statesmen, including parlimentarians, to the questions of vital importance for the peoples of the two countries and of the whole world.

14

ADDRESS ON FRENCH
TELEVISION
SEPTEMBER 30, 1985

On September 30, Mikhail Gorbachev received Yves Mourousi, Alain d'Anvers, and Dominique Bromberge, journalists of the French television company TF-1, on the occasion of his upcoming official visit to France.

Below is the text of Mikhail Gorbachev's address to the French television viewers and his replies to the questions the TF-1 representatives sent him.

Good evening, ladies and gentlemen,

Good evening, dear friends,

I am glad to have an opportunity to meet the French television viewers on the eve of my visit to your country. I must say that I am looking forward with much interest to this new meeting with France, her people, political leaders, and public figures.

I share the opinion of the President of the Republic that the forthcoming meeting is of a special character for many reasons. We will certainly judge it by its results, but now I will say that we are preparing for the meeting with a sense of high responsibility, and, on our part, will do our utmost for it to be fruitful.

As far as bilateral relations are concerned, we are convinced that development of Soviet-French cooperation accords with the vital interests of both peoples. The best proof of that is historical experience. When Russia and France, and the Soviet Union and France have cooperated, this served the best interests of both of them, just as of the whole of Europe and of the whole world, for that matter. And, on the contrary, alienation and enmity were detrimental to our national interests and affected the international atmosphere adversely.

One cannot strike out of history the fact that Soviet people and Frenchmen were brothers-in-arms in the struggle against fascism. We would betray the memory of the fallen in that sacred struggle if we forgot how the French pilots of the Normandie-Nesman regiment fought heroically against the fascists in Soviet skies, and how the Soviet partisans fought in the ranks of the Maquisard on French soil.

Twenty million Soviet people died in that terrible war, and they died for our and your freedom. Frenchmen, too, sacrificed their lives for your and our freedom. More than twenty thousand Soviet anitfascist fighters are buried in France. I know that their memory is revered in your country. The Soviet people are grateful to you for your feelings of respect.

But it is not only that joint victory that brings the Soviet and French peoples close together. Our cooperation in many fields – in economics and trade, literature and the arts – has deep roots down through the ages. All this is indicative of good fundamentals, good traditions, and deep roots to our relations. Development and strengthening thereof – and I say this with great confidence – serves our common interests. It is most important not only to continue, but also to deepen the dialogue, accord, and cooperation between the Soviet Union and France.

On the whole, as it seems to us, our relations are shaping up quite well. The volume of trade has grown fourfold in ten years. We are gratified by that. And I believe this also serves the best interests of France. Yet our economic relations could be more active and diversified. Such is our belief. The same goes for cooperation in science and technology, where an impressive symbol was the joint flight of Soviet and French cosmonauts. The exchanges in the field of culture and education, tourism, and public contacts are fruitful.

I hope that the forthcoming Soviet-French meeting will give a fresh impetus to the development of political, trade, economic, scientific, technical, cultural and other relations between the Soviet Union and France. But we view this meeting as a major event not only in bilateral relations. Accords and cooperation, as was recorded in the Principles of Soviet-French relations in 1971, are designed to become a "Permanent policy in their relations and a permanent factor in international life."

Another reason for the urgency of my meeting with President Mitterrand is the worsening of the international situation. There is little consolation in what is happening in the world today. At any rate, judging by deeds rather than by words, international tensions are growing. The threat of nuclear-missile catastrophe is not declining. We must face this bitter truth. Mountains of arms have been stockpiled. Yet their production and modernization are being stepped up. Europe is literally crammed with military bases and deadly weapons. Today it is an understatement to say that it is a "powder keg." It is a much more explosive concentration of the latest means for destruction of human beings. But even this proves not enough: new gigantic armament programs and most dangerous strategic concepts are drawn up feverishly and realized. Although Europe is too small and too fragile for from strength policies. As, for that matter, is the whole of our planet earth.

I am saying all this in the belief that today nobody has the right to be a passive observer of what is going on. So much distrust and suspicion have accumulated in the world that it will, perhaps, take quite a lot of effort and time to dismantle the barriers. But without that, without an appropriate – what I would call a psychological – change of attitude, and, certainly, without political will it shall be difficult to change the situation for the better, if possible at all. The destiny of every nation, of every person, whether an ordinary citizen or a political leader, is being decided in foreign policy now.

To survive and ensure a future for our children and grandchildren, we must curb the forces of madness, the forces of war and militarism. The flames of war should be doused before they flare up.

Can it be done? We believe that this is possible. We already have positive experience on which to base ourselves – the success of détente. And that success has preserved its vital force. Consistent observance of all provisions of the Helsinki Final Act can again improve the climate in Europe and clear away the clouds which have gathered over the continent.

Once Voltaire dreamt of the triumph of reason as an indispensable condition for normal human life. This call by the great son of France is particularly topical today when the crossbow and sword have been replaced with nuclear weapons. We will have time enough to find out whose ideology, whose views and laws are more moral and 2whose economy is more rational. History will have enough time for a peaceful competition of ways of life to ensure for people an opportunity to make a voluntary choice, on their own, to determine which social system is more to their linking. Yes, we are different, but nothing can be done about that; such is the will of history.

As far as the Soviet Union is concerned, it is doing and will further do everything in its power to live in peace with the nations belonging to other systems. Moreover, this is precisely the principle which underlies our approach to the solution of international problems. We are guided by that also in our domestic policy.

Now I will speak briefly about our domestic affairs. About 277 million people live in the Soviet Union today. Experience of history has convinced us that the peoples of Russia made the right choice in 1917 by accomplishing the Revolution, by destroying exploitation, social and national oppression. The Soviet people are proud of their country's achievements, and, in particular, of the fact that for more than fifty years now there has been no unemployment in the country, and the right to work is enshrined in the Constitution and secured by a system of corresponding social and economic measures. There is no deficit in our national budget.

Our people, just like any other, want to live better and are gratified that in the past two decades real per-capita incomes have doubled, and that staple foodstuff prices have not increased. More than two million apartments are built in the Soviet Union every year. Housing is provided free of charge, and the rent accounts for an average 3 percent of a family's budget. The health of people and their spiritual development will remain our major concern. Mind you, we have succeeded in achieving a good deal in this field. There are more than 6 million engineers, 1.5 million scientific workers, and more than a million physicians in our country. A system of free public education and health care has been established and is functioning.

The Soviet Union integrates more than a hundred peoples and nationalities. The assertion of the principle of equality of peoples in all spheres of society's life was one of the principal gains of the Revolution. Of today's 15 Union Republics and 38 autonomous administrative units, many were backward outlying regions at the time the Revolution was accomplished. Nowadays they not only enjoy equal economic and political rights, but also have created powerful economies of their own and made great strides in science, culture, and education.

Soviet people see not only their achievements and successes but their weaknesses and shortcomings. You possibly know that all issues are discussed in our society widely, openly, democratically. We consider it important to focus attention precisely on unsolved problems and are striving to accelerate the economic and social development of our country and to improve people's lives. We are sensitive to negligence and irresponsibility. And, of course, we devote prime attention to seeing to it that the norms of social justice, the democratic rights of citizens and Soviet laws are strictly observed.

All these efforts are approved of by our people – moreover, the people demand of us, their leaders, that we pursue precisely such a line. I know this from the many thousands of letters I get from people and from personal meetings and contacts with hundreds and hundreds of Soviet people.

To put it in a nutshell, we know the existing problems well. Some questions have been or are being solved while others require time, resources, and persistant efforts. We have now fundamentally taken up the questions of scientific and technological progress and of improving economic management and management methods. We have the possibilities to solve the new tasks. There are highly qualified cadres, natural resources, and a science-based production potential.

The main point is that our political course is supported widely by all sections of the population. We intend to bring further measures to improve the state of affairs up for discussion by the whole people.

Generally, we shall come to our Party's forthcoming 27th Congress with a definite program of action to perfect Soviet society and with plans for the coming five years and for the period to the end of the century. We will peer with our mind's eye into the third millennium. The prospects that are opening up are vast. Suffice it to say that the amount of work to be done in industry alone in the forthcoming fifteen years is equal to that which we have done over the almost seven decades of Soviet power.

I am saying that not only to acquaint French TV audiences with our everyday work and cares. It seems important to me that in France and other countries, people should have a clear idea of our system of priorities. If the main thing of us, the Soviet people, is to develop the economy, social relations, and democracy, this also determines our interests in the international arena and our foreign-policy interests—above all, the interest in peace—and in a stable international situation which would make it possible to concentrate attention and resources on peaceful creative work.

We are determined opponents of the arms race on earth and of transferring that race to outer space. It is essential to stop this dangerous process and to set about tackling disarmament without delay.

I want to emphasize that we are not only making statements, but are also acting precisely in that direction. We have renounced first use of nuclear weapons unilaterally, have introduced a moratorium on all nuclear explosions, and suspended the deployment on medium-range missiles in Europe. We have told the whole world that we shall not be the first to march into outer space with weapons. Our country is ready for other radical solutions as well.

And what does all this mean? Just try, without bias, to think what is being done and said in reply to our initiatives. New nuclear explosions have been carried out, an antisatellite weapon has been tested, and a feverish drumming-up of distrust for our initiatives is under way. It is impossible to get rid of the impression that some people have been frightened by the very possibility of accords in Geneva, and by the prospect that production of weapons will perhaps have to be curtailed and military appetites moderated. But we shall see what we shall see. Our patience will suffice us. But I want to be frank: al this is very far from a search for ways to improve the international situation.

As you see, quite a number of issues have accumulated in the world—issues disquieting and urgent. I intend to discuss them with the President of France most seriously. I trust that our dialogue will be fruitful. I am convinced that the Soviet Union and France have a real possibility to make a tangible contribution to the cause of mutual understanding and cooperation among peoples. It is with this hope that I am going to France.

On behalf of the Soviet people, I wish all the TV viewers, all men and women of France, and all French families happiness, prosperity, and peace.

The best of wishes to you all.

D'Anvers: Please accept our thanks for receiving us, Mr. Gorbachev. We are glad to meet you here regardless of the views you profess. You are a man of the modern age, a man of your time.

Gorbachev: I hope our meeting will come off in the spirit of mutual understanding and of that traditional friendship which is characteristic of relations between our countries.

Question: You know that not everything will be easy during your visit to France. you are awaited in Paris both with interest and with, I could say, a certain wariness. They want to see what kind of man Mr. Gorbechev is. Also, questions of Soviet-French relations will be discussed regarding both defense policy and human rights. What do you think on this score? Will you now have to revise some positions?

Answer: Why am I going to France on my first foreign visit to the West? I have already tried briefly to answer this question in my address to the viewers.

We are aware, of course, that there are likely to be people in France who, perhaps, even frown at the way our relations are shaping up—and those relations are becoming dynamic, making progress and gaining momentum. What I have in mind is both political dialogue and the broadening of economic ties and traditional cultural contacts. We proceed from the assumption that this meets the vital interests of the Soviet people and the vital interests of the French people. This is the decisive thing; the rest are details. Perhaps there are those in France who criticize us. I think that, perhaps, those critics would even like to detract from these good tendencies in the development of Soviet-French relations. But it is not to them that we are looking. I repeat, we are going to France because we think that this meets the vital interests of our countries, the goals of improving the international situation as a whoole, and hence the interests of other peoples. Today, more than ever before, we need an active political dialogue to remove the overlayers of past years. We are different, true, and have different political systems and different views of human values, but we also have much in common. First of all, I think, what we have in common is a desire to live in a real world and to find ways to work together and cooperate in different fields—all the more so since all of us are worried today by the escalation in the threat of nuclear conflict, by the arms race.

We have a need—a real necessity—for such exchanges and for discussing various questions. And I think that France is a very important partner for the Soviet Union in this sense. It is proceeding from these considerations and this understanding that we are going to France.

Question: Mr. General Secretary, Soviet-French relations undoubtedly saw a period of cooling—I mean the years 1983 and 1984. Was this an interim, now a thing of the past, or will something of it survive?

Answer: Let us look ahead and fill our relations, our political dialogue, our economic and trade cooperation, and our cultural exchanges with new content, broaden our cooperation, find and identify common interests and possibilities for joint or parallel actions in the interests of France and the Soviet Union, in the interests of the other nations.

You know, way back in 1922, Vladimir I. Lenin said words which I have written down and decided to quote to you today. Perhaps I should have done so when I answered your first question, why we are going to France.

Question: Mr. General Secretary, Soviet-French relations undoubtedly saw a period of cooling—I mean the years 1983 and 1984. Was this an interim, now a thing of the past, or will something of it survive?

Answer: Let us look ahead and fill our relations, our political dialogue, our economic and trade cooperation, and our cultural exchanges with new content, broaden our cooperation, find and identify common interests and possibilities for joint or parallel actions in the interests of France and the Soviet Union, in the interests of the other nations.

You know, way back in 1922, Vladimir I. Lenin said words which I have written down and decided to quote to you today. Perhaps I should have done so when I answered your first question, why we are going to France. Lenin said in 1922: "Any rapprochement with France is extremely desirable for us...." I think that the meaning of these words of Lenin and of the idea carried by them effectively holds just as true today.

Question: Regardless of what government France will have?

Answer: You know, every nation decides for itself what government to have, and, respecting the sovereignty—the sovereign right of every nation—we must reckon with it in our foreign policy. We have much trust and respect for the friendly people of France and will seek to maintain and develop relations with the incumbent government and with any government which may come into office tomorrow.

There are periods in relations between states when something darkens. In our case, when we discuss Soviet-French relations, I would concentrate more on what brings our peoples closer together. I think that this is the capital which enables us to build confidently on today's relations, look ahead confidently and invigorate our relations. This, I think, will promote both the interests of our countries and the cause of peace. Let us look forward.

Question: You met with Mr. Marchais recently. Is it not paradoxical that at a time when the French Communists have withdrawn from the government and when they are criticizing the French government, you are paying your first visit to Mr. Mitterand in France.?

Answer: I do not think it is. What is taking place in France is the business of the French, their internal affair. I know that those political forces which are governing the country today—I mean the Socialist Party and those who are allied with it—and also those who are in opposition, stand, to some extent or other, for the development of Soviet-French relations on the basis of traditions, on the basis of experience accumulated over the years. I think that it is a responsible position. Our approach is the same.

Question: It seems you have excellent relations with all the Social-Democratic governments in Europe, don't you?

Answer: We have been cooperating energetically with Social-Democratic parties during the past few years on matters which today are worrying the peoples of the world—I mean questions of war and peace. You must have noted that meetings with delegations of Socialist and Social-Democratic parties have accounted for a sizable share of my meetings and talks during the past few months.

We think that our ideological differences are no obstacle to cooperation in tackling such urgent issues as those of war and peace, and we, for our part, say so openly. We have good relations and maintain useful contacts with the Social-Democrats in West Germany, Sweden, and Finland, and with the Socialist parties of Japan and Austria. Generally speaking, we are open for cooperation with all the forces which have an interest in reversing the dangerous tendencies in the world situation and an interest in leading the world onto the road of cooperation, interaction, and mutual understanding.

Question: You seem to have been showing special interest in Europe lately. Is this a true impression?

Answer: The Soviet leadership has always kept sight of our relations with Western European countries in pursuing its foreign policy — I would even say, has kept them in the focus of attention.

This is understandable. You and we live in this Europe. I think that Western European countries have no less interest in developing relations with the Soviet Union and that the Soviet Union is no less prominent in their foreign policies than they are in Soviet foreign policy. We have some traditions. We have history from which we draw some lessons, from which we are learning. The Europeans will not be found wanting in wisdom. Whatever aspect of the development of human civilization we take, the contribution made by the Europeans is immense. We live in the same house, though some use one entrance and others another. We need to cooperate and develop communications within that house. I think it natural that the Soviet Union attaches much importance to this cooperation.

Question: A Gaullist approach?

Answer: I will not debate with you now over who should be credited with precedent. The question of interaction, cooperation, and establishment of relations with Western European countries has always played a substantial role in Soviet foreign policy. It was so long before de Gaulle, that major political figure, emerged.

Question: Yet reaction to the actions of western countries may vary. Indeed, when some officials of Soviet institutions were accused of spying and asked to leave France, no special reaction came from the Soviet Union. but when the British recently charged a group of Soviet officials with spying, the reaction of the Soviet aide was strong and energetic. One has gotten the impression that the Soviet aide acts according to the principle "an eye for an eye, a tooth for a tooth." Do you divide the Europeans into good and bad?

Answer: I think you will reserve for the Soviet Union the sovereign right to make decisions on every case as it sees fit. In so doing, we take account of both the interests of the Soviet Union and the overall situation.

Question: What do you think of the European project known as "Eureka"?

Answer: I want to go to Paris and to learn in detail about "Eureka." Perhaps, later we will continue an exchange of opinions on this question.

Question: Speaking a priori, do you prefer the "Eureka" project to the "Star Wars" plans of the Strategic Defense Initiative?

Answer: A priori, we prefer nonmilitarization of space to its militarization. This is the main thing. If the "Eureka" project is pursuing peaceful goals – and this is just what we want to clarify in our conversations with the President and other French officials – we will think over our attitude to that project.

Question: You have written a letter to President Reagan. Have you put forward any new proposals?

Answer: Yes, we have.

Question: Could you tell us anything about these new proposals?

Answer: I think the Americans have already spoken about the main issues. They always call upon us to do everything in a confidential form, but their patience lasts them only as long as a meeting lasts. As soon as contact is over, the world learns within ten minutes what has taken place at that "confidential meeting." At the least, the world gets the basics. That is why you must already have an idea on this matter. But I think that we will yet have discussions in France on this subject.

Question: What all this amounts to is a 40 percent reduction in nuclear arms arsenals, does it not?

Answer: I'd put off answering this question. These problems are now being presented in Geneva, and I would not like to answer your question before our delegation to the Geneva talks has presented our proposals in their entirety.

Question: Do you think that your forthcoming meeting with President Reagan in Geneva in a few weeks can become something more than just a getting-to-know-you?

Answer: It would be too great a luxury for the leaders of such countries as the Soviet Union and the United States of America in today's tense situation with the peoples of the world expecting definite, constructive steps primarily from the great powers, to go to Geneva just to exchange a handshake, to look at each other and to smile pleasantly in front of TV cameras. We invite our partners—I mean the President of the United States of America and his colleagues—to make thorough preparations for our meeting in Geneva—to lay as soon as possible during those preparations and at the meeting itself, solid bricks in the edifice of future peace. We must build peace—but a different peace and different relations—proceeding from realities. We have our interests, France has hers, and the United States of America has its interests. But who can say that the other nations of the world have no interests? And all those interests are coming across each other on the world scene. To think that only one country or group of countries can act on that scene means to have a wrong idea of today's world. I think that much is caused by this lack of comprehension. Realities must be reckoned with: they are a serious matter.

Question: Mr. General Secretary, lately you have been showing some signs of pessimism. You said in your address to the French people that the threat of nuclear catastrophe is not abating. You also said in one of your interviews earlier that perhaps it would be too late, and that the world situation was growing explosive. Talking in this way, you had in mind mostly the SDI. But the SDI as yet is a thing of the future. Why, then, do you think that the threat to peace now is graver than it was?

Answer: This is the most crucial question which must be answered precisely now.

When we say that we have reached a point beyond which events may get out of hand, it is not a sign of pessimism, it is a manifestation of the responsibility of the Soviet state and its leadership for the destinies of peace. There are those who stand to lose if the peoples grasp the situation as it is. but we have now reached a pont as a result of scientific and technological progress when the arms race can spill over into space. We have reached a point when weapons of new types—not even nuclear, but no less awesome and efficient, if we may talk about efficiency in such a case—can be developed.

Frankly, right now it is difficult enough to begin talks. You must have noticed that a sort of militarization of political consciousness is taking place. And what happens if the militarization of space begins tomorrow and if space-strike weapons are developed? What should the logical answer of the other side to such actions be? By no means a beginning to disarmament in strategic weapons and other nuclear systems. We should face realities squarely and see how the situation is shaping up. These are very serious matters, and they must not be camouflaged with demagoguery. If you'll excuse my saying so. As a matter of fact, the destinies of the peoples—the destinies of peace—are at stake. They may emerge processes which will altogether block possibilities for seeking a peaceful settlement to problems. Ways must be looked for to counter that challenge.

If anyone introduces weapons to space, such constraints as the ABM treaty, the accord on the limitation of strategic weapons, and others will go overboard. That is why we have really approached a very critical point in the development of the international situation. It is not a pessimistic position, but a realistic appraisal of a real situation. And it prompts a need to look for solutions to lead the development of international relations onto a different road, onto the path of peaceful cooperation; to stop the arms race; to begin reductions in nuclear armaments; and eventually to eliminate them. And I must say that the matter hinges not only on the position of the Soviet Union and the United States of America—other countries also bear responsibility. Today one cannot sit it out on the sidelines: one must take a stand. The times demand that every responsible government or politician destined, so to speak, to lead one state or another should today take a clear stand on these issues.

Question: You have been General Secretary of the CPSU Central committee for several months now. some people view you as a leader for the next quarter-century. What would you like to change in the Soviet Union right now?

Answer: I can hardly add anything to what I have already said and what is known in France. We view the situation in the country as follows. On the one hand, we have traveled a great road and made immense economic, social, and political progress. In a historically short period, we have managed to carry out major plans and introduce radical changes in a vast country, once backward in terms of economy and education, and populated by many peoples. But we can no longer be satisfied with this progress. Perhaps this attitude is logical if we bear in mind that as man develops, his needs — material, cultural, and intellectual — keep growing. Our society must change to meet these needs to an ever-growing dynamism in the economy, in the social and the cultural and intellectual spheres. This is the main goal toward which we are working now.

Question: You are seen by many as a man of change. Why, then, are there no changes in the Soviet Union on a matter which, we believe, is damaging the reputation of the Soviet Union abroad: namely, human rights.

The names of Sakharov and Scharansky are mentioned in France, and a campaign is being conducted so that Soviet Jews could leave the country if they wish. why not take all this into account?

Answer: I could put it as follows: let us in the Soviet Union manage our affairs ourselves and you in France manage yours. But I will nevertheless answer your question. The issue of human rights is no problem to us, and we are ready to debate it anywhere, in any audience, and with any representatives. We have plenty to say on this issue which is now being played up artificially by Western propaganda and exploited to poison relations between nations and states.

As regards economic and social rights, we could demonstrate the state in which they are in the most developed Western countries, including France, and the situation in our country. Relevant facts are common knowledge. As for political rights, I could say that our Supreme Soviet has more worker and peasant deputies than all the parliaments of the developed capitalist countries put together. It would be interesting to stage an experiment, at least for half a year or for a year, and send workers to the parliaments of your countries. We would then see what happens. But workers, as a rule, are kept away—yet, in our country, they are in key positions everywhere, from rural Soviets to the Supreme Soviet.

Of course, we have people which by some logic or another have fallen out with the Soviet form of government, with socialism, and profess some different ideology. Problems in such cases arise when one individual or another comes into conflict with the law. That was what happened to the Scharansky mentioned by you. He breached our laws and was sentenced by a court for that.

You mentioned the "Jewish question." I would be glad to hear of Jews enjoying anywhere such political and other rights as they have in our country. The Jewish population, which accounts for 0.69 percent of the entire population of the country, are represented in its political and cultural life on a scale of at least 10 to 20 percent. Many of them are people well known countrywide.

When it is a question of reunification of families, we agree to this and settle such questions. There are exceptions when individuals in point know state secrets. But does not France have legislation protecting the interests of the state? It does. I know so. We will continue to resolve these questions without fuss, through a humanitarian approach.

Question: And a last question, just in passing: Is it true that there are four million political prisoners in the Soviet Union?

Answer: Absurd! It calls to mind, you know, Goebbels's propaganda. I am amazed that you, Mr. Mourousi, an educated and up-to-date man, could ask such a question. I repeat: it is absurd.

Question: Mr. Gorvachev, you seem to be practicing a new method of communication, a new method of leadership. Is there a "Gorbachev style"? If so, how would you define that style?

Answer: I think there is no "Gerbachev style." I have already said so. As to our methods of work—particularly the style of my work—it is not something which appeared yesterday or a month, two, or three ago. I have been working like this all my life. And many of my comrades have been working precisely the same way.

The style we are cultivating in our party we define as a Leninist style of work. It is characterized by such things as extensive communication with the working people, publicizing our work, and analysis of the real processes which underlie policy making. It is everything which Lenin taught our party. I am an enthusiastic champion of precisely such an approach. The example set by Lenin is the best possible example. We are following the road of Lenin and using his style.

Question: A new generation of Soviet leaders have risen to power with you, Mr. Gorbachev. For instance, at the end of last week, we heard that the Soviet Head of Government had been replaced. What can this new generation of Soviet leaders give your country in addition to style?

Answer: I think what is taking place is a normal process. There is nothing out-of-the-ordinary in it. Every generation makes its contribution to progress, to molding political, cultural, and intellectual values. I think that the present generation of leaders in the Soviet Union will make their contribution. This will concern primarily large-scale work to upgrade Socialism. We know what is to be done to bring out to a fuller extent the best aspects inherent in that social system. And it is man with his needs who is the centerpiece of all our aspirations.

Every effort will be taken to make our economic system, our political system, the system of socialist democracy more dynamic. Our attention—the most rapt attention possible—will be devoted particularly to bringing out the importance of the human factor in full measure.

Question: You come to Paris the day after tomorrow. If you have an evening off, what would you prefer? Going to the Picasso Museum, seeing Shakespeare's *Julius Caesar,* a concert, an opera? In short, what is your preference?

Answer: Since I know the program and since it does not give me an evening off—let alone a day off—I have no such problem.

But generally speaking, when you visit another country, it is always interesting to learn about its past, too. But I must say that I have no less interest—or even more interest—in the present-day life of every society, every country, every people, their problems, traditions and interests. Perhaps this is natural for a politician.

Question: Mr. General Secretary, probably we would have a

thousand other questions, but we must conclude our interview. We want to thank you again for granting this exclusive interview to French television.

Answer: I was happy to meet with representatives of French television. I think our conversation with you makes it possible to say that we can meet, that we can discuss all matters calmly.

We are interested in further development of relations with the friendly people of France. This is a matter that requires reciprocity. We must move toward each other. It is from such a viewpoint that we regard our forthcoming visit, too. This is a good opportunity for upgrading our relations and showing their prospects for the future.

15

ADDRESS
TO THE
FRENCH PARLIAMENT
OCTOBER 3, 1985

PARIS. Mikhail Gorbachev, General Secretary of the CPSU Central Committee, member of the Presidium of the Supreme Soviet of the USSR, met today with MPS, members of the Foreign Affairs Committees, and Franco-Soviet Friendship Groups of the National Assembly and the Senate at Lassay Palace.

E. A. Shevardnadze, Member of the Politburo of the CPSU Central Committee and Minister of Foreign Affairs of the USSR; I. V. Arkhipov, First Vice-Chairman of the USSR Council of Ministers; N. D. Komarov, First Deputy Minister of Foreign Trade of the USSR, Y. P. Velikhov, Vice-President of the USSR Academy of Sciences; members of the Foreign Affairs Commissions of the Chambers of the USSR Supreme Soviet A. M. Alexandrov, V. V. Zagladin and L. M. Zamyatin; Deputy Minister of Foreign Affairs of the USSR A. G. Kovalev; and USSR Abmassador to France Y. M. Vorontsov were present at the meeting on the Soviet side.

Mikhaili Gorbachev was greeted warmly by Louis Mermaz, the President of the National Assembly of France, and Alain Poher, the President of the French Senate.

In his speech, Louis Mermaz pointed out the long-standing traditions of friendship and cooperation between the two countries. Cooperation between France and the Soviet Union has been and remains an example which must inspire countries with different socioeconomic systems, he said. Our people fought side-by-side during the years of World War II. This strengthened our friendship. In the 1960s Franco-Soviet relations to a great extent promoted the commencement of the spirit of Helsinki. Our cooperation has been and can be of great mutual benefit in the future and contribute to the progress of the peoples of France and the Soviet Union, and of the whole of mankind.

We sincerely believe in the Soviet Union's striving for peace. It is with great interest that we are studying your proposals on a moratorium on nuclear tests and on the United states and the Soviet Union reducing by 50 percent their nuclear arms capable of reaching each other's territory, because we have always held that the two great nuclear powers should set the example in this field.

The contacts maintained by Members of Parliament of the two countries over many years have facilitated the strengthening of Franco-Soviet relations, Louis Marmaz pointed out. Good relations between France and the Soviet Union will facilitate, to a certain extent, the favorable development of events in Europe and beyond. The French Members of Parliament are prepared to continue the direct and constructive dialogue.

Then the Members of Parliament were addressed by Mikhail Gorbachev.

Esteemed Presidents,

Esteemed Deputies and Senators,

Ladies and Gentlemen,

I am gratified by the opportunity to address the French parliament, to meet with you—the elected representatives of the French people. I would like to avail myself of this opportunity to thank the President of the Republic for his kind invitation to visit your country.

Today is the second day of our delegation's visit. Important meetings have been held and an exchange of views has been started on topical questions of bilateral relations and international affairs. Of course, as yet it is early to sum up the results of the talks with President Mitterrand and other French statesmen. But it is obvious already that both sides are showing desire to impart a new impulse to the development of relations between our countries and, considering the existing realities, to bring closer our positions on international problems.

In talking with the President of the Republic and addressing you today, I strive naturally for the essence, the main direction of the Soviet state's foreign policy to be understood better and more fully in France. Like the foreign policy of any state, it is determined first of all by internal requirements.

Permit me to dwell briefly on this question. I believe you know what a long and, in many respects, difficult road has been traversed by my country in the years of Soviet government. From Czarist Russia we inherited extreme economic backwardness. Within a very short period of time, if the yardstick of history is applied, the Soviet Union has turned into a mighty – in all respects modern – power with a high level of popular culture. We put an end to unemployment and ensured for the population such social boons as free provision of housing, medical services, and education. I will name a few figures illustrating our country's economic development. In the years since the war alone, our national income has grown more than 16 times over and industrial output 24 times over. In the same period, the real income of Soviet people has sextupled.

Pride in our success does not make us complacent. We see that at the present stage society's increased maturity sets before us much more far-ranging tasks which, in many ways, are new ones by their content. We are fully aware also of the shortcomings that exist in our work, of the existing difficulties and problems, quite often sufficiently serious ones. The main task that we set ourselves today can be expressed in a brief formula: to accelerate society's social and economic development.

This goal requires that many things be raised to a higher level – the scientific and technical base of the national economy, the methods of management and people themselves, their awareness, skills, and qualifications. In short, we have set off on a road to achieving a new qualitative state in society.

Our main task is to make the economy more efficient and dynamic, to make the lives of people spiritually richer, more full-blooded and meaningful, to develop the system of socialist self-government by the people.

It is not difficult to understand that not only reliable peace, but a calm, normal international situation are paramount conditions for attaining these ends. And it is these priorities that determine our foreign policy; a policy in which, naturally, we strive to take account in full measure of the interests and requirements of other peoples, all the realities of the present epoch.

Our world, a multifaceted and contradictory world, is rapidly approaching the end of the century and the millennium. It has more than its fair share of complex problems of political, economic and social nature. The coexistence on our planet of two social systems, each of which is living and developing according to its own laws, has long become a reality.

But we must see the other reality as well. And that reality is that the interconnection and interdependence of countries and continents is becoming increasingly closer. This is an inevitable condition of the development of the world economy, of scientific and technological progress, the acceleration of the exchange of information and the movement of people and things — on the earth and even in space. In short, the entire development of human civilization is becoming more interconnected.

Alas, it is not always that the gains of civilization are a boon for people. All too often and too vigorously, the achievements of science and technology are also being used for the creation of means of annihilating human beings, for the development and stockpiling of ever-more-terrible types of weapons.

In these conditions, Hamlet's famous question — "To be or not to be" — is being set already not before a single individual, but before mankind. It develops into a global problem. There can be only one answer: mankind, civilization must survive at all costs. But our survival can be ensured only if we learn to live together, to get along on the small planet by mastering the difficult art of showing consideration for each other's interests. This we call the policy of peaceful coexistence.

We are strong enough to give crushing rebuff to any attempt to encroach on our people's security and peaceful work. Yet we hold that it is not by force of arms, but only and exclusively by force of example that one must prove the corrections of one's ideology, the advantages of the system that each people has chosen of its own will. Such is our firm conviction.

I spoke yesterday to the President about our perception of the main axis of contradictions, the struggle of the two tendencies in a world politics. We regard as extremely dangerous the view, no matter how it is being justified, that the tasks facing the international community can be solved by the creation and stockpiling of ever-new and more destructive types of arms: on earth and in space. We also regard as dangerous actions that preserve and aggravate international tension. The latter is incandescent as it is — so incandescent that now it has become extremely difficult to reach agreement not only in complex, urgent matters but even on relatively simple problems. If we do not stop the present tendencies, tomorrow we will not be able to overcome their monstrous inertia. It will become even more difficult tot alk.

That is why we consider it so important right now, immediately, before it is too late, to stop the "infernal train" of arms race, to start reduction of arms, improve the international situation, and develop peaceful cooperation among peoples. This is a mutual interests: this is everybody's task. Nobody can permit himself to sit it out on the sidelines.

The Soviet Union, as you probably know, has not only been issuing calls, but also acts in this direction.

We have suspended further deployment of medium-range missiles in Europe unilaterally and have called on the United States to respond in kind. We have stopped all nuclear explosions and called on the United States to respond in kind. Quite naturally, we address this call to the other nuclear powers as well.

The Soviet Union proposes a start to a reduction in the armed forces and armaments of both sides in Central Europe, and to start with a reduction of Soviet and American troops. Moreover, we are prepared to reduce more troops than the Americans.

As for space, we are for its use exclusively for peaceful purposes and call persistently for the reaching of agreement on this issue because a transfer of the arms race into space will make reduction of nuclear arsenals objectively impossible. As you know, we have submitted to the United Nations a proposal on international cooperation in the peaceful exploration of outer space.

And now I would like to inform you of the new steps taken by the Soviet Union. They pursue the same aim: to stop the baleful process of the arms race and ward off the war danger hanging over mankind.

First: A few days ago, we proposed to the government of the United States of America to come to terms on total prohibition of space strike arms for both sides and to reduce really radically—by 50 percent—the nuclear arms capable of reaching each other's territory.

In other words, we propose a practical solution to the very

same tasks that were agreed upon by both sides early this year as being the aims of the Geneva talks: not only to stop the arms race, but to lower the level of armaments drastically and at the same time avert an arms race in space.

There is hardly any need to say how all this would strengthen strategic stability and mutual trust.

I can inform you that our delegation in Geneva has been instructed to present concrete proposals on this question and has been authorized to give the participants exhaustive explanations.

I am saying all this because a multitude of versions and false rumors are already circulating in the West concerning our proposal, and it is time for some clarification.

Second. concerning medium-range nuclear weapons in Europe. With the aim of making easier agreement on their speediest mutual reduction (as we are often told, in Western Europe, too, there is great interest in this), we consider it possible to conclude a corresponding agreement separately, outside of direct connection with the problem of space and strategic arms. This road, as it appears to us, may turn out to be practical.

In this context, I consider it important to explain our position on such an issue as the place of the nuclear potential of France and Britain in the European balance of forces. This potential is growing rapidly, and we can no longer ignore it. It was said from the French side that the nuclear forces of France are not subject to discussion without her participation. This stands to reason. It follows from this that it is time to start between us direct dialogue on this theme and try to find an acceptable way out through joint effort. Of course, the Soviet Union is prepared for such a direct dialogue with France, just as with Britain.

I want to stress at this point that we will consider the security interests of France in the most attentive manner. And today, as it appears to us, the question of a reduction in her armaments is not on the agenda.

Third. You know that we have announced a moratorium on deployment of medium-range missiles in Europe. The number of SS-20 missiles that the Soviet Union has standing ready in the European Zone is now 243. This means that it accords precisely with the level of June 1984, when the additional deployment of our missiles was started in response to the deployment of American medium-range missiles in Europe. The SS-20 missiles that were deployed additionally in the process have been withdrawn from stand-ready and the stationary installations that housed these missiles will be dismantled within the next two months. This is verifiable. As to our reply measures in respect of the territory of the United States itself, they continue to remain in force.

I would also like to explain the meaning which we give to the term "European Zone." This is the zone in which medium-range missiles capable of striking targets on the territory of Western Europe are deployed.

It should be noted that we have already totally phased out the old and very powerful SS-5 missiles and are continuing to phase out SS-4 missiles. This means that, on the whole, the number of medium-range carrier missiles in the European Zone of the Soviet Union is now much smaller than ten or even fifteen years ago. In accepting this self-limitation, we proceed from the broad interests of European security. I think that Europe is now entitled to expect a move in response by the United States—the termination by it of further deployment of its medium-range missiles on the continent of Europe.

You see what serious steps the Soviet Union is taking. In combination with our previous actions, our latest proposals, as it seems to us, are a package of constructive and realistic measures which would bring about a genuine breakthrough in the development of international relations. A breakthrough in favor of peace, security, and cooperation among nations.

This, if you please, is our program for improving the explosive international situation that threatens peace. We expect that in response to our proposals, the West, too, will traverse its part of the road.

I should like to stress that the realization of the program proposed by us would also signify substantial advance toward an aim that is so desired by all the nations and is so important to them: prohibition and total liquidation of nuclear arms and total delivery of mankind from the threat of nuclear war.

There can be no victors in a nuclear war. It seems that all responsible politicians are in agreement on this point. It is high time to draw a practical conclusion from this: to stop the nuclear arms race. And we believe that this demand will be supported by all honest, realistically thinking political forces, public figures, all people who cherish their homeland, their lives, the lives of their children and grandchildren.

The task of totally prohibiting chemical weapons and liquidating their stockpiles is becoming ever more urgent. At the Conference on disarmament in Geneva, the Soviet Union is participating actively in the drafting of a relevant convention. We are meeting our partners in the talks halfway on a number of substantial aspects, including verification. I am sure that it is quite possible to reach agreement on reliable verification.

Incidentally, the following thought also prompts itself. If we reached agreement on the nonproliferation of nuclear arms, why not apply the same method to chemical weapons? This task would be in the general channel of efforts to achieve a total ban on them. The Soviet Union would be prepared to take part in the drafting of an international accord on nonproliferation of chemical weapons. We are also prepared to do everything in our power for the creation of a zone in the center of Europe free from chemical weapons.

As I speak here, in Paris, in the heart, it can be said, of Western Europe, I cannot but speak about some substantial problems of European security, about how we in the Soviet Union view them.

I will start with the most general question. What, after all, is security in Europe? It is the absence of war and the threat of war. The interdependence, the intertwining of the destinies of peoples, despite the difference of the social roads chosen by them, is felt in Europe with special force. Because of geographical density and oversaturation with armaments, Europe, like no other continent, is vulnerable to armed conflict—the more so, nuclear weapons.

This means that Europe's security cannot be ensured by military means, by military force. This is an absolutely new situation and means a departure from traditions, from a mentality and manner of action that took centuries—even milleniia to form. Human thought does not adjust to something new right away. This applies to all of us. We feel this. We have started a rethinking and adjusting in full conformity with the new realities in many customary problems, including the military and political spheres. We would also want such a rethinking to take place in Western Europe and beyond.

So far, fear of unacceptable retribution is one of the obstacles to war, to the use of military force. Everybody understands, though, that lasting peace cannot be built on fear alone. But the entire question is: where to search for the alternative to fear, or, to use military language, deterrence?

We see what attempts are now being made to find a way out — by using new arms in the so-called "Star Wars." This is an illusion, and an extremely dangerous one at that. It is naïve, in general, to search for a solution to the problem of security in the perfection of shield and sword. Security in Europe, just as international security as a whole, can be achieved only on the road of peaceful coexistence, relaxation of tension, disarmament, strengthening of trust, and development of international cooperation.

This is a long and difficult road, the more so that it requires the overcoming of mutual suspicions, mistrust, and prejudices accumulated over decades. But there is no other road if we want to live. And, like any long road, it begins with the first steps, which often are the most difficult to make. We understand this and want to help ensure solution of the task — for ourselves and for you. It is this desire that motivates the proposals that I have already mentioned.

This desire for peace applies also to the conference in Stockholm, which is discussing the important problem of mutual trust in military matters. As it appears to us, the contours of future accords are beginning gradually to take shape there. They include making more definite and imparting maximum effectiveness to the principle of not using force. They comprise a definite set of confidence-building measures in the military field — what we might call safety fuses to prevent an erroneous interpretation of the actions of the other side in conditions of aggravation of the military confrontation. A number of states — first of all, neutral — propose agreement on mutual exchanges of annual plans for military activity, subject to notification. We are prepared for such an accord in the hope that it will help overcome suspicion and impede covert preparations for war.

The ideas of setting up nuclear-free zones in various parts of the world, including our continent—in the north of Europe and in the Balkans—are spreading ever wider. We support these ideas and are ready to take part in the appropriate guarantees where they are required. We view as useful the idea of creating a corridor free of nuclear arms along both sides of the line dividing the two military-political groupings. We also hold that nations that do not possess nuclear arms and do not have them on their territory have full right to reliable guarantees of their security based on international law, guarantees that nuclear arms will not be used against them.

Many aspects of European cooperation are recorded in the Helsinki Final Act. We hold that it is a serious achievement and retains its importance fully. When the tenth anniversary of the Helsinki Accords was marked, all the participants in the All-European Process declared for its continuation. The Soviet Union is prepared to take the most vigorous part in this continuation.

Every European country has contributed a share of its national experience to the Helsinki process. This is a common asset of the peoples of Europe, and it should be protected and multiplied by joint effort.

The political climate in Europe depends in no small measure on the development of economic ties between West and East. Here, too, an innovative approach is needed. The reaching of the targets for industrial, technical, and scientific progress that face each country today could be made much easier by effective international division of labor. We in the Soviet Union are ready for this cooperation, and for search for new forms of coproduction and cooperation. It goes without saying that this implies principles of mutual advantage, equality, and a serious approach.

The establishment of more businesslike relations between the CMEA and the EEC also appears to us useful. The countries of the Council for Mutual Economic Assistance have displayed in this respect a constructive initiative which appears to have been met favorably. It is important for it to produce concrete results. Here, as has already been stated, in the measure in which the EEC countries act as a "political unit," we are prepared to find a common tongue with them on definite international problems as well. This arrangement could be made in various forms, including parliamentary ties, among them with those who represent the European Parliament.

Without all European countries uniting efforts, it will not be possible really to solve either such an acute problem as preserving and improving the environment on our continent. In many of its areas, figuratively speaking, the land is beginning to burn under our feet, the rain falling from the sky is acid, if not fiery, while the sky itself cannot be seen because of smoke. European rivers and seas are becoming pitifully polluted. At one time, it seems, we all did not act with sufficient farsightedness and generated such problems that now simply defy solution within national frameworks. Here truly there is a field in which we all must become aware of our continent's common destiny.

Much can be done in the broad sphere that is called "humanitarian." The preservation by common effort of the cultural values of the past, cultural exchanges that mutually enrich one of the cradles of mankind's spiritual values—Europe—does this not deserve the closest attention? It is with interest that we are preparing for such an extraordinary event as the "cultural forum" opening in a few days in Budapest. In this sphere, too, lies expansion of information about each other's lifestyle, and cultivation of feelings of mutual sympathy and respect. The mutual study of each other's languages is of much importance from this point of view. Extensive exchanges of school pupils, students, and teachers is a promising area. It is very important for the young generations to have correct perceptions of each other because it is they who will build a peaceful Europe. The pooling of efforts in the struggle against disease—old and new—is a task of immense importance.

The Soviet Union attaches the most serious importance to human-rights guarantees. All that is needed is to free this issue from hyprocrisy and speculation, from attempts at interference in the internal affairs of other countries. Such problems as the position of migrant workers, mixed marriages, and reunification of families stand rather acute in Europe today. We are for approaching such problems in a positive and humane spirit with full respect for the sovereign rights of all nations.

Ladies and Gentlemen,

I believe that in the present situation it is especially important not to emulate medieval fanatics and not to spread ideological differences to international relations. Stability in these relations, less susceptibility of them to political situations will likewise consolidate stability in Europe as a whole.

We do not think, for instance, that there is a taboo forever on contacts in some form between the Warsaw Treaty and the North Atlantic Alliance as organizations, not to speak of overcoming Europe's division into opposing groupings in the more or less foreseeable future. As is known, this is exactly what we and our allies are proposing. But, as we see it, even in conditions of existence of two blocs, it is possible to create such a modus vivendi as would blunt the acuteness of the present confrontation.

And, of course, it is important today—as never before—to develop more intensive political dialogue between East and West, to use all the already-established forms of such dialogue—regular meetings at various levels, including, of course, the highest, political consultations, broad contacts between the scientific and cultural communities.

We regard the development of parliamentary ties as a very important matter as well. I would like to emphasize this point especially as I am speaking within these walls. This includes, naturally, the development of parliamentary ties with France. The Deputies of the National Assembly and Senate of France can be assured that they are welcome guests in Moscow. I state this on behalf of the Supreme Soviet of the Soviet Union.

Such, in the most general outline, are our views on how really it is possible to achieve—and within a comparatively short period of time, at that—an improvement in the situation on our continent and to increase Europe's role in overcoming the present stretch of confrontation.

I will add yet another moment. The need for more active interaction to eliminate the seats of conflict and tension existing in various areas has never been greater than now. The fact that the Soviet Union and France, despite their belonging to opposing military-political groupings, have much in common in the approach to a number of presently existing regional problems and situations, is one of the examples of opportunities for such interaction. For instance, the situation in the Middle East, Central America, South Africa, and so on. Our contacts with the French leaders confirm this.

In proposing an expansion of good-neighborliness and cooperation with Western europe, we have no intention at all of belittling the importance of a possible contribution to this goal by Canada, which belongs to NATO, and at the same time has signed the Helsinki Act. Neither does our European policy have an anti-American bias.

Since one hears much speculation on this theme, permit me to look at it in greater detail. The very way the question is posed — that by improving relations with Western Europe we want to drive a wedge, to set it a loggerheads with the United States — is absurd. First, we want to have good relations not only with Western Europe, but with the United States; Just as, for that matter, also, with China, Japan and other countries. We are not pursuing a Metternich-like policy of "balance of power," of setting one state against another, knocking together blocs and counterblocs, creating "axes" and "triangles," but a policy of global détente, of strengthening world security and developing universal international cooperation. Second, we are realists and we understand how strong are the time — historical, political, and economic — linking Western Europe and the United States.

Esteemed deputies,

The best minds of mankind have warned about the danger of our consciousness lagging behind rapid change in social being. This is especially topical today. Man is beginning to explore the galaxy. But how much remains undone on earth?

Not a single nation, not a single state is capable of solving the existing problems alone. And the old baggage of disunity, confrontation, and mistrust impedes unification.

I know that far from everyone in this hall accepts our world outlook, our ideology. As a realist, I am not trying to convert anyone to our creed. Any philosophy is approached by individuals and peoples themselves, achieving it only through much suffering, only on accepting it with their minds and hearts. But despite all differences in political and philosophical views, in ideals and values, we must remember one thing: we all are keepers of the fire of life handed over to us by earlier generations.

Each had its own mission, and each, in its own way, enriched world civilization. The giants of the Renaissance and the great French Revolution, the heroes of the October Revolution in Russia, of victory and the Resistance—they all have fulfilled their duty to history.

And what about our generation? It has made great discoveries, but has also found recipes for self-destruction of the human race. On the threshold of the third millennium, we must burn the black book of nuclear alchemy. May the twenty-first century become the first century of life without fear of universal death.

We will fulfill this mission if we unite our efforts. The Soviet Union is prepared to make its contribution to ensuring a peaceful, free and flourishing future for Europe and all the other continents. We will not stint our efforts for this.

BOOK TWO

THE COMING
CENTURY OF PEACE

16

ADDRESS
TO THE PEOPLE
OF THE UNITED STATES

Esteemed citizens of the
United States of America,

I see a good augury in the way we are beginning the New Year, which has been declared the year of peace. We are starting it with an exchange of direct messages—President Reagan's to the Soviet people and mine to you.

This, I believe, is a hopeful sign of change which, though small, is nonetheless a change for the better in our relations. The few minutes that I will be speaking to you strike me as a meaningful symbol of our mutual willingness to go on moving toward each other, which is what your President and I began doing at Geneva. For a discussion along those lines we had the mandate of our peoples. They want the constructive Soviet-American dialogue to continue uninterrupted and to yield tangible results.

As I face you today, I want to say that Soviet people are dedicated to peace—that supreme value equal to the gift of life. We cherish the idea of peace, having suffered for it. Together with the pain of unhealing wounds and the agony of irretrievable losses, it has become part and parcel of our flesh and blood. In our country there is not a single family or a single home that has not kept alive the memory of their kith and kin who perished in the flames of war—the war in which the Soviet and American peoples were allies and fought side by side.

I say this because our common quest for peace has its roots in the past, and that means we have an historic record of cooperation which can today inspire our joint efforts for the sake of the future.

The many letters I have received from you and my conversations with your fellow countrymen—senators, congressmen, scientists, businessmen and statesmen—have convinced me that in the United States, too, people realize that our two nations should never be at war, that a collision between them would be the greatest of tragedies.

It is a reality of today's world that it is senseless to seek greater security for oneself through new types of weapons. At present, every new step in the arms race increases the danger and the risk for both sides, and for all humankind.

It is the forceful and compelling demand of life itself that we should follow the path of cutting back nuclear arsenals and keeping outer space peaceful. This is what we are negotiating about at Geneva, and we would very much like those talks to be successful this year.

In our efforts for peace we should be guided by an awareness of the fact that today history has willed our two nations to bear an enormous responsibility to the peoples of our two countries and, indeed, the peoples of all countries, for preserving life on Earth. Our duty to all humankind is to offer it a safe prospect of peace, a prospect of entering the Third Millennium without fear. Let us commit ourselves to doing away with the threat hanging over humanity. Let us not shift that task onto our children's shoulders.

We can hardly succeed in attaining that goal unless we begin saving up, bit by bit, the most precious capital there is— trust among nations and peoples. And it is absolutely essential to start mending the existing deficit of trust in Soviet-American relations.

I believe that one of the main results of my meeting with President Reagan is that, as leaders and as human beings, we were able to take the first steps toward overcoming mistrust and to activate the factor of confidence. The gap dividing us is still wide, to bridge it will not be easy, but we saw in Geneva that it can be done. Bridging that gap would be a great feat—a feat our people are ready to perform for the sake of world peace.

I am reminded of the title of a remarkable work of American literature, the novel *The Winter of Our Discontent*. In that phrase let me just substitute "hope" for "discontent." And may not only this winter but every season of this year and of the years to come be full of hope for a better future, a hope that, together, we can turn into reality. I can assure you that we shall spare no effort in working for that.

For the Soviet people, the year 1986 marks the beginning of

a new stage in carrying out our constructive plans. Those are peaceful plans; we have made them known to the whole world.

I wish you a happy New Year. To every American family I wish good health, peace and happiness.

January 1, 1986

17

NUCLEAR DISARMAMENT BY THE YEAR 2000

THE NEW YEAR 1986 has started to elapse. It will be an important year, one can say a turning point in the history of the Soviet state, the year of the Twenty-seventh Congress of the CPSU. The Congress will chart the guidelines for the political, social, economic and spiritual development of Soviet society in the period up to the next millennium. It will adopt a program for accelerating our peaceful construction.

All efforts of the CPSU are directed toward ensuring a further improvement in the life of the Soviet people.

A turn for the better is also needed in the international arena. This is the expectation and the demand of the peoples of the Soviet Union and of peoples throughout the world.

Being aware of this, at the start of the new year the Politburo of the CPSU Central Committee and the Soviet Government have adopted a decision on a number of major foreign policy actions of a fundamental nature. They are designed to promote to a maximum degree an improvement in the international situation. They are prompted by the need to overcome the negative, confrontational trends that have been growing in recent years and to clear the ways toward curbing the nuclear arms race on Earth and preventing it in outer space, toward an overall reduction of the risk of war and trust building as an integral part of relations among states.

I.

Our most important action is a concrete program aimed at the complete elimination of nuclear weapons throughout the world and covering a precisely defined period of time.

The Soviet Union is proposing a step-by-step and consistent

process of ridding the Earth of nuclear weapons, to be implemented and completed within the next fifteen years, before the end of the century.

The twentieth century has given humanity the gift of the energy of the atom. However, this great achievement of the human mind can turn into an instrument of the self-annihilation of the human race.

Is it possible to solve this contradiction? We are convinced it is. Finding effective ways toward eliminating nuclear weapons is a feasible task, provided it is tackled without delay.

The Soviet Union is proposing a program of ridding humankind of the fear of a nuclear catastrophe, to be carried out beginning in 1986. And the fact that this year has been proclaimed by the United Nations the International Year of Peace provides an additional political and moral incentive for this. What is required here is rising above national selfishness, tactical calculations, differences and disputes, whose significance is nothing compared to the preservation of what is most valuable—peace and a safe future. The energy of the atom should be placed at the exclusive service of peace, a goal that our socialist state has invariably advocated and continues to pursue.

It was our country that as early as 1946 was the first to raise the question of prohibiting the production and use of atomic weapons and to make atomic energy serve peaceful purposes for the benefit of humanity.

How does the Soviet Union envisage today in practical terms the process of reducing nuclear weapons, both delivery vehicles and warheads, leading to their complete elimination? Our proposals can be summarized as follows.

Stage One. Within the next five to eight years the USSR and the USA will reduce by one half the nuclear arms that can reach each other's territory. On the remaining delivery vehicles of this kind each side will retain no more than 6,000 warheads.

It stands to reason that such a reduction is possible only if the USSR and the USA mutually renounce the development, testing and deployment of space strike weapons. As the Soviet Union has repeatedly warned, the development of space strike weapons will dash the hopes for a reduction of nuclear weapons on Earth.

The first stage will include the adoption and implementation of the decision on the complete elimination of intermediate-range missiles of the USSR and the USA in the European zone, both ballistic and cruise missiles, as a first step toward ridding the European continent of nuclear weapons.

At the same time the United States should undertake not to transfer its strategic and medium-range missiles to other countries, while Great Britain and France should pledge not to build up their respective nuclear arms.

The USSR and the USA should from the very beginning agree to stop any nuclear explosions, and call upon other states to join in such a moratorium as soon as possible.

We propose that the first stage of nuclear disarmament should concern the Soviet Union and the United States because it is up to them to set an example for the other nuclear powers to follow. We said that very frankly to President Reagan of the United States during our meeting in Geneva.

Stage Two. At this stage, which should start no later than 1990 and last for five to seven years, the other nuclear powers will begin to engage in nuclear disarmament. To begin with, they would pledge to freeze all their nuclear arms and not to have them in the territories of other countries.

In this period the USSR and the USA will go on with the reductions agreed upon during the first stage and also carry out further measures designed to eliminate their medium-range nuclear weapons and freeze their tactical nuclear systems.

Following the completion by the USSR and the USA of the fifty per cent reduction in their relevant arms at the second stage, another radical step is taken: All nuclear powers eliminate their tactical nuclear arms, namely the weapons having a range (or radius of action) of up to 1,000 kilometers. At the same stage the Soviet-American accord on the prohibition of space strike weapons would have to become multilateral, with the mandatory participation of major industrial powers in it.

All nuclear powers would stop nuclear-weapons tests.

There would be a ban on the development of nonnuclear weapons based on new physical principles, whose destructive capacity is close to that of nuclear arms or other weapons of mass destruction.

Stage Three will begin no later than 1995. At this stage the elimination of all remaining nuclear weapons will be completed. By the end of 1999 there will be no nuclear weapons on Earth. A universal accord will be drawn up that such weapons should never again come into being.

We have in mind that special procedures will be worked out for the destruction of nuclear weapons as well as the dismantling, re-equipment or destruction of delivery vehicles. In the process, agreement will be reached on the numbers of weapons to be destroyed at each stage, the sites of their destruction, and so on.

Verification with regard to the weapons that are destroyed or limited would be carried out both by national technical means and through on-site inspections. The USSR is ready to reach agreement on any other additional verification measures.

The adoption of the nuclear disarmament program that we propose would undoubtedly have a favorable impact on the negotiations conducted at bilateral and multilateral forums. The program would identify specific routes and reference points, establish a specific time frame for achieving agreements and implementing them and would make the negotiations purposeful and goal oriented. This would break the dangerous trend whereby the momentum of the arms race is greater than the progress of negotiations.

In summary, we propose that we should enter the Third Millennium without nuclear weapons, on the basis of mutually acceptable and strictly verifiable agreements. If the United States Administration is indeed committed to the goal of the complete elimination of nuclear weapons everywhere, as it has repeatedly stated, it is being offered a practical opportunity to begin this in practice. Instead of wasting the next ten to fifteen years by developing new, extremely dangerous weapons in space, allegedly designed to make nuclear arms useless, would it not be more sensible to start eliminating those arms and finally bring them down to zero? The Soviet Union, I repeat, proposes precisely that.

The Soviet Union calls upon all peoples and states and, naturally, above all nuclear states, to support the program of eliminating nuclear weapons before the year 2000. It is absolutely clear to any unbiased person that if such a program is implemented, nobody would lose and everybody stands to gain. This is a problem common to all mankind and it can and must be solved only through common efforts. And the sooner this program is translated into practical deeds, the safer life will be on our planet.

II.

Guided by the same approach and the desire to make another practical step within the context of the program of nuclear disarmament, the Soviet Union has taken an important decision.

We are extending by three months our unilateral moratorium on any nuclear explosions, which expired on December 31, 1985. Such a moratorium will remain in effect even longer if the United States for its part also stops nuclear tests. We propose once again to the United States to join this initiative, whose significance is evident to practically everyone in the world.

It is clear that adopting such a decision was by no means simple for us. The Soviet Union cannot display unilateral restraint with regard to nuclear tests indefinitely. But the stakes are too high and the responsibility too great for us not to try every possibility of influencing the position of others through the force of example.

All experts, scientists, politicians and military men agree that the cessation of tests would indeed block off the channels for upgrading nuclear weapons. And this task has top priority. A reduction of nuclear arsenals alone, without a prohibition of nuclear-weapons tests, does not offer a way out of the dilemma of nuclear danger, since the remaining weapons would be modernized and there would still remain the possibility of developing increasingly sophisticated and lethal nuclear weapons and evaluating their new types at test ranges.

Therefore, the cessation of tests is a practical step toward eliminating nuclear weapons.

I wish to say the following from the outset. Possible references to verification as an obstacle to the establishment of a moratorium on nuclear explosions would be totally groundless. We declare unequivocally that verification is no problem, so far as we are concerned. Should the United States agree to stop all nuclear explosions on a reciprocal basis, appropriate verification of compliance with the moratorium would be fully ensured by national technical means as well as through international procedures—including on-site inspections whenever necessary. We invite the United States to reach agreement to this effect.

The USSR is strongly in favor of the moratorium becoming a bilateral, and later a multilateral action. We are also in favor of resuming the trilateral negotiations involving the USSR, the USA and Great Britain on the complete and general prohibition of nuclear-weapons tests. This could be done immediately, even this month. We are also prepared to begin without delay multilateral test ban negotiations within the framework of the Geneva Conference on Disarmament, with all nuclear powers taking part.

Nonaligned countries are proposing consultations with a view to making the 1963 Moscow Treaty banning nuclear-weapons tests in the atmosphere, in outer space and underwater apply also to the underground tests, which are not covered by the Treaty. The Soviet Union is agreeable to this measure too.

Since last summer we have been calling upon the United States to follow our example and stop nuclear explosions. Washington has as yet not done that despite the protests and demands of public opinion, and contrary to the will of most states in the world. By continuing to set off nuclear explosions, the U.S. side continues to pursue its elusive dream of military superiority. This policy is futile and dangerous, a policy which is not worthy of the level of civilization that modern society has reached.

In the absence of a positive response from the United States, the Soviet side had every right to resume nuclear tests starting already on January 1, 1986. If one were to follow the usual "logic" of the arms race, that, presumably, would have been the thing to do.

But the point is that it is precisely that notorious logic that has to be resolutely repudiated. We are making yet another attempt in this direction. Otherwise the process of military rivalry will become an avalanche and any control over the course of events would be impossible. To submit to the force of the nuclear arms race is inadmissible. This would mean acting against the voice of reason and the human instinct of self-preservation. What is required are new and bold approaches, a new political thinking and a heightened sense of responsibility for the destinies of the peoples of the world.

The U.S. Administration is once again given more time to weigh our proposals on stopping nuclear explosions and to give a positive answer to them. It is precisely this kind of response that people everywhere in the world will expect from Washington.

The Soviet Union is addressing an appeal to the United States President and Congress, to the American people. There is an opportunity for halting the process of upgrading nuclear arms and developing new weapons of that kind. It must not be missed. The Soviet proposals place the USSR and the United States in an equal position. These proposals do not attempt to outwit or outsmart the other side. We are proposing to take the road of sensible and responsible decisions.

III.

In order to implement the program of reducing and eliminating nuclear arsenals, the entire existing system of negotiations has to be set in motion and the highest possible efficiency of disarmament machinery ensured.

In a few days the Soviet-American talks on nuclear and space arms will resume in Geneva. When we met with President Reagan last November in Geneva, we had a frank discussion on the whole range of problems that constitute the subject of those negotiations, namely on space, strategic offensive arms and intermediate-range nuclear systems. It was agreed that the negotiations should be accelerated and that agreement must not remain a mere declaration.

The Soviet delegation in Geneva will be instructed to act in strict compliance with that agreement. We expect the same constructive approach from the U.S. side, above all on the question of space. Space must remain peaceful. Strike weapons should not be deployed there. Neither should they be developed. And let there also be a most rigorous control, including opening the relevant laboratories for inspection.

Humanity is at a crucial stage of the new space age. And it is time to abandon the thinking of the Stone Age, when the chief concern was to have a bigger stick or a heavier stone. We are against weapons in space. Our material and intellectual capabilities make it possible for the Soviet Union to develop any weapon if we are compelled to do this. But we are fully aware of our responsibility to the present and future generations. It is our profound conviction that we should approach the Third Millennium not with the "Star Wars" program but with large-scale projects of peaceful exploration of space by all humankind. We propose to start practical work on such projects and their implementation. This is one of the major ways of ensuring progress on our entire planet and establishing a reliable system of security for all.

To prevent the arms race from extending into space means to remove the obstacle to deep cuts in nuclear weapons. There is on the negotiating table in Geneva a Soviet proposal on reducing by one half the relevant nuclear arms of the Soviet Union and the United States, which would be an important step toward a complete elimination of nuclear weapons. Barring the possibility of resolving the problem of space means not wanting to stop the arms race on Earth. This should be stated in clear and straightforward terms. It is not by chance that the proponents of the nuclear arms race are also ardent supporters of the "Star Wars" program. These are the two sides of the same policy, hostile to the interests of people.

Let me turn to the European aspect of the nuclear problem.

It is a matter of extreme concern that in defiance of reason and contrary to the national interests of the European peoples, American first-strike missiles continue to be deployed in certain West European countries. This problem has been under discussion for many years now. Meanwhile, the security situation in Europe continues to deteriorate.

It is time to put an end to this course of events and cut this Gordian knot. The Soviet Union has for a long time been proposing that Europe should be freed from both intermediate-range and tactical nuclear weapons. This proposal remains valid. As a first radical step in this direction we are now proposing, as I have said, that even at the first stage of our program all intermediate-range ballistic and cruise missiles of the USSR and the USA in the European zone should be eliminated.

Achieving tangible practical results at the Geneva talks would give meaningful material substance to the program designed to totally eliminate nuclear arms by the year 2000, which we are proposing.

IV.

The Soviet Union considers as fully feasible the task of completely eliminating, even in this century, such barbaric weapons of mass destruction as chemical weapons.

At the talks on chemical weapons within the framework of the Geneva conference on disarmament certain signs of progress have recently appeared. However, these talks have been unreasonably protracted. We are in favor of intensifying the talks in order to conclude an effective and verifiable international convention prohibiting chemical weapons and destroying the existing stockpiles of those weapons, as agreed with President Reagan at Geneva.

In the matter of banning chemical weapons, just as in other disarmament matters, all participants in the talks should take a fresh look at things. I would like to make it perfectly clear that the Soviet Union is in favor of an early and complete elimination of those weapons and of the industrial base for their production.

We are prepared for a timely declaration of the location of enterprises producing chemical weapons and for the cessation of their production and ready to start developing procedures for destroying the relevant industrial base and to proceed, soon after the convention enters into force, to eliminating the stockpiles of chemical weapons. All these measures would be carried out under strict control, including international on-site inspections.

A radical solution to this problem would also be facilitated by certain interim steps. For example, agreement could be achieved on a multilateral basis not to transfer chemical weapons to anyone and not to deploy them in the territories of other states. As for the Soviet Union, it has always strictly abided by those principles in its practical policies. We call upon other states to follow that example and show equal restraint.

V.

Along with eliminating weapons of mass destruction from the arsenals of states, the Soviet Union is proposing that conventional weapons and armed forces become subject to agreed reductions.

Reaching agreement at the Vienna negotiations could signal the beginning of progress in this direction. Today it would seem that a framework is emerging for a possible decision to reduce Soviet and U.S. troops and subsequently freeze the level of armed forces of the opposing sides in Central Europe. The Soviet Union and our Warsaw Treaty allies are determined to achieve success at the Vienna Talks. If the other side also wants this, 1986 could become a landmark for the Vienna Talks too. We proceed from the understanding that a possible agreement on troop reduction would naturally require reasonable verification. We are prepared for it.

As for observing the commitment to freeze the number of troops, in addition to national technical means permanent verification posts could be established to monitor any military contingents entering the reduction zone.

Let me now mention such an important forum as the Stockholm Conference on Confidence and Security-Building Measures and Disarmament in Europe. It is called upon to place barriers against the use of force or covert preparations for war, whether on land, at sea or in the air. The possibilities have now become evident.

In our view, especially in the current situation, it is essential to reduce the number of troops participating in major military maneuvers notifiable under the Helsinki Final Act.

It is time to begin dealing effectively with the problem still outstanding at the conference. It is known that the bottleneck there is the issue of notifications regarding major ground force, naval and air force exercises. Of course, those are serious problems and they must be addressed in a serious manner in the interests of building confidence in Europe. However, if their comprehensive solution cannot be achieved at this time, why not explore ways for their partial solution? For instance, reach agreement now about notifications of major ground force and air force exercises, postponing the question of naval activities until the next stage of the conference.

It is not an accident that the new Soviet initiatives in considerable part are directly addressed to Europe. In achieving a radical turn toward the policy of peace, Europe could have a special mission. That mission is erecting a new edifice of détente.

For this Europe has a necessary historical experience, which is often unique. Suffice it to recall that the joint efforts of the Europeans, the United States and Canada produced the Helsinki Final Act. If there is a need for a specific and vivid example of new thinking and political psychology in approaching the problems of peace, cooperation and international trust, that historic document could in many ways serve as such an example.

VI.

Ensuring security in Asia is of vital importance to the Soviet Union, which is a major Asian power. The Soviet program for eliminating nuclear and chemical weapons by the end of the current century is in harmony with the sentiments of the peoples of the Asian continent, for whom the problems of peace and security are no less urgent than for the peoples of Europe. In this context one cannot fail to recall that Japan and its cities Hiroshima and Nagasaki became the victims of nuclear bombing and Vietnam a target of chemical weapons.

We highly appreciate the constructive initiatives put forward by the Socialist countries of Asia and by India and other members of the nonaligned movement. We view as very important the fact that the two Asian nuclear powers, the USSR and the People's Republic of China, have both undertaken not to be the first to use nuclear weapons.

The implementation of our program would fundamentally change the situation in Asia, rid the nations in that part of the globe, too, of the fear of nuclear and chemical warfare, and bring the security in that region to a qualitatively new level.

We regard our program as a contribution to a search, together with all Asian countries, for an overall comprehensive approach to establishing a system of secure and durable peace on this continent.

VII.

Our new proposals are addressed to the whole world. Initiating active steps to halt the arms race and reduce weapons is a necessary prerequisite for coping with the increasingly acute global problems: Those of deteriorating human environment and of the need to find new energy sources and combat economic backwardness, hunger and disease. The pattern imposed by militarism—arms instead of development—must be replaced by the reverse order of things—disarmament for development. The noose of the trillion-dollar foreign debt, which is now strangling dozens of countries and entire continents, is a direct consequence of the arms race. The over two hundred and fifty billion dollars annually siphoned out of the developing countries is an amount practically equal to the size of the mammoth U.S.

military budget. Indeed, this coincidence is far from accidental.

The Soviet Union wants each measure limiting and reducing arms and each step toward eliminating nuclear weapons not only to bring nations greater security but also to make it possible to allocate more funds for improving people's lives. It is natural that the peoples seeking to put an end to backwardness and achieve the level of industrially developed countries associate the prospects of freeing themselves from the imperialist burden of foreign debt, which is draining their economies, with limiting and eliminating weapons, reducing military expenditures and switching resources to the goals of social and economic development. This theme will undoubtedly figure most prominently at the international conference on disarmament and development to be held next summer in Paris.

The Soviet Union is opposed to making the implementation of disarmament measures dependent on the so-called regional conflicts. Behind this dependency is both the unwillingness to follow the path of disarmament and the desire to impose upon sovereign nations what is alien to them and what would make it possible to maintain profoundly unfair conditions, whereby some countries live at the expense of others, exploiting their natural, human and spiritual resources for the selfish imperial purposes of certain states or aggressive alliances. The Soviet Union, as before, will continue to oppose this. It will continue consistently to advocate freedom for the world's peoples, peace, security, and a stronger international legal order. The Soviet Union's goal is not to whip up regional conflicts but to eliminate them through collective efforts on a just basis, and the sooner the better.

Today, there is no shortage of statements professing commitment to peace. What is really in short supply is concrete action to strengthen its foundations. All too often peaceful words conceal war preparations and power politics. Moreover, some statements made from high rostrums are in fact intended to eliminate any trace of that new "spirit of Geneva" which is having a salutary effect on international relations today. It is not only a matter of statements. There are also actions clearly designed to incite animosity and mistrust and to revive confrontation which is antithetical to détente.

We reject such a way of acting and thinking. We want 1986 to be not just a peaceful year but one that would enable us to reach the end of the twentieth century under the sign of peace and nuclear disarmament. The set of new foreign policy initiatives that we are proposing is intended to make it possible for humanity to approach the year 2000 under peaceful skies and with peaceful space, without fear of nuclear, chemical or any other threat of annihilation and fully confident of its own survival and of the continuation of the human race.

The new resolute measures now taken by the Soviet Union for the sake of peace and of improving the overall international situation give expression to the substance and the spirit of our internal and foreign policies and their organic unity. They reflect the fundamental historic law which was emphasized by Vladimir Ilyich Lenin. The whole world sees that our country is holding even higher the banner of peace, freedom and humanism raised over our planet by the Great October Revolution.

On the questions of preserving peace and saving humanity from the threat of nuclear war, no one should remain indifferent or stand aloof. This concerns all and everyone. Each state, large or small, socialist or capitalist, has an important contribution to make. Every responsible political party, every social organization and every person can also make an important contribution.

No task is more urgent, more noble and humane, than uniting all efforts to achieve this lofty goal. This task is to be accomplished by our generation without shifting it onto the shoulders of those who will succeed us. This is the imperative of our time. This, I would say, is the burden of historic responsibility for our decisions and actions in the time remaining until the beginning of the Third Millennium.

The course of peace and disarmament will continue to be pivotal to the foreign policy of the CPSU and the Soviet state. In actively pursuing this course, the Soviet Union is prepared to engage in wide-ranging cooperation with all those who stand on positions of reason, good will and an awareness of responsibility for assuring the human race a future without wars or weapons.

18

A JOINT
SOVIET–AMERICAN
STATEMENT

By MUTUAL agreement, General Secretary of the CPSU Central Committee Mikhail Gorbachev and President of the United States Ronald Reagan met in Geneva on November 19-21, 1985. Attending the meeting on the Soviet side were member of the Politburo of the CPSU Central Committee and Foreign Minister of the USSR Eduard Shevardnadze; First Deputy Foreign Minister of the USSR Georgy Kornienko; the USSR Ambassador to the United States Anatoly Dobrynin; head of the Propaganda Department of the CPSU Central Committee Alexander Yakovlev; head of the International Information Department of the CPSU Central Committee Leonid Zamyatin; Assistant to the General Secretary of the CPSU Central Committee Andrei Alexandrov. Attending on the American side were U.S. Secretary of State George Shultz; the White House Chief of Staff Donald Regan; Assistant to the President for National Security Affairs Robert McFarlane; U.S. Ambassador to the USSR Arthur Hartman; Special Advisor to the President and the Secretary of State for Arms Control Paul H. Nitze; Assistant Secretary of State for European Affairs Rozanne Ridgway; Special Assistant to the President for National Security Affairs Jack Matlock.

These comprehensive discussions covered the basic questions of Soviet-U.S. relations and the current international situation. The meetings were frank and useful. Serious differences remain on a number of critical issues.

While acknowledging the differences in the sociopolitical systems of the USSR and the USA and their approaches to international issues, some greater understanding of each side's view was achieved by the two leaders. They agreed about the need to improve U.S.-Soviet relations and the international situation as a whole. In this connection the two sides have confirmed the importance of an ongoing dialogue, reflecting their strong desire to seek common ground on existing problems.

The General Secretary of the CPSU Central Committee and the President of the United States agreed to meet again in the nearest future. The President of the United States accepted an invitation by the General Secretary of the Central Committee of the CPSU to visit the Soviet Union and the General Secretary accepted an invitation by the President of the United States to visit the United States of America. Arrangements for and timing of the visits will be agreed upon through diplomatic channels.

At their meetings, agreement was reached on a number of specific issues. Areas of agreement are registered below.

I.

The sides, having discussed key security issues, and conscious of the special responsibility of the USSR and the U.S. for maintaining peace, have agreed that a nuclear war cannot be won and must never be fought. Recognizing that any conflict between the USSR and the U.S. could have catastrophic consequences, they emphasized the importance of preventing any war between them, whether nuclear or conventional. They will not seek to achieve military superiority.

The General Secretary and the President discussed the negotiations on nuclear and space arms.

They agreed to accelerate the work at these negotiations, with a view to accomplishing the tasks set down in the joint Soviet-U.S. agreement of January 8, 1985, namely to prevent an arms race in space and to terminate it on Earth, to limit and reduce nuclear arms and enhance strategic stability.

Noting the proposals recently advanced by the Soviet Union and the U.S., they called for early progress, in particular in areas where there is common ground, including the principle of fifty per cent reductions in the nuclear arms of the U.S. and the USSR appropriately applied, as well as the idea of an interim agreement on medium-range missiles in Europe. During the negotiation of these agreements, effective measures for verification of compliance with obligations assumed will be agreed upon.

The sides agreed to study the question at the expert level of centers to reduce nuclear risk, taking into account the issues and developments in the Geneva negotiations. They took satisfaction in such recent steps in this direction as the modernization of the Soviet-U.S. hotline.

General Secretary Gorbachev and President Reagan reaffirmed the commitment of the USSR and the U.S. to the Treaty on the Nonproliferation of Nuclear Weapons and their interest in strengthening, together with other countries, the nonproliferation regime and in further enhancing the effectiveness of the treaty, *inter alia*, by enlarging its membership.

They note with satisfaction the overall positive results of the recent review conference of the Treaty on the Nonproliferation of Nuclear Weapons.

The USSR and the U.S. reaffirm their commitment, assumed by them under the Treaty on the Nonproliferation of Nuclear Weapons, to pursue negotiations in good faith on matters of nuclear arms limitation and disarmament in accordance with Article VI of the Treaty.

The two sides plan to continue to promote the strengthening of the International Atomic Energy Agency and to support the activities of the agency in implementing safeguards as well as in promoting the peaceful uses of nuclear energy. They view positively the practice of regular Soviet-U.S. consultations on nonproliferation of nuclear weapons which have been businesslike and constructive and express their intent to continue this practice in the future.

In the context of discussing security problems, the two sides reaffirmed that they are in favor of a general and complete prohibition of chemical weapons and the destruction of existing stockpiles of such weapons. They agreed to accelerate efforts to conclude an effective and verifiable international convention on this matter.

The two sides agreed to intensify bilateral discussions on the level of experts on all aspects of such a chemical weapons ban, including the question of verification. They agreed to initiate a dialogue on preventing the proliferation of chemical weapons. The two sides emphasized the importance they attach to the Vienna negotiations on the mutual reduction of armed forces and armaments in Central Europe and expressed their willingness to work for positive results there.

Attaching great importance to the Stockholm Conference on Confidence and Security-Building Measures and Disarmament in Europe and noting the progress made there, the two sides stated their intention to facilitate, together with the other participating states, an early and successful completion of the work of the conference. To this end, they reaffirmed the need for a document which would include mutually acceptable confidence and security-building measures and give concrete expression and effect to the principle of nonuse of force.

II.

General Secretary Gorbachev and President Reagan agreed on the need to place dialogue on a regular basis and intensify it at various levels. Along with meetings between the leaders of the two countries, this envisages regular meetings between the USSR Minister of Foreign Affairs and the U.S. Secretary of State, as well as between the heads of other ministries and agencies. They agreed that the recent visits of the heads of ministries and departments in such fields as agriculture, housing and protection of the environment have been useful.

Recognizing that exchanges of views on regional issues, including those on the expert level, have proven useful, they agreed to continue such exchanges on a regular basis.

The sides intend to expand the programs of bilateral cultural, educational and scientific-technical exchanges, and also to develop trade and economic ties. The General Secretary of the Central Committee of the CPSU and the President of the United States attended the signing of the agreement on contacts and exchanges in scientific, educational and cultural fields.

They believe that there should be greater understanding

among our peoples and that to this end they will encourage greater travel and people-to-people contact.

They agree that matters concerning individual citizens should be resolved in the spirit of cooperation.

The two leaders also noted with satisfaction that, in cooperation with the government of Japan, the Soviet Union and the United States have agreed to a set of measures to promote safety on air routes in the North Pacific and have worked out steps to implement them.

They acknowledged that delegations from the Soviet Union and the United States have begun negotiations aimed at resumption of air services. The two leaders expressed their desire to reach a mutually beneficial agreement at an early date. In this regard, an agreement was reached on the simultaneous opening of consulates-general in New York and Kiev.

Both sides agreed to contribute to the preservation of the environment—a global task—through joint research and practical measures. In accordance with the existing Soviet-U.S. agreement in this area, consultations will be held next year in Moscow and Washington on specific programs of cooperation.

The two leaders agreed on the utility of broadening exchanges and contacts including some of their new forms in a number of scientific, educational, medical and sports fields (*inter alia*, cooperation in the development of educational exchanges and software for elementary and secondary school instruction; measures to promote Russian language studies in the United States and English language studies in the USSR; the annual exchange of professors to conduct special courses in history, culture and economics at the relevant departments of Soviet and American institutions of higher education; mutual allocation of scholarships for the best students in the natural sciences, technology, social sciences and humanities for the period of an academic year; holding regular meets in various sports and increased television coverage of sports events). The two sides agreed to resume cooperation in combatting cancer diseases.

The relevant agencies in each of the countries are being

instructed to develop specific programs for these exchanges. The resulting programs will be reviewed by the leaders at their next meeting.

The two leaders emphasized the potential importance of the work aimed at utilizing controlled thermonuclear fusion for peaceful purposes and, in this connection, advocated the widest practicable development of international cooperation in obtaining this source of energy, which is essentially inexhaustible, for the benefit of all mankind.

November 21, 1985

19

PRESS CONFERENCE
IN GENEVA

Mikhail Gorbachev, General Secretary of the Central Committee of the Communist Party of the Soviet Union, held a press conference for journalists covering the Soviet-American meeting at the Soviet Press Center in Geneva on November 21, 1985.

OUR TALKS with the President of the United States of America, the first in the past six and a half years, have just ended. This has been, beyond a doubt, a significant event in international life. The importance of this meeting will become even more obvious if one considers not only Soviet-American but international relations in general, which are experiencing a special, I would say, difficult, period.

First, a few words about what had preceded the Geneva meeting. It had been awaited with impatience all over the world. People linked with it their great hopes for an improvement of the world situation and a lowering of international tension, which has reached a danger point. True, there were some doubts: Hasn't the confrontation of the two powers gone too far for counting on any accords at all? All that was there, you know it as well as we do.

As far as the Soviet side, the Soviet Union, is concerned, we fully realized the actual situation and did not nourish the slightest illusion regarding American policy. We saw how far the militarization of the economy and even the political thinking in that country had gone.

But we also understood that the situation in the world is too dangerous to neglect even the slightest chance of setting things right and moving toward a more stable and secure peace.

Well in advance of the meeting, within months of it, we had begun to sort of pave the way to it and create a propitious climate for this meeting. Back in the summer we unilaterally suspended all nuclear explosions, expressing our readiness to immediately resume the talks about a general nuclear test ban. We also reaffirmed our unilateral moratorium on the testing of anti-satellite weapons and, as you know, put forward radical proposals for a reduction of nuclear arsenals. Our proposals to prevent the arms race from spreading into space were accompanied by proposals for starting the broadest possible international cooperation in the peaceful exploration and use of space for the good of all nations.

I repeat, even before the meeting, we were doing everything so as to lay the groundwork for mutual understanding and make the political atmosphere healthier. In the period leading up to the Geneva summit, the Political Consultative Committee of the Warsaw Treaty member states held a session in Sofia which heard the socialist nations speak out for peace, détente and cooperation, for an improvement of the international situation in the interests of all peoples of the Earth, and against the arms race and confrontation.

And although our moves, prompted by a sense of responsibility for the fortunes of peace, fetched no proper response from our partners in the talks to be held in Geneva, we stood firm by a constructive position. We found it necessary to try and reverse the dangerous course of events by the force of arguments, the force of example, the force of common sense. The very complexity of the international situation convinced us that a direct conversation with the U.S. President was necessary. Because of the tremendous role that both the Soviet Union and the United States of America play, these states and their political leaders naturally have just as tremendous a responsibility to bear. Our conclusion was this: The time has come to learn the great art of living together in the face of a nuclear danger to all. Both the Soviet people and, I think, the American people, are equally interested in learning this art. This is something that all of the world's peoples are interested in.

We have always felt that people in all countries aspire to peace, and not only want peace to be preserved but the situation to be improved and real progress to be made in the struggle to halt the arms race. This desire is growing stronger and this is a fact of tremendous importance. Two major conclusions can be drawn from it.

On the one hand, it is an encouraging fact that everything we do meets the hopes and aspirations of a vast number of people in the world, regardless of where they live and whatever their political views, religious persuasions and traditions. On the other hand, this fact not only encourages us but imposes many duties on us, and a special responsibility.

What characterizes the present stage of development of the international situation? In a nutshell, it is growing responsibility for the future of the world. The peoples have realized this tremendous responsibility, and they are doing everything they can to live up to it.

This means that states and political leaders should be guided by these characteristics in their practical policies. The absence of a policy adequate to the needs of the moment, needs which are felt by all the peoples of the world, cannot be replaced by all sorts of propaganda wrappings. The people have quickly learned to see what is what and put everything in its proper place.

This is my profound conviction. This is how my colleagues in the political leadership of the Soviet Union and I understand the situation, and we have therefore focused our attention on a constructive search for a better and more tranquil world.

I was greatly impressed by the letters I received from the Soviet Union, the United States, Australia, Europe, Asia and Africa. They were from children, women, men, war veterans. I would like to emphasize that in those letters I could clearly hear the voice of the world's youth, those to whom the future belongs, who are just making a start in life and assuming upon themselves responsibility for the world's future.

Now about the meeting itself.

It was largely a private meeting with President Reagan. When the U.S. President and I were saying goodbye to each other a short while ago, we decided to count the number of confidential meetings we had had. We decided that there were five or six. Most of our meetings lasted for an hour, some a little longer. This is not simple arithmetic. Our discussions were straightforward, lengthy, sharp and at times very sharp. Nevertheless, I think they were productive to some extent. Of course, they took a great deal more time than planned: They occupied most of the time of these two days.

This allowed us to discuss a broad range of problems while looking into each other's eyes. We spoke political language, open and straightforward, and I think that was the most important thing.

These discussions and also the plenary sessions and broad contacts between all members of the delegations and experts at appropriate levels—these were internationally known authorities on both the Soviet and American sides—made it possible to accomplish in two days a tremendous amount of work.

We acquainted the President with our views and assessment of the situation in the world. The point of reference in our analysis is as follows: During the past few decades dramatic changes have taken place in the world which require a new approach and a new assessment of many things in foreign policy. There is a very important thing about the international situation today which we and the United States must take into account in our foreign policy. What I mean is this. Today it is not only a matter of confrontation of the two social systems but of a choice between survival and mutual destruction.

In other words, the objective course of world affairs has placed the problem of war and peace and the problem of survival in the center of world politics. I would like to emphasize that I am using the word "survival" not because I want to dramatize the situation or escalate fear but because I want all of us to feel deeply and realize the realities of the modern world.

The problem of war and peace is a problem of paramount importance, a burning problem of concern to all of us living on this planet. I would like to emphasize that this problem is now in the center of world politics. We must not avoid looking for a solution to this crucial problem. This is our firm belief. This is the will of the Soviet people. This is also the will of the American people and of all the peoples of the world. This is what I wanted to say in the first place.

Second, we once again drew the attention of the American side to the following factors of which I have already spoken. These factors are so important, and we attach such serious attention to them that we deemed it necessary to mention this again in Geneva—namely, it is a fact that it is already very difficult for us to commence a productive dialogue and talks on questions relating to stopping the arms race and nuclear disarmament. It will be even more difficult to do so tomorrow.

That is why it was necessary to hold a meeting, a responsible dialogue. All of us have come up to a point at which it is necessary to stop, to have a look around, to think better of it and to decide, on the basis of realities, on the basis of a wide approach to determining national interests, what is to be done in the world in the future. In the course of the meetings and talks I wanted to comprehend the stand of the present U.S. Administration on this cardinal issue—the question of war and peace.

All of us have read a lot on this score. Generally speaking, you journalists have also said quite a lot about this. But for the decision-makers it is essential to understand the starting point for the shaping of the partners' policy, the initial design of the foreign policy of the present U.S. Administration. It took a lot of work, a lot of effort to appraise everything objectively, with great responsibility and with a broad outlook, and to find an answer to this very important question.

This analysis has shown that, despite all the differences in the sides' approaches and appraisals which came into the open during this serious and necessary job—it was impossible to go to the summit without having done this job—it seems to me we saw that we have elements in common that can serve as the starting point for improvement in Soviet-U.S. relations. I mean the understanding of the fact that a nuclear war is inadmissible, that it cannot be waged and is unwinnable. This idea was voiced more than once both by us and by the American side. It is only logical to conclude from this that the problem of security is the central issue in relations between our countries at the present stage. We emphatically stand for achieving agreements ensuring equal security for both countries.

We are aware that consistent strengthening of mutual trust and general improvement of the political atmosphere, in which one could hope for the development of a political dialogue, for a fruitful discussion of the economic and humanitarian problems and the problems of contacts and reciprocal information, will become possible exactly on this basis. Herein lies the key to the problem of preserving life on Earth, to changing the political atmosphere toward one of goodwill.

We told the President that we did not and would not seek to gain military superiority over the USA. Furthermore, I repeatedly tried, both tête-à-tête and at the plenary meetings, to express our profound conviction that a lower level of security for the United States of America compared with that of the Soviet Union would not benefit us because this would lead to mistrust and generate instability. We are counting on an analogous approach by the USA to the questions relating to our country. At the same time, we told the President that we would never allow the USA to gain military superiority over us. In my view, this is a logical formulation of the question. Both sides had better get accustomed to strategic parity as a natural state of Soviet-U.S. relations. What we should discuss is how to lower the level of this parity through joint efforts, i.e. ways to carry out real measures to reduce nuclear armaments on a mutual basis. This is a field of action worthy of the leaders of such great states as the Soviet Union and the United States of America, as well as leaders of other states, because it is an issue of concern to all of us.

But this perfectly logically leads up to the following conclusion of fundamental importance. Neither of us, the United States of America nor the Soviet Union, should do anything that might open the door for the arms race in new spheres, specifically, in space. If the door into space is opened for weapons, the scope of military confrontation would grow immeasurably and the arms race would acquire an irreversible character, which to a certain extent can be predicted even now, getting totally out of control. In that case each side would all the time have the feeling that it has fallen behind in something, so it would be frantically looking for ever new countermoves. All this would spur on the arms race, not only in space but on Earth, too, for such countermoves should not necessarily be taken in the same sphere. They just have to be effective.

I use the same line of reasoning now as I did talking to the President. If such a situation does arise, I repeat that the possibility of agreement on any restraint upon military rivalry and the arms race will grow extremely problematic. I would like to return to the point which I have already made: The distinctive feature of the present situation is that we have come to a certain brink. So unless the existing problems are considered and thought out with genuine responsibility, wrong conclusions by politicians may lead to such steps which will have the most dire consequences for all nations.

Of course, neither the differences between our countries nor our rivalry will disappear, but we must do everything so that this does not overstep reasonable bounds and lead to military confrontation. Let each of the two social systems prove its advantages through example.

We have a good idea of not only the weak but also the strong aspects of American society and of other advanced nations. We are aware of their accomplishments and their potential. And, of course, we know our own potential even better, including those aspects of it which still require materialization. In other words, we are for competition with the U.S. and, I might add, for active competition. It is history itself rather than mere theoretical reckoning and speculations that has confirmed the viability of the policy of peaceful coexistence.

Much in the development of relations between the USSR and the U.S. depends on the way each side apprehends the surrounding world. We think that here it is particularly important to have a clear understanding of the historical realities and to take them into account in policy-making. I refer here both to the Soviet and to the American leadership.

Today's world is a highly diversified assembly of sovereign states, of nations with their own interests, aspirations, policies, traditions and dreams. Many of them have just embarked on the road of independent development. Their first steps come in the impossibly difficult conditions left over from the days of colonialism and foreign domination. Some of them, having gained political sovereignty, are seeking now to obtain economic independence. They see that they have the resources and the manpower, or the things which, given the adequate time to work through, can secure a better life for them. Why, these are whole great continents. So it is only natural that each nation should seek to exercise its sovereign rights in the political, economic and social fields.

One may like or dislike this policy, but it does reflect the inner processes in each particular country and the interests of each given nation which possesses that sovereign right. This is the right to choose the way, the system, the methods, the forms and the friends. This right belongs to each nation. I don't know how international relations can possibly be built without the recognition of this right.

When I was in Great Britain last December, I recalled a phrase by Palmerston. It had settled in my memory when I was studying international relations in the law department of Moscow State University. Palmerston said that Britain had no eternal enemies or eternal friends, but only eternal interests. I told Margaret Thatcher then that I agreed with that judgement. But if Palmerston and you, the present political leader of Britain, admit that you do have such interests, you must admit that the other nations and other countries have interests of their own.

When about two hundred states are involved in the international arena, each of them strives to promote its own interests. But to what extent are these interests promoted? It depends on taking into account the interests of others in the course of cooperation. But to look upon the world as somebody's private domain is an approach which we renounce. We have always said so—10 years ago and today, and we will be saying so tomorrow. We have no dual policy here. We pursue an honest and frank policy. We have been doing so, we shall continue to do so.

The causes of tension, conflicts in some regions, even wars between various states in one or another part of the world are found both in the past and in the present socioeconomic conditions of those countries and regions. To present the whole thing as if those contradictory knots have been born of the rivalry between East and West is not only erroneous but also extremely dangerous. I said this to the President and to the American delegation.

If today, for example, Mexico, Brazil and several other

states fail to pay not only their debts but also interest on those debts, one can imagine what processes are taking place in those countries. This may strain the situation and lead to an explosion. Will they again be talking about the "hand" of Moscow? But one simply cannot subject the whole world to such judgements on these issues in so irresponsible a manner. These banalities can still be found somewhere, but they are inadmissible, particularly at such meetings as the one we are having. That is why we said right away: Let us not tell each other banalities, for a lot of these were uttered on the eve of and in the course of preparations for the meeting. It was a real skirmish that proceeded, not without the help of you journalists. (Animation in the hall.)

Of course, the Soviet Union and the United States are two mighty powers with their own global interests and with their own allies and friends. They have their priorities in their foreign policies. Yet the Soviet leadership regards it not as a source of confrontation but rather as the origin of a special, greater responsibility for the destiny of peace shouldered by the Soviet Union and the United States and their leaders. This is how we see it. Of course, we can argue about the situation in one or another part of the world. Our conclusions may be different, often contradictory, particularly when the matter concerns any particular event and the causes of any particular conflicts. In principle, we are not against discussing any particular regional problems to find ways promoting their settlement. We discussed them and agreed with the President to continue to exert joint efforts, something that has been reflected in the final Joint Statement. Yet we always emphasize—and I want to say it now again—we are against any kind of interference in the internal affairs of other states. Such is our conception of Soviet-American relations which we brought to the meeting and presented to the President and the American delegation. It was presented in a more detailed manner, but I have just tried to convey its essence to you.

We believe that improvement of Soviet-U.S. relations is quite possible. Many problems have accumulated, I would say, whole obstructions that should be cleared away. Soviet leaders have the political will to tackle this job. But it should be done jointly with the American side. It is known that when geologists and miners come up against cave-ins and find themselves in a critical situation, rescue teams converge to save people.

In order to save our relations from being further strained, to prevent them from moving toward confrontation and to turn them toward a normal course, toward improvement, this work should be done through joint efforts. We are ready for this. I told the U.S. President that it would be a big mistake if we fail to use the chance that has presented itself for changing the situation in Soviet-U.S. relations toward normalization, and this means toward improvement of the situation in the world as a whole.

I would like to return again to the main issue which was pivotal to the Geneva meeting, as it were. There was not a single meeting of the delegations, not a single confidential meeting, where questions of war and peace and arms control did not hold a central place. These were the pivot of the Geneva meeting. We explained to the U.S. side that the "Star Wars" program would not merely give an impulse to the arms race involving weapons of all types, but that it would also put an end to any restrictions on the arms race. In reply, we were told again and again that the large-scale antimissile system with space-based elements was allegedly defensive in character. We were asked: What would you tell the Soviet people after Geneva if you refused to effect a reduction in offensive arms? We gave an answer to that, and I repeat it: This isn't so. We are prepared for a sweeping reduction in nuclear arms providing the door is firmly closed on starting an arms race in space. On that condition, we are ready to cover the first stage on the basis of the principle of a 50 per cent reduction in nuclear arms and then, drawing the other nuclear powers into this process, to move further on the road of radical reduction.

There is a certain part of the world, and perhaps there are even some politicians and journalists, who have a positive reaction, so to speak, to the SDI. It is alleged that this is a weapon of defense, a shield. This is absolutely not so. As a matter of fact, although mountains of weapons have been stockpiled in the world, the arms race is under way and we cannot for all our efforts cope with this process, put it under control, curb or reverse it. In this highly complicated situation the United States proposes that we start a race in space. Who could guarantee that we would then be able to organize any effective talks? I think no man in his right mind would guarantee this. The American side is reluctant to admit that the SDI means bringing weapons to space. Weapons. They would fly over people's heads in waves—American and Soviet weapons. We would all watch this sky and expect something to fall from there. We told the American side—let us imagine the consequences of even an accidental collision in space. Say, something has become separated from a missile, the nose part has gone off on its own and the vehicle has broken away to collide with a space weapon subsystem. There would be signals which could be interpreted as perhaps an attempt by the other side—I don't even say which side, ours or theirs—to destroy these weapons. All computers would be switched on while politicians would not be able to do anything sensible. Shall we allow such things to prevail over us? We can imagine many such situations. I told the U.S. President: We understand that this idea has captivated him as a man and we can understand this to some extent or another. However, what we cannot understand in this respect is his position as a politician responsible for such a mighty state, for security matters. We think that after the talks we had the American side will weigh in earnest everything we said on this score.

The meeting has shown once again that the Americans do not like our logic, while we cannot find logic in their arguments. They say: Believe us, if the Americans were the first to deploy the SDI, they would share their experience with the Soviet Union. I then said: Mr. President, I call on you to believe us. We have said that we would not be the first to use nuclear weapons and we would not attack the United States. Why then do you, while preserving the defense capability on Earth and underwater, intend to start the arms race also in space? You don't believe us? This shows that you don't. Why should we believe you more than you believe us? Especially since we have reasons not to believe you, since we invite you to leave space in peace and start disarmament on Earth. All this is comprehensible to everybody.

In general, it is to be hoped this is not all the American side has to say. The talk with the President was serious. We attentively listened to each other's arguments and recorded all these things. If the United States found the will and resolution to give the matter new thought and evaluate all the pernicious aspects and implications of the "Star Wars" program, this would give the go-ahead to the effective handling of the international security issue and ending the arms race. In saying this, I mean that this refers to control matters as well. There is a lot of speculation around this issue, with the Soviet stand being deliberately misrepresented. However, the truth is that the Soviet Union is open for verification. Provided an accord is reached to ban deploying weapons in space, we are prepared to open our laboratories, on a reciprocal basis, in order to monitor such an agreement. However, what has been proposed looks like this: Let us open our laboratories and monitor the progress of the arms race in space. It's naive and, besides, the premise is wrong and unacceptable.

If the American side also stopped all tests of nuclear weapons and we signed a relevant agreement, there would be no problems with control, including international verification, on our side of this issue too.

If both sides agree to cut their nuclear weapons by 50 per cent, then of course it will be necessary to verify this process, and we are interested in this no less than the Americans.

I want to say just a few words to the effect that at this stage differences have been revealed in the positions with regard to the 50 per cent cut in nuclear weapons. We have our reservations concerning the draft submitted by the American side, and the Americans have theirs with regard to our drafts. But we do not dramatize these differences and are ready to seek a mutually acceptable solution if of course an arms race in space is not started. The proposals of the two sides are a foundation for seeking mutually acceptable solutions. There can be compromises here. This will require time and clarification of the situation. We are prepared to look for these solutions proceeding from the basic principle that we are not striving to achieve military superiority and that we stand for equal security.

There was an exchange of views on humanitarian problems at the meeting. This has resulted in corresponding agreements reflected in the Joint Statement. I'll remind you that understanding has been reached on some questions of bilateral Soviet-American relations and on extending contacts in science, culture, education and information. An exchange of students, TV programs and sports delegations will be broader. An understanding in principle has been reached on concluding an agreement on air links. I think that information has already come from Moscow that it seems this problem too was removed yesterday.

I would like to draw your special attention to the fact that it has been decided to jointly appeal to a number of states concerning cooperation in the field of thermonuclear synthesis. This is a very interesting idea. Its realization can turn a new page in a very important sphere—providing a practically inexhaustible source of energy to humankind. This is an area for joint activity. This calls for tremendous efforts on the part of scientists, for tremendous efforts of experts and for new solutions. All this will advance technological progress and technology.

I think that from the point of view of the political results and consequences of the Summit, it is important to take one more factor into account. We have witnessed the great political effect of the meeting. It has shown and heightened the world public's interest in the problems of Soviet-American relations, in the danger of the arms race and in the necessity of normalizing the situation.

I have to mention several episodes in this connection. The day before yesterday a group of the leaders of U.S. peace movements, led by prominent politician Jesse Jackson, visited our mission. I want to say that we have always regarded them as worthy and respected American citizens representing the millions of people living in the USA who have signed a message to President Reagan and to me with wishes for the success of the meeting and with specific proposals aimed at strengthening peace, including the call to stop nuclear tests. The American World War II veterans who participated in the Elbe Linkup came to Geneva, and representatives of many mass organizations of other countries, children's organizations included, were also here these last few days. At my request, they were received by the Soviet delegation. It was a moving meeting. It is needless to say here that we constantly felt the powerful support and solidarity of our socialist friends and of the nonaligned countries. Even before the Summit the leaders of six states—India, Mexico, Argentina, Tanzania, Greece and Sweden—introduced a proposal to freeze all types of nuclear weapons. We highly appreciate their initiative. A large group of Nobel Prize winners advanced proposals all of which, save one, I was ready to support right away. That wish, or demand, was that we should not leave Geneva until we have reached an accord. It was risky to agree to this. Otherwise, it might have taken us too long before we could go home. (Animation among the audience.) At this moment I would have thought differently. I would have, most likely, supported this proposal, too. (Laughter and applause among the audience.)

Ladies and gentlemen, comrades,

It so happens at the sharp, crucial turns of history that moments of truth are as necessary as the breath of life. As a result of the intensifying arms race, the international situation has become too dangerous, and too many stories on this score are spun to scare people. It has really become necessary to dispel this fog and to test words by deeds. The best way to do this is to have a frank talk, that kind of talk which is presupposed by a summit meeting, especially considering our states' role and responsibility in the world. Issues are discussed here on a different plane, where it is no longer possible to try to evade the truth. So, when we speak about the general results of the meeting, any hard-and-fast appraisal would hardly be right. Of course, it would have been much better if in Geneva we had reached accord on the crucial, key issue—the problem of terminating the arms race. Regrettably, this has not happened.

For the time being, the American side has proved to be unprepared for major decisions. But I think that it was impossible to complete this process within two days anyway, even if it had taken such a course. We have a mechanism. But at the same time the meeting is too important an event to be appraised by any simplified standards. It has made it possible to get a better idea of the character of our differences, to remove—at least, I think and hope so—some of the biased ideas with regard to the USSR and to the policy of its leadership, and to get rid of part of the amassed prejudices. This may have a favorable effect on the further course of developments. It is impossible to restore trust at once. This is no easy process. We paid attention to the assurances by the American President that the USA does not seek military superiority and does not want a nuclear war. It is our sincere wish that these statements be confirmed by deeds.

We would like to regard the summit as the commencement of a dialogue with a view to effecting changes for the better both in Soviet-American relations and in the world in general. In this sense I would appraise the meeting as one creating opportunities for progress.

Such is, in general outline, our appraisal of the results and significance of the Geneva meeting. And this gives me ample reason to look into the future with optimism as I am leaving hospitable Geneva. Common sense must prevail. See you again! (Applause.)

*   *   *

Mikhail Gorbachev then answered journalists' questions.

Question: (BBC, Great Britain). Mr. General Secretary, in your opinion, what are the prospects for relations between the USSR and the USA and for the international situation as a whole after the Geneva meeting?

Answer: For the most part, I optimistically look to the future. If we all continue to act in the spirit of responsibility both in Soviet-American relations and in international relations as a whole, which was nevertheless felt at the Geneva meeting, we shall find answers to the most burning issues and approaches to their solution. I am deeply convinced of this.

Question: (Soviet Television). You have mentioned the

need for a new approach in international relations today, even for a new way of thinking. What do you regard as the essence of such a new approach, a new way of thinking?

Answer: Yes, I am convinced that at this stage in international relations, which is characterized by a greater interrelationship of states, by their interdependence, a new policy is required.

We feel that the new approach makes it incumbent that the realities of today's world should nourish current policy for any state. This is the most important prerequisite for the constructiveness of a state's foreign policy. This is what will lead to an improvement of the situation in the world.

The problem of war and peace is the focal point of world politics. It is a special concern of all nations.

All countries—developed capitalist, socialist and developing—have economic problems, social problems and ecological problems. These problems can be more successfully solved on the basis of cooperation and mutual understanding. It takes a dialogue, it calls for more cooperation, it takes a pooling of efforts.

Take the problems of the developing world. We cannot fence ourselves off from them. And the new policy, based on realities, obliges us all to look for answers to the problems of this multitude of states which are striving for a better life.

The most important point—and I return to it—is that everything should be done to stop the arms race. An awareness of this is growing. Unless this problem is solved, all our other hopes, plans and actions can be undermined.

I am convinced that with the old approach, based on purely egoistic interests—although this is presented as the defense of national interests—there will be no movement forward. A new policy is required that will correspond to the present stage, taking into account the realities pushed to the fore by the very course of world development.

Question: (NBC, USA). During World War II the United States and the Soviet Union fought together against fascism and defeated it. Considering your talks with President Reagan, do you think that the Soviet Union and the United States of America can again become allies in the struggle against hunger in Africa, against international terrorism, against the pollution of the environment, against such diseases as cancer?

Answer: I thank you for your recalling an important stage of our common history. We remember it, we do not forget it. I think that as a result of the Geneva meeting opportunities will open up for broad cooperation between our countries and peoples. And when I say between our countries and peoples, I do not oversimplify the situation.

I know the depth of the differences now separating us. I'm conscious of the real state of current Soviet-American relations. But I am convinced that cooperation is possible, including on the problems you mentioned. I do not want to dwell now on the nuances of these problems. We shall be able to release huge funds to come to the aid of the developing countries.

Today, in Latin America alone, an enormous number of people, half of them children, are starving or are undernourished. A reduction of world arms spending by just 5 to 10 per cent would make it possible to remove this problem.

So all this deserves our giving thought to this problem.

I welcome your question and answer it affirmatively, although this does not mean that there are not certain nuances here in approaching the problems you mentioned.

Question: (NBC television network, USA). You have said that you are disappointed with President Reagan's response regarding the SDI. There are as many weapons now, after the meeting, as before it. Can it be said that the world has become safer after the Geneva summit, and if so, why?

Answer: I would venture claiming that although the amount of weapons has remained unchanged since before the meeting, the world has grown safer. Anyway, it seems to me that the meeting itself and its results are a definite contribution to the cause of security, since the meeting constitutes the beginning of the road to dialogue and understanding, or to the things that work for the benefit of security. In this sense, Geneva has certainly produced such an effect.

Question: (Pravda). What concrete, practical steps could be undertaken by the Soviet Union and the United States to secure the earliest end to the arms race?

Answer: Although I have devoted all of my speech here to this subject, I will say again: We must stop.

If we keep the arms race out of space, both our proposals and those proposed by the American side will allow us to move ahead, to look for compromises and to seek parity at a lower level. There is a good mechanism for this: the Geneva talks.

I would also add that we hope that the U.S. Administration still has not had its final say concerning the prohibition of all nuclear-weapons tests. The whole world is for such a ban. There is still time for the American side to consider the situation. A positive decision would be a momentous step stimulating the termination and reduction of the arms race.

I think that further intensification of the political dialogue between the USSR and the United States of America will likewise contribute to this process. We have agreed to expand it, and I think that the participation of the top leaders of our countries in this political dialogue will be instrumental in curbing the arms race.

Here is another point. The things dealt with at the Geneva talks, or the objectives and the subject of these talks, are a cause of all nations. Responsible politicians and, first of all, the leaders of states must adopt a firm and constructive stand on this issue. That would be a move of colossal importance.

I think that the overwhelming majority of politicians are in favor of speeding up the search for solutions in Geneva and of finding ways to stop the arms race and to proceed to disarmament.

Question: (GDR Television). What are, in your opinion, the most important results of the meeting? And another question: What is the significance of top-level political dialogue?

Answer: To answer your question, I would first of all point out that the Geneva meeting is an important stage in Soviet-American relations. It lays the groundwork for the search for ways to improve and normalize them in all directions. If this search continues in the future joint efforts of the two sides, it will help improve the situation in the world. This is what I would call the political result.

At the Geneva meeting attention was focused on the issues which concern all nations of the world. The Joint Statement by the leaders of the Soviet Union and the United States saying that nuclear war is impossible, that it should never be started, that they are not seeking military superiority and that they will impart a fresh impetus to the Geneva talks—is of great importance in itself if it is consistenty implemented with practical moves.

Now the second question. I think that the meeting has shown that under any conditions the thing to be done is to try and maintain a political dialogue which helps compare mutual positions, to understand each other better and to look for mutually acceptable solutions to the most distressing problems of today's world on this basis.

Question: (The Italian newspaper *Il Mattino*). The Soviet Union suffered heavy material and human losses during the Second World War. This notwithstanding, don't you think that 40 years after the end of the war the Soviet Union could help with the unification of the two German states?

Answer: I think that this question was very thoroughly discussed and considered at the conference in Helsinki. The Helsinki process and the Final Act signed by all states of Europe, as well as by the USA and Canada, are our common achievement. The Helsinki process deserves being supported and developed in every way. That is why it is the results of the Helsinki Conference that provide an answer to your question.

Question: (Swiss Radio). You stressed the deep distinction in the stand of the USSR and the USA on "Star Wars." Will this not hamper progress at the Geneva talks?

Answer: I do not want to repeat what I have said before. Our stance can be expressed in a few words. We adhere to a constructive line at the Geneva negotiations. We shall do our best to come to decisions to stop the arms race and to effect a radical reduction of nuclear armaments so as to really achieve, at one of the subsequent stages, the elimination of nuclear weapons with the participation of all nuclear powers. It is our strong belief that this is possible if the door to an arms race in outer space is bricked up.

Question: (Associated Press). You spoke about the President's personal allegiance to the "Star Wars" program and said that you had discussed the SDI in detail. What was his attitude to your arguments? How did he react to them? Do you see any chance to get things moving in this field?

Answer: I think that after the meeting the American side has ample reason to think over everything we have said. We hope for understanding of our arguments. In our view, their logic is in line with the spirit of the January accord, namely, that as a result of the Geneva talks we must take the road of drastic reductions of nuclear armaments provided an arms race in space is prevented.

This objective was jointly determined by us earlier. The U.S. President states that the SDI is a shield. I hope that we have convincingly shown that it is a space weapon which can be used against missiles, against satellites and against targets on Earth. It is a new type of weapon. A new sphere of the arms race is thereby opened. This is unacceptable. This would complicate the whole situation and would make the atmosphere at the Geneva talks problematic.

That is why I appreciate the fact that it was stressed at the level of the U.S. President and the General Secretary of the CPSU Central Committee that the work at the negotiations in Geneva would be speeded up on the basis of the January accord.

Now it is already a point of view confirmed by the signatures of not only the ministers of foreign affairs but also of the leaders of the two states. We view this as a certain signal and hope.

Question: (BBC). If you do not succeed in coming to agreement on stopping the arms race in space, would the Soviet Union be able to compete with American technology in this field or will it fall behind?

Answer: You have touched on a very interesting subject. I

tried to explain to the President in a very open and straightforward talk that, as it seems to me, much in American policy in respect to the Soviet Union is built on delusions. On the one hand, some hope that the continued arms race will wear out the Soviet Union economically, weaken its influence in the world and so give the United States of America a free hand. History has put such prophets to shame. And that was at a time when our society had a different potential from what it has today and had smaller opportunities. Now we have immense potential, and delusions regarding us only stand in the way of a realistic policy.

On the other hand, there have been delusions in terms of military calculations. There was an attempt to outdo us. They phased in intercontinental ballistic missiles. Our response followed. A little later, but it did follow. Next came independently targetable nuclear warheads. The response followed. We always found the way to respond.

Now, as it seems to me, the illusions in the U.S. military establishment have affected, to some extent, political quarters, perhaps, the President, too. I do not maintain this, yet that is the impression we have formed.

Some people in the U.S. apparently believe that the Americans have a certain edge on us in some aspects of technology, computer technology and radioelectronics. Again there is a desire, seizing upon that edge, to secure military superiority. Once more some are quoting President Johnson, who once said that the nation that would dominate space would dominate the Earth as well. There are some people who have their fingers itching to obtain world supremacy and look down upon the world. Those are old ambitions of bygone years. The world has changed very much in many ways.

So, speaking of the so-called technological superiority that the SDI is supposed to bring with it and thus put the Soviet Union into an awkward predicament, I want to say that this is yet another delusion. We would find the way to respond.

That is just what I told the President. Please note that there are no simpletons here.

If the President is so much committed to the SDI, we,

understandably, consider it our duty to thoroughly analyze the "Star Wars" program.

And so we did. Especially since there has been a kind of invitation from the American side: Let us see, let us analyze it, let us talk not of how to prevent space from being militarized, but of what kind of weapon to take into space. We are against that. We are against an arms race in space.

We have looked into another aspect of the matter. Suppose, the Americans do not accept our arguments and do not appreciate our goodwill and our appeal to find a way to end the arms race and cut the available stocks of nuclear weapons, that is, if they continued to move in the same direction. We would, of course, find a way to respond.

The Soviet leadership gave appropriate instructions to competent organizations and scientists at one time, and we can say that our response would be effective, less expensive and could come within shorter time limits.

But that is not our political choice. Our choice is to prompt the U.S. to think over the entire situation, after all, and pursue a responsible policy based on common sense and the mood and aspirations of people rather than compound what is the most dramatic problem of international relations.

Question: (Czechoslovakian Television and the newspaper *Rude Pravo*). In what particular, practical fields do you perceive chances for developing Soviet-American relations after meeting with President Reagan?

Answer: I think the political dialogue will be furthered, and it will be conducted at various levels. We agreed to exchange visits, something that in itself must be welcomed. We will have more opportunities to promote bilateral cooperation in those spheres which we agreed upon. Apparently, we will continue and expand our consultations on regional problems and the situations in various parts of the world.

Finally, we proceed from a premise that both in our country and in the U.S. business community there is still a good deal of mutual interest—I know this for certain—in improving relations. If things go that way, the scope of economic cooperation may be expanded. We are prepared to invite U.S. businesses to take part in implementing some big projects. Our plans are vast. We are doing a lot to expand our cooperation with the Western Europeans. And we welcome it.

I conveyed to the President the idea that one cannot underestimate economic relations, and not just because they cannot do without us, or that we cannot do without the USA. We can do well without the USA, and, I hope, America can do well without us. But this is the material base for a political relationship, for its being made healthier, for enhancing the atmosphere of confidence.

Honestly speaking, economic ties engender mutual dependence. This mutual dependence is then reflected in the solutions to political problems. I think that it would be both to the advantage of the Soviet Union and the United States of America to continue furthering economic ties. But please don't think we are begging for this.

Question: (The Lebanese newspaper *Al Nahar Arab Report*). Did you discuss the situation in the Middle East, above all, that in Lebanon while speaking about regional problems? What is your forecast for the situation there after the Summit?

Answer: During the meeting we dealt with the situation in such regions as Central America, the Middle East and Africa. However, most of the time was devoted to discussing the principled aspects of these issues. We agreed to continue political consultations and expand the scope of cooperation in dealing with regional problems.

Question: (Soviet author Yulian Semyonov). Mikhail Sergeyevich, you have spoken about the need to learn the art of living together. My experience as an author tells me that since the sad times of McCarthy, the films and television of the United States have unfortunately been portraying the Soviet people to the American people as something like monsters. Don't you think that after the Geneva meeting it would be very important if in the USA they abandoned that kind of biased thinking and looked in a more impartial manner upon the Soviet people, as partners of the American people?

Answer: Here is what I am going to tell you, Comrade Semyonov. Don't you try to make political leaders shoulder all the burdens. (Animation in the hall.) We agreed to further cultural contacts—which include films—so please meet them and negotiate with them. One must act in the spirit of Geneva, meaning work for an improvement in Soviet-American relations.

20

A REPORT
TO THE USSR SUPREME
SOVIET SESSION
ON THE RESULTS
OF THE GENEVA SUMMIT
AND THE INTERNATIONAL
SITUATION

COMRADE deputies,

Major questions of the domestic and foreign policies of the Soviet state have been submitted for discussion at the current session of the USSR Supreme Soviet.

The laws on the state economic and social development plan of the USSR and on the state budget for 1986, passed by this session, are extremely important to our country, to its present and future, to every work collective, to every Soviet family. The new year, 1986, ushers in not merely the first year of the Twelfth Five-Year Plan period but a qualitatively new stage in the development of Soviet society.

The 1986 plan reflects the strategic policy of the Party toward accelerating the country's socioeconomic development. It provides for higher rates of growth of the national income, industrial and agricultural production, and labor productivity. Efficiency in the use of material resources will increase. Priority is given to developing the branches that are called upon to ensure scientific and technical progress and improve the quality of products.

Measures have been set forth for speeding up the reconstruction, refurbishing and modernization of production that will perfect management and the economic mechanism. A further rise in the people's well-being is envisaged.

It is important, Comrades, that all of us constantly take into account the specific features of the plan for 1986.

An even pace for all five years should be set as early as the first year of the five-year plan period. Proceeding from this, rates for developing the national economy for 1986 have been envisaged so that their implementation, as intensity gradually grows in subsequent years, will facilitate the implementation of assignments for the five-year period on the whole. This will help avoid the situation that occurred during the previous five-year period when reduced targets were fixed for the first years, while the major increment was planned for the final years. The negative results that this practice brought about are known.

The second specific feature of the plan is that it was shaped with the greatest consideration for the need to speed up scientific and technical progress. Proceeding from the directive of the June conference at the CPSU Central Committee, the plan includes, on a top-priority basis, assignments to accelerate the scientific and technical progress envisaged by resolutions on developing major directions in science and technology in branches of the national economy. Simultaneously, established principles in planning were largely revised. For the first time, the plan provides for generalized key indicators of the effectiveness of scientific and technical progress in the branches of the economy. These indicators are put in place with a view toward invigorating the practical work of ministries, amalgamations and enterprises, and toward ensuring advancement to the top levels of scientific and technical development.

The next specific feature of the 1986 plan is its orientation toward carrying out practical transfers to intensive methods of running the economy. This is dictated by life itself, by the complex situation of labor and material resources, and by the near exhaustion of extensive factors of economic growth. Next year, we are to achieve production growth through a maximum saving of resources. In other words, saving is actually becoming the main means of providing resources for the entire increment of production. Here are some figures that illustrate the point. Next year, 97 per cent of production growth will be gained through raised labor productivity. Metal consumption in the national income will drop by 2.7 per cent, and energy consumption will fall by three per cent.

And finally, an extensive transition to new methods of management has proved to be positive. Starting from January 1986, more than half of products manufactured by industry will be at enterprises working under the new conditions.

In general, Comrades, the policy is correct. Now we are to make it material—both in the process of further detailed elaboration of plans in the branches, republics, territories and regions, in amalgamations and enterprises, and, naturally, in concrete practical work. This aspect should be emphasized also because many workers in the center and in the provinces, including at planning and economic bodies, are not fully aware of the importance of assessing and resolving in a new way the country's economic, social and financial problems.

The current session is held at a crucial period immediately preceding the Party congress. The April Plenary Meeting of the Central Committee of the CPSU charted the course toward accelerating the social and economic development of society, marked the beginning of substantive changes in approaching the fulfillment of economic and political tasks, and set a new rhythm for all the work of Party, state and local government bodies and all our cadres and workers' collectives.

The Party's political course, both in domestic matters and international problems, has found its fullest reflection in the theoretical and political documents of paramount importance that will be submitted for consideration to the Twenty-seventh Congress of the CPSU. These are the draft of the new edition of the CPSU program, the proposed changes in the Party rules, and the Draft Guidelines for the Economic and Social Development of the USSR for 1986-1990 and in the Period till the Year 2000.

The Party is determined to be responsive to the people, and the first results of vast discussions show that the documents submitted for consideration evoke the profound satisfaction of the Soviet people. Our optimism, our confidence that the chosen road is correct and that what has been planned will certainly be fulfilled stems from the vigorous support for the Party's strategic course, supported by word and deed.

As you know, comrade deputies, the Central Committee of the Party and the Soviet Government have undertaken of late a number of important measures aimed at speeding up the switching of the economy toward intensive development and enhancing the efficiency of the management of the national economy. Further practical measures are being taken toward putting things in order, strengthening labor and state discipline, enforcing strict economy and combatting drunkenness and alcoholism.

In other words, vast, intensive work has been started in all spheres of public life, and it is beginning to bear fruit.

The new factors that are introduced into our life have now stirred up the Soviet people, boosted their creativity and showed once again the vastness of the resources and possibilities inherent in the socialist system.

We can now say with certainty that things have begun to look up. The growth rate of production is rising and other economic indicators are improving. Despite setbacks in a number of sectors of the national economy at the start of the year, the Soviet people managed to put the situation right and to ensure the fulfillment of economic plan targets. Change for the better is taking place in the agrarian sector of the country as well.

Immense credit for what has been achieved goes to our heroic working class, which sparing neither effort nor energy and overcoming difficulties has done everything possible to meet the plan targets. The positive results achieved are representative of the strenuous work of the collective farmers and all the other workers in the agroindustrial complex. Our achievements embody the creative thought of scientists, engineers and the people's intelligentsia. Soviet young people, who boldly and energetically come to grips with difficult and complex tasks and vigorously support the ongoing changes in our society, linking to it their own future, have pioneered and initiated many important undertakings.

We also associate these changes with the activization of the work of the Party, government and trade union bodies, and of all our cadres.

In short, comrade deputies, a good deal is being done. However, it would be an error to overestimate all this—and it is not our custom anyway. We are at the start of the road we have planned, the road which is arduous and difficult and which calls for a combination of a creative approach to the tasks posed by practice with a purposefulness and a high sense of discipline and dedication. We have immense reserves and opportunities and we must work hard to tap them and to use them to maximum benefit. This is to be done in every area of economic and cultural development, primarily in those in which the situation remains complex and which are slow to catch up and gain momentum.

Now that the current five-year period is drawing to a close, one should work hard so that we may start the next year with a confident and dynamic advance, ensure that the targets planned will be reached, and create the prerequisites for a further qualitative transformation of the country's productive forces.

Comrades, the plan for 1986 shows patently the peaceful, constructive nature of our concerns. Our foreign policy aspirations, the international policy of the Soviet state, are closely linked with this peaceful trend of domestic policy.

The foreign policy guidelines of the April Plenary Meeting of the CPSU Central Committee have become a concrete manifestation of Leninist foreign policy at the present stage. The plenary meeting has emphasized the need to intensify to the utmost the Soviet Union's peaceful policy on the broadest front of international relations. It has called for doing everything to ensure that the forces of militarism and aggression shall not prevail. It has emphasized the urgency of ending the arms race, of stepping up the process of disarmament, declared for the development of equal, proper, civilized relations between states and for the widening and strengthening of mutually-advantageous economic ties.

The directives of the plenary meeting were dictated by the times, the specificities of the situation and the demands of the socialist policy of peace and progress. In its assessment the Politburo of the CPSU Central Committee proceeded from the premise that the degree of the unpredictability of events grows as a result of the continuing arms race. The possibility of the militarization of outer space signifies a qualitatively new leap in the arms race. It would inevitably result in the disappearance of the very notion of strategic stability—the basis for the preservation of peace in the nuclear age. A situation would develop in which fundamentally new decisions, irreversible in their consequences, would in fact be taken by computers without the participation of the human mind and of political will, without taking into account the criteria of ethics and morality. Such a development of events could result in a universal catastrophe—even if the initial impulse were given by an error, miscalculation, or technical malfunctioning of sophisticated computer systems.

In other words, the development of world events has approached the point when especially responsible decisions are required, when lack of action or delay is criminal: For the point at issue today is the preservation of civilization and life itself. That is why we have believed and continue to believe that all necessary measures should be taken to break the vicious circle of the arms race, so as not to miss a single chance of reversing the course of events for the better. The question today is acute and definite in the extreme: It is necessary to rise above narrow interests, to realize the collective responsibility of all states in the face of the danger that looms over the human race at the threshold of the Third Millennium.

The April Plenary Meeting of the CPSU has instructed us to take precisely this line in the implementation of our foreign policy. This line is fully in keeping with the interests of the Soviet people and the peoples of socialist states. And, as we have become convinced, it has met with understanding in other countries. During a brief period of time marked by important international events, the Soviet Union has striven to interact in the interests of peace with a great number of states. We have been and are proceeding from the view that the period of dangerous tension can be ended only by the efforts of all countries, big and small.

Political and economic ties with countries of the socialist community have been intensified and deepened considerably in the past months. Long-term programs of cooperation in the sphere of economy and scientific and technical progress have been drawn up. A mechanism for effective, concrete ties has been created. Coordination of foreign policy activity has become more intensive. The meetings of the leaders of fraternal countries in Moscow, Warsaw, Sofia and Prague have become important milestones on the road of the further rallying of the socialist community. Ties with all the socialist countries develop and strengthen.

Cooperation with states that have gotten rid of colonial oppression, that participate in the nonaligned movement, assumes a broader nature. Important steps have been taken in the development of relations with many of those countries. This is a factor of great importance in the turbulent ocean of present-day international relations, a factor that operates in favor of peace, equality, freedom and the independence of peoples.

The Soviet Union is making an effort to improve ties with capitalist states as well. I will single out the recent Soviet-French summit in Paris, in the course of which substantial steps were undertaken toward the further development of bilateral cooperation, consolidation of European and international security and return to détente.

We will continue to build our foreign policy on a multiple foundation, on the basis of firm and stable bilateral relations with all countries. But the reality of today's world is such that there are states which—due to their military, economic, scientific and technical potential, and international position—bear a special responsibility for the character of world development, its course and consequences. It is primarily the Soviet Union and the United States which have this responsibility, I stress responsibility—not privilege.

Looking at things from this position, the Soviet-American summit held last week is, as the Politburo of the Central Committee of the CPSU assesses, an important event—not only in our bilateral relations, but in world politics on the whole. I have already shared my first impressions of the talks with the U.S. President at the press conference in Geneva. The meeting's final document—the Joint Statement—is known too.

Today, speaking at the session of the USSR Supreme Soviet, I would like to appraise the results and significance of the Geneva meeting in the context of the present-day situation, with due account taken for past experience and prospects for the future and for the tasks that we have to tackle.

First of all I must say that the road to the Geneva dialogue was long and arduous for many reasons. The U.S. Administration, which came to office in the early 1980s, openly assumed a course of confrontation while rejecting the very possibility of a positive development of Soviet-American relations. I think everyone remembers even today the pitch of anti-Soviet rhetoric of those years and the power politics practiced by the U.S. ruling circles.

The mutual efforts over many years to achieve the essential minimum of trust in those relations were committed to oblivion, and virtually every thread of bilateral cooperation was snapped. Détente itself was branded as being contrary to the interests of the United States of America.

Having assumed a course for reaching military superiority over the USSR, the Administration went ahead with programs for nuclear and other rearmament of the USA. U.S. first-strike missiles began to be deployed in Western Europe. In this way a situation was taking shape that was fraught with high-level military and political uncertainties and concomitant risks.

Lastly, there appeared a "Star Wars" program, the so-called "Strategic Defense Initiative." They in Washington became obsessed with it without giving much thought to those grave consequences which were bound to ensue if this idea were translated into practice. The plan to introduce weapons in outer space is extremely dangerous to all the peoples of the world, to all without exception.

But we knew something else as well: Such U.S. policies would inevitably clash with reality. And it happened. The Soviet Union together with its allies unequivocally declared that they would not allow military superiority over themselves.

Confusion emerged even among U.S. allies in the face of Washington's apparent disregard for the interests of their security, and its readiness to bank all on the pursuit of the will-o'-the-wisp of military superiority. In the United States itself this course generated serious doubts. The proclamation of the "Star Wars" preparation plans sounded alarm bells throughout the world.

It was miscalculation on the part of those who thought that their line of confrontation would determine world development. I will add, perhaps, in this connection, that dreams of world domination are basically wrong—both in what concerns the objective and in what concerns the means. As with designs of perpetual motion motors born out of a lack of knowledge of the elementary laws of nature, so imperial claims grow out of notions about the world which are far removed from present-day reality.

While giving a firm rebuff to the U.S. line of disrupting military-strategic equilibrium, the Soviet Union advanced large-scale peace initiatives and displayed restraint and constructiveness in the approach to the key issues of peace and security.

Our initiatives, and there are quite a number of them, clearly showed what we are seeking to achieve in the world arena, what we are urging the United States and its allies to do. These actions by the USSR found the enthusiastic approval of the world public. They were highly valued by the governments of many countries.

Under the influence of these factors, Washington was compelled to maneuver. Signs of demonstrative peacefulness appeared in the U.S. Administration's statements. They were not backed by deeds, but their very appearance was symptomatic.

Early this year an agreement was reached, at our initiative, on new talks between the USSR and the United States, talks to encompass the entire complex of space and nuclear armaments in their interrelationship, and aimed at preventing an arms race in outer space and terminating it on Earth.

The atmosphere of Soviet-American relations, and to some extent the international behavior of the United States, started to undergo changes which in fact, naturally, had to be taken into account when considering the possibility of holding a summit meeting.

By adopting this decision, we firmly proceeded from the premise that central to the talks would be the questions that determine our relations and the world situation in general—security issues. At that, we took into account political and strategic realities in Europe and the world, the opinion of our friends and allies, the views of the governments and public circles of many countries and their persistent calls on the Soviet Union to do everything possible so that the summit meeting would be held. We understood how many hopes were pinned on the meeting all over the world, and we undertook concrete steps to improve the international climate and to make it more favorable for the meeting.

We have put forward concrete and radical proposals in the Geneva negotiations on nuclear and space arms. What is their substance?

We have first of all proposed prohibiting space strike arms completely. We did so because the beginning of an arms race in outer space, and even only the deployment in near-Earth space of antimissile systems, will not contribute to the security of any state. Hidden behind a space "shield," offensive nuclear systems will become even more dangerous.

The appearance of space strike arms could turn the present strategic balance into a strategic chaos, could cause the arms race to proceed feverishly in all directions, and could undercut one of the fundamental pillars of its limitation—the ABM Treaty. As a result, mistrust in relations between states will grow and security will diminish considerably.

Further, in the conditions of the complete prohibition of space strike weapons we have proposed halving all nuclear systems of the USSR and the U.S. capable of reaching each other's territory and limiting the total number of nuclear warheads on such systems belonging to either side by a ceiling of 6,000. These are radical reductions of thousands of nuclear warheads.

Such an approach is fully justified. It embraces all those systems which form the strategic correlation of forces. It also makes it possible to take due account of the nuclear threat which really exists with respect to either side, regardless of how and from where nuclear warheads can be delivered to a territory, whether by missile or plane, from one's own territory or the territory of one's allies.

We regard the reduction of nuclear systems of the USSR and the U.S. by 50 per cent as a beginning. We are prepared to go further, right down to the complete elimination of nuclear weapons—a process in which other states having nuclear weapons should, naturally enough, be involved too.

It does not take much to realize that the race in nuclear arms is a source of special concern to European nations. We understand well why this is so. Europe is overflowing with nuclear systems. The Soviet Union stands for completely removing nuclear weapons, both medium-range and tactical ones, from Europe. However, the U.S. and its NATO partners do not agree to that. Then we proposed to start at least with provisional decisions and then to work toward further reductions. We are convinced that our proposals accord with the hopes of European nations for lessening the nuclear threat and enhancing European security.

I would like to emphasize the principled aspect of the matter: In the three areas of the negotiations—space, strategic offensive arms and medium-range nuclear systems—we do not propose to the U.S. anything that would lessen its security. Moreover, our proposals make it possible to resolve such issues which the American side elevates to the rank of its "special concerns."

For example, much is said about the Soviet intercontinental ballistic missiles. Our proposals provide for a reduction of the number of such missiles and the limitation of the share of their warheads in the overall number of nuclear munitions. Or, here is another example. There has been quite an outcry in the West around the Soviet SS-20 missiles. We propose reducing them substantially in the context of solving the problem of nuclear medium-range weapons in Europe.

Britain and France's nuclear weapon systems are presented as a stumbling block. It is said that they cannot be discussed at the Soviet-American talks. Well, we are prepared to seek a solution to this, too. We propose to start a direct exchange of opinions with those countries about their nuclear arms.

The Soviet proposals are met with a broad and positive response in the world. They are backed by the prestige of the Warsaw Treaty member states, which unanimously supported our constructive stand. Joint statements of the leaders of six countries—Argentina, Mexico, Tanzania, India, Sweden and

Greece—are largely consonant with our approach. The Soviet initiative was received with approval and hope by communist and workers' parties, large public organizations of different countries and continents, scientists of world renown, prominent politicians and military leaders. It evoked the positive response of most of the parties of the Socialist International.

What is more, there were thousands of letters from Soviet and foreign citizens that were addressed to me on the eve of the Geneva meeting and during it. I wish to take the opportunity to express gratitude to their authors for their good wishes, for their advice and support, and for their profound and sincere concern over safeguarding peace.

The Americans advanced their counterproposals on the eve of the meeting. This was a positive fact in itself. One of our numerous initiatives evoked a favorable response.

A lot was written in the press about the essence of these counterproposals. I shall not repeat their contents. I shall only say that these are indeterminate and largely inequitable proposals. They are based on a one-sided approach and are clearly prompted by a striving for the military superiority of the United States and NATO as a whole.

But the main thing is that the United States' stand does not envisage a ban on the creation of space strike arms. Quite the contrary, it seeks to legalize their creation. The stand assumed by the U.S. side in the question of "Star Wars" is the main obstacle to agreement on arms control. And this is not only our opinion. The governments of France, Denmark, Norway, Greece, the Netherlands, Canada and Australia refused to take part in the so-called "Strategic Defense Initiative." On the eve of the Geneva meeting the United Nations General Assembly adopted a resolution urging the leaders of the USSR and the USA to work out effective agreements aimed at the prevention of an arms race in space and its termination on Earth. It is only the United States and some of its allies that deemed it possible not to support this clear call of the world community. A fact, as it is said, that needs no comment.

It should also be recalled, perhaps, that there were powerful political forces at work in the United States, doing whatever they could to thwart the meeting or at least to make it meaningless and to nullify its importance. I think such steps as the test of an ASAT system, the entrance of the battleship *Iowa* with long-range cruise missiles into the Baltic, the speedy deployment of Pershings in West Germany, the decision on the development of binary chemical weapons and, finally, the adoption of a new all-time record military budget are fresh in the memory of many people.

Moreover, the President was already on his way to Geneva when a letter from the U.S. Defense Secretary, pleading with him not to make any agreements with the Soviet Union which would reaffirm the treaties on the limitation of strategic offensive weapons and on antimissile defense systems, was made public. In other words, the Defense Secretary wanted the USA to have a completely free hand to act in every venue of the arms race on Earth and in space.

And indeed, was the Pentagon alone standing in the way? We did not overlook either the "mandate" given to the U.S. President by the forces of the American extreme right-wing represented by their ideological headquarters, the Heritage Foundation. The President was instructed to carry on the arms race, not to give the Soviet Union any opportunity to convert resources to socioeconomic development programs and to seek eventually to crowd the USSR out of international politics. Those gentlemen went so far as to formulate for the U.S. Administration the task of forcing us to alter our system, to revise our Constitution! These are familiar tunes, Comrades. We have heard all this on more than one occasion. In short, there were quite a few attacks.

Yet we decided in favor of meeting the U.S. President. We took that decision because we had no right to disregard even the slightest chance to reverse dangerous world developments. We took that decision in the awareness that if we failed to start a direct and frank discussion now, tomorrow it would be a hundred times more difficult, if at all possible.

It is beyond question that differences between us are immense. But the interrelationship and interdependence between us in the present-day world is similarly immense. The crucial times we are living through leave the leaders of the USSR and the USA, the peoples of the USSR and the USA, no alternative to learning the great art of living together.

During our first one-on-one conversation with the President—and those conversations featured prominently at the Geneva meeting—it was stated directly that the Soviet delegation had come to seek solutions to the most urgent problem in the area of international affairs, the problem of averting nuclear war and curbing the arms race. That, as I told the President, was the main meaning of our meeting and that was what would determine its results.

I must stress that the Geneva talks were sometimes very acute and, I would say, frank to the utmost. It was impossible either to hoodwink each other there or to get away with political or propaganda stereotypes—too much depends on the pivotal questions of war and peace.

The American side stubbornly insisted at the meeting on going ahead with the SDI program. We were told that the point was the development of purely defensive systems, which were not even weapons as such. We were also told that those systems would help to stabilize the situation and to get rid of nuclear weapons altogether. There was even the proposal that in some foreseeable future these systems would be "shared" with us and that the two sides should open the doors of their laboratories to each other.

We frankly told the President that we did not agree to these evaluations. We had thoroughly analyzed all those questions and our conclusion was unequivocal. Space weapons are not at all defensive. They can breed the dangerous illusion that it is possible to deliver a first nuclear strike from behind a space "shield" and to avert, or at least weaken, retaliation. And what are the guarantees that space weapons in themselves would not be used against targets on Earth? There is every indication that the U.S. space-based ABM system is being conceived precisely as a component of an integrated offensive complex rather than as a "shield."

Naturally, we cannot agree to the allegation that the programed space systems are not weapons altogether. Neither can we rely on the assurances that the United States will share with us what they will develop in that field.

So if the doors of the laboratories have to be opened, it is only to verify compliance with a ban on the development of space strike weapons but not to legalize these weapons.

We are told about a desire to remove the fear of missiles and to achieve the total elimination of nuclear weapons. This desire can only be welcomed and it is fully in accord with the goals of our policy. But it is far easier to eliminate these weapons without developing space strike systems. Why spend tens and hundreds of billions of dollars and pile up mountains of space weapons in addition to nuclear armaments? What is the point?

I asked the President if the American leadership believed in all seriousness that at a time when American space weapons were being developed we would reduce our strategic potential and help the United States with our own hands to weaken this potential. No hopes should be pinned on this. Quite the contrary will happen: To regain the balance, the Soviet Union will have to improve the efficiency and accuracy and to raise the yield of its weapons so as to neutralize, if necessary, the electronic space machinery of "Star Wars" that is being developed by the Americans.

And will the Americans feel more secure if our weapons in space will be added to the echelons of space weapons planned by Washington? Indeed, the USA cannot really hope to achieve a monopoly in outer space. At least, not seriously.

However, the American Administration is still tempted to try out the possibility of achieving military superiority. At present, too, by designing an arms race in outer space, they hope to surpass us in the field of electronics and computers. But we will find a response, just as it happened several times in the past. The response will be effective, sufficiently prompt and, perhaps, less costly than the American program. We put this idea across to the President.

I think that in order to achieve a real turn in our relations, which would meet the interests of the USSR, the United States and the interests of the peoples of the world, what is required are new approaches, a fresh look at many things and, what is most important, political will on the part of the leadership of the two countries. The USSR—and I emphasized that in Geneva—does not feel enmity toward the United States, and it respects the American people. We are not building our policy on the desire to infringe on the national interests of the United States. I will say more: We would not like, for instance, a change of the strategic balance in our favor. We would not like that because such a situation will enhance the suspicion of the other side, will enhance the instability of the overall situation.

Life is developing in such a way that both our countries will have to grow accustomed to strategic parity as a natural state. We will have to come to a joint understanding in which the level of arms of either side can be considered relatively sufficient from the point of view of its dependable defense. We are convinced that the level of such sufficiency is well below what the USSR and the United States actually have at the present time. And this means that tangible practical steps in arms limitation and reduction are quite possible. These are measures which will not diminish the security of the USSR and the U.S. or the overall strategic stability in the world. On the contrary, they will enhance them.

What can be said about other questions discussed at the meeting?

I will begin with the problem of regional conflicts. Both sides expressed concern over the continuing existence of such "trouble spots." It is easy to understand why. Such conflicts are a dangerous thing, especially in light of the threat of their escalation in this nuclear age.

However, it can be said that our approaches to their causes and ways for settling such conflicts are not simply different— they are diametrically opposite. The United States, which is used to thinking in terms of "spheres of interests," reduces these problems to East-West rivalry. But these days it is an anachronism, a relapse into imperial thinking, which denies the right of a majority of nations to think and take decisions independently.

The deep-lying causes of such conflicts are multifaceted—to an extent they are rooted in history, but mainly, in those social and economic conditions into which the emergent countries have been put. It is definitely not by chance that in discussing the problem of regional conflicts the U.S. does not mention the atrocities of apartheid in South Africa, the aggression staged by that country against its African neighbors, the wars fought by American puppets in Central America and Southeast Asia, Israel's banditry in the Middle East and many other things. Washington is trying to equate the legitimate governments of the states that follow the path of national liberation and social progress with counterrevolution.

It goes without saying that we could not accept such an interpretation of the situation. The President was told that we are for the recognition of the inalienable right of every people to freedom and independence, to an independent choice of their road. We wish this right not to be flouted by anyone. There should be no attempts at outside interference. Freedom, not tyranny, should prevail. We have been and remain on the side of peoples upholding their independence. This is our principled line.

The President touched upon the question of Afghanistan. It was confirmed again in this connection that the Soviet Union consistently declares for a political settlement of the situation around Afghanistan. We stand for friendly neighboring Afghanistan to be an independent nonaligned state, for establishing a practice of guaranteed noninterference in Afghanistan's affairs. The question of withdrawal of Soviet troops from that country will thus also be resolved. The Soviet Union and the Government of Afghanistan are wholly for this. And if anybody hinders an early resolution of that question, it is, above all, the United States, which is financing, backing and arming gangs of counterrevolutionaries and is frustrating efforts at the normalization of the situation in Afghanistan.

Matters of bilateral relations assumed an important place

at the talks. A certain invigoration that has started in this area of late has now been borne out with concrete agreements on exchanges and contacts in the sphere of science, education and culture and on the resumption of air services between the two countries.

The potential inherent in this will, naturally, be much easier to bring into play in full measure under conditions where security matters decisive for our mutual relations start being tackled. If we are to cooperate, this must be cooperation on an equal footing, without any discrimination and preliminary terms advanced, without attempts at interference in internal affairs of the other side. Our stand on this is firm and consistent.

How can the main results of the Geneva meeting be assessed?

The meeting was, undoubtedly, a significant event. It was direct, clear and concrete talk, and the possibility to compare positions was useful. Too many explosive, acute problems are heaped up, problems that needed to be considered in earnest in order to try to overcome the deadlock on them.

We appreciate personal contact established with the President of the United States. A dialogue of top leaders is always a moment of truth in relations between states. It is important that such a dialogue has been held. It is a stabilizing factor in itself in the present troubled times.

But we are realists and we must say outright that solution of the most important questions connected with an end to the arms race was not achieved at the meeting. The unwillingness of the U.S. leadership to give up the program of "Star Wars" has made it impossible to achieve in Geneva concrete arrangements on real disarmament, above all, on the cardinal problem of nuclear and space arms. The amount of arms stockpiled by both sides has not lessened as a result of the meeting. The arms race continues. This cannot but cause disappointment.

There remain major differences between the USSR and the United States on a number of other issues of principle concerning the situation in the world and developments in individual regions. But we are also far from belittling the significance of the Geneva Accords.

I will recall the most important of them. These are, above all, the common understanding, sealed in the Joint Statement, that a nuclear war cannot be won and must never be fought, and the pledge by the USSR and the United States to build their relations proceeding from this indisputable truth, and not to seek military superiority.

We believe that this understanding, jointly endorsed at the highest level, should actually underlie the foreign policy of the two states. Since it is acknowledged that a nuclear war, by its very nature, cannot help attain any rational end, therefore, the stronger the stimulus should be in favor of its prevention, the termination of the development and testing of weapons of mass annihilation and the complete elimination of the stockpiles of nuclear armaments. Still more, it is inadmissible to open new directions in the arms race. Of course, the Joint Statement is not a treaty, but it is a principled directive that commits the leaders of the two countries to much.

Further, the USSR and the United States clearly reaffirmed their pledge to facilitate in all ways the enhancement of the effectiveness of the nuclear nonproliferation regime and agreed on practical steps in this direction. This is of no little importance in the disquieting present-day international situation for maintaining world stability and diminishing the risk of nuclear wars.

The Joint Statement of the leaders of the two countries in favor of the universal and complete prohibition and elimination of such barbarous weapons of mass destruction as chemical weapons has basic importance. We express hope that the United States will observe that important understanding in practical politics as well.

The agreement of the leadership of the USSR and USA to contribute jointly with the other states participating in the Stockholm Conference to its early completion, with the adoption of a document which would include both concrete obligations on the nonuse of force and mutually acceptable confidence-building measures, goes far beyond the boundaries of Soviet-American relations.

It is only to be welcomed that the meeting produced a number of useful agreements in many areas on the development of bilateral cooperation between the USSR and the USA. I hope that they will provide a good base for increasing trust between our countries and peoples. Naturally, this will be so if a careful attitude is taken to all the achievements and if everything positive built into those achievements is developed, but not if artificial pretexts are made up to throw them overboard.

The importance of the agreement reached in Geneva to continue political contacts between the Soviet Union and the United States, including new meetings at the summit level, should be mentioned specifically.

To sum it all up, we have every right to say that the overall balance sheet of the Geneva meeting is positive.

Undoubtedly, the constructive and consistent policy of our country contributed in a decisive degree to the achievement of such an encouraging outcome. Simultaneously, it would be wrong not to say here also that the position of the American side at the meeting included certain elements of realism, which helped to resolve a number of questions.

Of course, the real importance of everything useful agreed upon in Geneva can only manifest itself in practical deeds. I want to state in this context that the Soviet Union for its part intends not to slow down the pace and to seek most resolutely and in the spirit of honest cooperation with the United States the folding up of the arms race and the overall improvement of the international situation. We hope that the USA will display a similar approach. Then, I am certain, the work done in Geneva will bear real fruit.

This is our evaluation of that event and its role in international relations. I can say with satisfaction that this evaluation is shared by our allies, the fraternal socialist countries, and is borne out with utmost clarity by a meeting of the leaders of the Warsaw Treaty member countries in Prague immediately upon the completion of the Soviet-American summit talks.

The participants in the Prague meeting stressed that the

situation, of course, remained difficult. Struggle for improving it is being carried on but conditions for that struggle have become better, as can already be stated today. The Geneva meeting is an important element of our long-term joint and closely coordinated efforts to ensure peace.

A natural question to ask is: What is to be done now in the light of the results of the Soviet-American dialogue in Geneva?

As I have already said, we attach much importance to the agreement reached in Geneva on new Soviet-American summit meetings. I want to stress that our approach to this question is not formal. What is important is not the mere fact of another meeting between the leaders of the two countries but its results. The peoples will expect a practical advance on the road mapped out in Geneva. It is precisely this that we will be seeking. We should already begin making preparations for the next Soviet-American summit meeting now, first and foremost in the area of practical politics.

Not to make it more difficult to achieve new agreements, both sides, we are convinced, should first and foremost refrain from actions subverting what was achieved in Geneva, refrain from actions which could block talks and detract from the existing constraints on the arms race. This calls, *inter alia*, for strict and honest compliance with the treaty on the limitation of ABM systems and also for the further mutual respect by the sides for the relevant provisions of the SALT II Treaty.

But the main thing, of course, is to create a possibility for actually ending the arms race and initiating practical reductions in the existing nuclear arms arsenals.

Is there such a possibility? It is our firm conviction that there is. True, at present there are differences on many points between our proposals and the American proposals on nuclear arms reductions. But we do not overdramatize this circumstance. Compromises are possible here and we are prepared to look for them.

Undoubtedly, given such a course of developments, questions of dependable verification, in which the Soviet Union has a direct interest, could be resolved. One cannot rely on promises here, especially since the case in point is disarmament and the country's defenses.

But to resolve all these questions, it is absolutely essential to slam the door shut through which weapons could get into space. Without this, radical reductions in nuclear armaments are impossible. I want to state this with utmost responsibility on behalf of the Soviet people and their supreme body of power.

Accord is possible if it respects the interests of both sides. The stubborn desire of the American side to go ahead with the development of space weapons can have only one result, the blocking of the possibility of ending the nuclear arms race. This outcome, naturally, could bitterly disappoint the peoples of the whole world, including, I am certain, the American people.

There is a real chance today to sharply lessen the threat of nuclear war and subsequently to remove altogether any possibility of such a war. It would be a fatal mistake to miss that chance. We hope that what was said about the SDI in Geneva was not the last word of the American side.

We have come to terms with President Reagan on instructing our delegations to the Geneva talks on nuclear and space arms to speed up negotiations, carrying them forward on the basis of the January agreement between the two countries. Thus, it was confirmed by both sides at the highest level that it is necessary to prevent an arms race in space, resolving this question in conjunction with the reduction of nuclear arms. This is what the Soviet Union will press for. This is what we call upon the United States to do. By honoring the pledge we have made jointly with practical actions, we will live up to the hopes of the peoples of the world.

As time goes on the question of terminating nuclear tests is becoming more and more acute. This is so primarily because with an agreement an end would be put to the development of new types of nuclear weapons and the modernization of existing types. Further, without testing, without renovation, the gradual process of the withering away of nuclear arsenals and the demise of nuclear weapons would begin. Lastly, it is so because it is impossible to permit nuclear blasts—and their number stands in the hundreds—to deface our beautiful planet and intensify concern over how the succeeding generations will live on it.

This is why the Soviet Union has announced a moratorium on all types of nuclear tests till January 1, 1986, and is ready to extend this moratorium, given reciprocity on the part of the United States. We expect the U.S. leadership to make a concrete and positive decision that would have a very favorable effect on the entire situation, would change it greatly and build up trust between our countries.

We have put this question to the American President in Geneva.

Silence was the answer we heard. Really, in essence there are no reasonable arguments against the prohibition of nuclear tests. Difficulties of verification are sometimes mentioned. But the Soviet Union clearly demonstrated the excellent possibility of exercising such verification with the help of national means. This year we registered an underground nuclear blast of a very low yield staged in the United States and unannounced by it. We are also ready to examine the possibility of establishing international control. In this context special attention should be devoted to the ideas formulated in the message of the leaders of six states who proposed to set up special stations on the territories of their countries to monitor the observance of a test ban agreement.

The entire world raises its voice in favor of terminating nuclear tests. Not so long ago the United Nations General Assembly passed a resolution calling for such a move. Only three countries—the U.S., Britain and France—voted against it. This is a deplorable move.

But there's still time. I think that the leaders of the United States and other nuclear powers will use the existing opportunity and, proceeding from the interests of peace, will show the necessary responsibility. I would like to remind them that our moratorium remains in effect, and we hope that the discussion of that issue at the session of the Supreme Soviet of the USSR will be regarded as an urgent call for a realistic and immediate prohibition of all nuclear tests.

On the whole the Soviet Union is coming up with an all-embracing complex of measures which completely blocks all avenues for the arms race, be it in space or on Earth, be it nuclear, chemical or conventional weapons. Concrete proposals on that score are well known—in Vienna, in Geneva and in Stockholm. They remain in effect and retain their timeliness and importance in full.

Europe should be mentioned separately. The task of preventing the level of military confrontation in Europe from growing any further is more urgent than ever before. The European home is a common home where geography and history have strongly bonded together the destiny of many countries and peoples.

It is only by a collective effort, by following the reasonable norms of international contacts and cooperation, that Europeans can preserve their home, can make it better and safer.

We proceed from the view that Europe, which gave the world so much in the sphere of culture, science, technology, and advanced social thought, is also capable of setting an example in the solution of the most complex problems of present-day international life. The basis for this was laid down in Helsinki ten years ago. It is our profound conviction that the whole world, including the United States, stands ultimately to gain from the positive developments in Europe. We have been and shall be working for the sake of the principles and policy of détente which is being consolidated more vigorously on the long-suffering European continent and for the overcoming of the roadblocks of the past and the consequences of the confrontation of recent years.

I would like to make a special mention here of trade and economic relations. The business circles of many Western countries would like to establish wider economic contacts with us. I heard this mentioned by very influential representatives of those circles. They were talking about readiness to conclude large contracts and to start vast joint projects. Those politicians who try to impose restrictions on this natural striving for businesslike cooperation in the hope of "punishing" someone, of inflicting damage on a partner, are simply acting, to my mind, unwisely.

The fallacy of this policy has long become obvious. It would be much more useful to exert efforts for a different purpose, for ensuring that trade, scientific and technical exchanges consolidate the material basis of confidence and accord.

We will continue to cooperate closely with our Warsaw Treaty allies and with all the other countries of the socialist community in the struggle for lasting peace and cooperation among nations in Europe and on other continents. The states participating in the Warsaw Treaty Organization will under no circumstances foresake the security of their peoples. They will pool their efforts to an ever-growing extent within the CMEA framework to accelerate scientific and technical progress and socioeconomic development.

Interaction with the nonaligned movement, including comprehensive cooperation with the Republic of India, whose people and leaders we hold in profound respect, has a great role to play in the improvement of international relations.

The Soviet leadership attaches serious importance to the Asian and Pacific region. The Soviet Union's longest borders are in Asia. There we have loyal friends and reliable allies, from neighboring Mongolia to socialist Vietnam. It is extremely important to ensure that this region is not a source of tension and an area of armed confrontation. We stand for the broadening of political dialogue among all the states in the region in the interests of peace, good-neighborliness, mutual trust and cooperation.

We welcome the stand of the People's Republic of China, which is opposed to the militarization of space, and its statement renouncing the first use of nuclear weapons.

We stand for better relations with Japan and it is our conviction that this is possible. It stems even from the mere fact that our countries are next-door neighbors. Also, the interests of the USSR and Japan cannot help coinciding in the vital matter of removing the nuclear threat.

We have established relations of equal cooperation with many states of Latin America, Africa and the Middle East. The Soviet Union will continue to work purposefully to develop these relations. We value especially our close contacts with socialist-

On the way to a private talk. Geneva, November 19, 1985.

Soviet Minister of Foreign Affairs Eduard Shevardnadze and U.S. Secretary of State George Shultz sign bilateral Agreement on Exchanges and Contacts in Science, Education and Culture in the presence of Mikhail Gorbachev and Ronald Reagan. Geneva, November 21, 1985.

Mikhail Gorbachev talks with Bernard Lown, U.S. Co-Chairman of the International Physicians for the Prevention of Nuclear War. The Kremlin, December 18, 1985.

Mikhail Gorbachev visits a synthetic textile factory in Kustanai (Kazakh Soviet Socialist Republic, Central Asia).

Greeting a group of workers famous for their skill and innovations.
The Kremlin, September 20, 1985.

Mikhail Gorbachev welcomes Malcolm Baldridge, U.S. Secretary
of Commerce in the Kremlin. December 10, 1985.

Mikhail Gorbachev in conversation with Andrei Gromyko. 1986.
Photo Courtesy of the author.

President and Mrs. Mitterrand in Moscow with Mikhail Gorbachev
and Mrs. Gorbachev.

Visiting Mother, Mikhail Gorbachev and Raisa Gorbachev flank Mr. Gorbachev's mother. The others are relatives and friends. 1986. Photo Courtesy of the author.

Mikhail Gorbachev in Vladivostok. 1986.

Mikhail Gorbachev and Anatoli Dobrynin with Armand Hammer (at left) and Dr. Robert Gale (arms folded). Dr. Gale went to the Soviet Union to treat Chernobyl workers exposed to radiation. 1986.

Mikhail Gorbachev and Stewart Richardson, of Richardson & Steirman in Moscow. He is holding a leatherbound copy of *The Coming Century of Peace*. 1986.

Raisa Gorbachev with children. 1986.

A recent portrait of Mikhail Gorbachev. 1986.

oriented countries on different continents.

The peoples of the whole world are today facing a host of questions which can only be resolved jointly and only under conditions of peace. A few dozen years ago serious ecological problems were virtually nonexistent. But already our generation is witnessing the mass extermination of forests, extinction of animals, contamination of rivers and other water bodies, and growing desertification. What will the world be like that future generations will see? Will they be able to live in it if the voracious destruction of nature is not stopped and if the economic, technical and scientific achievements of our time are not directed to meet the needs of ensuring conditions for the existence and progress of man and his environment but at perfecting weapons of destruction?

Or take energy. We are now living for the most part at the expense of the Earth's depths. But what was lying virtually on the surface is being exhausted, and the further development of these resources is growing more and more expensive and becoming more and more arduous. Moreover, this source is not eternal.

Dangerous upheavals can be caused by the growing gap between a handful of highly industrialized capitalist nations and those developing countries—and there is an overwhelming majority of them—whose lot is poverty, hunger and lack of hope. The gap between these two poles in the world is becoming ever wider, and relations between them ever more antagonistic. It cannot be otherwise unless the industrialized capitalist nations alter their self-serving policies.

Mankind is capable of resolving all these problems today if it pools its forces and intellect. Then it will be possible to scale new heights in the development of our civilization.

Militarism is an enemy of nations. The arms race, which whipped up the thirst for gain of the military-industrial complex, is sheer madness. It affects the vital interests of all countries and peoples. This is why, when instead of the elimination of nuclear weapons the project of the arms race into space is proposed to us as well, we respond with a firm "no." We say "no" because such a step means a new round in the mad squandering of funds. We say "no" because this means the heightening of the threat already looming darkly over the world. We say "no" because life itself calls not for a competition in armaments, but for joint action for the good of peace.

The Soviet Union is a decisive advocate of the development of international life in this direction.

On the initiative of the USSR work involving scientists from different countries has begun on the Tokomak thermonuclear reactor project, which opens up an opportunity to resolve the energy problem radically. According to scientists, it is possible to create as early as within this century a "terrestrial sun"—an inexhaustible source of thermonuclear energy. We note with satisfaction that it was agreed in Geneva to carry on with that important project.

It is our country that submitted to the United Nations an extensive and detailed program of peaceful cooperation in space, and for the development of a universal space organization to coordinate the efforts of countries in the exploration and development of space. There are truly boundless possibilities for such cooperation. They include fundamental research projects and the application of their findings in geology, medicine, materials studies and studies of the climate and the environment. They include the development of global satellite-aided communication systems and remote probing of the Earth. They, finally, include the development of new space technology, such as large orbital scientific stations and various manned spacecraft, their use in the interests of all the peoples, and the eventual industrialization of near-Earth space. All this constitutes a realistic alternative to the "Star Wars" plans. It is oriented toward a peaceful future for all humankind.

The Soviet Union was one of the active participants in the conclusion of an international convention to regulate the economic utilization of the resources of the world's oceans. The accomplishment of this task is also vastly important for ensuring the progress of human civilization and in broadening and multiplying the possibilities open to present-day society.

We offer the whole world, including the world of capitalist

states, a broad, long-term and comprehensive program of mutually beneficial cooperation, a program incorporating new opportunities which are being opened before mankind by the age of scientific and technical revolution. Cooperation between two such states as the Soviet Union and the United States could play a far from minimal role in carrying out this program.

Our policy is clearly a policy of peace and cooperation.

Comrades, the successes of our foreign policy are inherent in the nature of the socialist system. The Communist Party senses well and appreciates highly the nationwide support for its domestic and foreign policy. This support is manifested in the daily practical work of millions upon millions of people. The results achieved in the national economy mean not only an economic, but also an important moral and political result attesting to the rightness of our course.

We face important undertakings which are not easy. "However, difficulty does not imply impossibility," the great Lenin taught us. "The important thing is to be confident that the path chosen is the right one, this confidence multiplying a hundredfold revolutionary energy and revolutionary enthusiasm. . . ." The Party and the Soviet people have this confidence, which multiplies our strength.

We are confident that every Communist, every worker, every farmer, every engineer and scientist, every work collective, will be aware of high responsibility to the Motherland, will perform their duty.

We are confident that everything will be done at every work place to ensure that the plans of 1986 are successfully fulfilled and overfulfilled, that our country becomes still richer and mightier, and that the cause of peace on Earth is strengthened and victorious.

November 27, 1985

21

A MESSAGE
TO THE
U.N. SECRETARY GENERAL
AND PARTICIPANTS IN THE
U.N. GENERAL ASSEMBLY
COMMEMORATIVE SESSION

Esteemed Mr. Secretary General,

I greet you and all those who attend the UN General Assembly's anniversary session to mark forty years of the United Nations Organization.

The United Nations owes its birth to the victory over fascism and militarism won by the freedom-loving peoples. It is only natural that the UN Charter proclaims in its very first lines the United Nations' determination to save succeeding generations from the scourge of war, to practice tolerance and live in peace with one another as good neighbors.

The UN Charter, which became valid on October 24, 1945, the date recognized as the inauguration of the UN, has stood the test of time. The Organization has become an important factor in the system of international relations. The United Nations also has contributed to helping humanity avoid another world war for the past forty years.

Today, however, it is more essential than ever before to say that the principal task set by the UN Charter has not yet been accomplished. The guarantees for a durable peace have not been created. Today the joint efforts of states and peoples are needed more than ever to deliver humanity from the threat of a nuclear catastrophe.

What is needed above all for this purpose in practical terms is to put an end to the arms race on Earth and keep it out of space.

What is also required are fresh efforts to calm regional sites of tension and to remove the last vestiges of colonialism in all its manifestations.

The United Nations has many other pressing tasks: To facilitate, through real disarmament measures, the release of resources for the purposes of development, and the overcoming of backwardness, hunger, disease and poverty. The reshaping of international economic relations on a just and democratic basis and ensuring genuine human rights and liberties, most notably the right to a peaceful life, should also serve these purposes.

We speak about all this because we are firmly convinced that because the Organization's fortieth anniversary is such an important event, the prime attention of its member states should be directed at making UN activities still more effective and fruitful.

The Soviet Union, one of the founders of the United Nations and a permanent member of its Security Council, will make every effort, as always, to facilitate the world organization's successful fulfillment of its lofty mission in strict compliance with its Charter.

Mikhail Gorbachev
October 25, 1985

22

A SPEECH
BEFORE NOBEL PEACE
PRIZE WINNERS

IT IS with pleasure that I accept an address signed by outstanding scientists who are Nobel Prize winners. I would like to say right away that the Soviet leadership views this address as a document of tremendous significance to all humankind. The appeal it makes for the two great powers to secure a turn for the better in international affairs, put an end to the arms race and prevent the militarization of outer space is fully consonant with the sentiments in our country and the practical intentions of its leadership.

Our time is, without exaggeration, a crucial moment in history. Humankind has now reached a point which calls for particular wisdom in decision-making, care in considering moves, discretion in action and regard not only for our own country's national interests but also for the interests of the entire world community. I think it is the realization of this fact that also underlies the initiative made by the Nobel Prize winners.

In the USSR we believe that there is no task more important and pressing today than to close the channels for the continued stockpiling of nuclear arms, the increasingly sophisticated kinds of these weapons, while shutting the door securely on armaments in outer space. This is consistent with the views and proposals we are taking to the Soviet-American meeting in a few days.

Our approach to this meeting is open and fair. We go to Geneva completely aware of the responsibility resting on the leaders of all countries but, primarily, of the USSR and the United States. We go there for serious and productive work and, I should say, with our hands not empty.

The Soviet Union stands for the meeting to help in actually resolving the key issues of our times, those of enhancing international peace and security, improving relations between the USSR and the United States, checking the arms race and preventing its extension to outer space.

We are deeply convinced that it is especially important

today that every thinking person be fully aware of one's personal responsibility for warding off the war threat. And it is only natural for scientists, who perhaps have a clearer idea than others of the likely aftermath of a nuclear war, to raise their voice against wars, be they terrestrial wars or "star" wars. This is also how I interpret the message conveyed by you. Our country highly values the humanist tradition of true scientists who have always taken an active stand on the issue of war and peace, a tradition initiated by Niels Bohr, Albert Einstein and Frederic Joliot-Curie.

Our time is truly the "gold age" of science. The bounds of knowledge are extending exceptionally fast. All the way from the microcosm to outer space, human reason is penetrating such depths and secrets of nature as seemed out of reach only a short time ago. Making full use of the results of this cognition would make it possible to enrich man's material and intellectual life in terms of quality.

And isn't it a terrible paradox of the twentieth century that achievements in science directed to developing weapons of mass annihilation threaten the very existence of the human race?

The issues of war and peace have been put in the foreground by the objective course of development itself.

Scientists' influential say and competent opinion can, and are called upon, to play a big role in awakening the people to reality and urging them on to vigorous action to stop and reverse the arms race and start reducing armaments.

You are right in stressing in your message that courage today is required not in preparing for war but in achieving peace. This is even more true since the arms race has reached a critical point. Even today advances in military technology have made arms control extremely difficult. We have come right down to a line beyond which the situation may become altogether uncontrollable.

Whether strike weapons will make it to outer space or be barred from it is an all-important question. The answer to it is decisive in the course of developments in the world for many years ahead. Can there be any peaceful future and strategic stability if yet another mortal danger, one from space, emerges in addition to the missiles already in silos and under the ocean?

Imagine what the world will be in this case in ten or twenty years. Waves of all manner of strike weapons will be rushing overhead everywhere, from the edge of the atmosphere at an altitude of a hundred kilometers to geostationary orbits, above all people inhabiting our planet.

The Soviet people, who have lived for forty years surrounded by American "forward-based" weaponry, strongly reject the very possibility of its spread to outer space and the very prospect of having it overhead, above their homes.

And how will ordinary Americans, who have not yet gotten accustomed to having others' weapons on their borders, either on Earth or in space, feel in this case? I think that tension in relations between our countries will escalate to a point unprecedented even by today's standards and will be even more difficult to control.

The militarization of outer space will put a heavy psychological burden on people in all countries and bring about an atmosphere of universal instability and uncertainty.

The question arises: What's the purpose of all this? By the way, it is appropriate to ask this question as well: Doesn't the very fact of deployment of weapons by one state in outer space, above the territory of other states, constitute a breach of their sovereignty?

Soviet people in their letters often ask what the Soviet Union will do if the United States, in spite of everything, embarks on the development, testing and deployment of a multi-tier antimissile defense. We have already said that the USSR will find an effective answer which, in our opinion, will meet the demand of maintaining strategic equilibrium and its stability. But if this happens, the case in point will be a new round of the arms race.

As is known, there were no weapons in outer space until now. If they appear there it will be an exceptionally difficult undertaking to bring them back from space. And it is totally unsubstantiated to expect that the development of space strike weapons will lead to the disappearance of nuclear weapons on Earth. The history of the development of new types of weapons and the existing realities are convincing testimony to the contrary.

Does the logic that it is necessary to arm oneself to the teeth in order to disarm make sense at all? In other words: Why should one develop missiles to destroy missiles when there is a different, more dependable and safer way and, what is most important, a way leading directly to the goal. This is to reach accords on the reduction and subsequent complete elimination of the existing missiles.

It is clear from all points of view and from the position of common sense as well that the second way is the only reasonable one. We are for it.

You know that our country is prepared to see halved the number of warheads capable of reaching the territory of the United States and the USSR. We have stopped all tests of nuclear weapons. We have unilaterally reduced medium-range missiles in Europe as well. We are ready to sign a treaty of nonaggression, to agree to the establishment of zones free from nuclear and chemical weapons.

All these steps of ours, just like many proposals that are now on the negotiating table, taken together and individually provide an opportunity to improve the international situation substantially, to lessen the threat of nuclear conflict and to pave the way toward complete nuclear disarmament. We realize perfectly well that to live with the perpetual threat of nuclear weapons is a dismal prospect for humankind.

What alternative to that does the Strategic Defense Initiative provide? In our firmly held view, only an unlimited and mutually accelerating race in so-called "defensive" and "offensive" arms.

I have more than once had to characterize the SDI politically. I won't stress yet another time its clearly imperial tilt toward trying to ensure superiority—both military and technological—over other states.

I will dwell on another aspect. It is said that the SDI will ensure a breakthrough in the field of technology. But even if we assume that its realization will promote scientific and technological progress, the question still remains: At what price will this be achieved? It is absolutely clear that the price will be the development of new suicidal arms systems. More and more people, in the U.S. also, are coming to understand this.

We are in favor of an essentially different way of speeding up the progress in science and technology. We are for competition in technology and constructive cooperation in the conditions of a durable and just peace.

Isn't outer space itself a highly promising arena of international cooperation? We have just now started exploring it in the interests of science and man's practical activity. But how much has been achieved within a short period of time! The first sputnik, the first man in space, the first man on the Moon, the landings on Venus and Mars, an excellent map of Venus.

These are just initial steps. And it is necessary to make the exploration of boundless expanses of outer space a joint undertaking of states.

We have submitted for the United Nations' consideration an extensive program of peaceful cooperation in space. The USSR proposes to create a world space organization, which would be the center for coordinating the efforts of all countries in this enterprise.

This means fundamental scientific research and the launching of interplanetary ships, for instance to Mars, for these purposes.

This means the application of the results of space research in the spheres of biology, medicine, materials science, weather forecasting, studies of the climate and nature, for the creation of a global satellite communication system and remote sensing of the Earth's surface and making studies of the world ocean.

This, finally, means creation by joint efforts and use in the interests of all peoples of new space equipment, including large orbital scientific stations, various manned ships and, in the future, the industrialization of near-Earth space.

Naturally, we are prepared for peaceful cooperation in

space on a bilateral basis, too, with those states that show interest in it. This fully applies to the United States as well.

You remember the Soyuz-Apollo linkup in 1975 which fascinated humankind. Something is being done now, too: We are conducting studies of Venus and Halley's Comet jointly with American scientists in the framework of the international project called "Vega." We take part in the search and rescue program from space jointly with other countries.

This, however, is just a small fraction of what could be done jointly. It is unreasonable to let such opportunities slip by.

By all indications, much interest is being shown among the American public, scientists and in the U.S. Congress in the resumption of cooperation, and specific projects are being advanced. We are prepared to consider serious proposals of this kind.

Both military programs and peaceful projects in space, including research, are costly undertakings. So, the greater the reasons to choose the alternative of peaceful cooperation.

The mastering of thermonuclear synthesis is a promising area of international cooperation. This will provide humankind with a virtually unlimited source of energy, a sort of man-made Sun.

As is known, the idea of a controlled thermonuclear reaction was first advanced by Academician Igor Kurchatov in his well-known lecture in Great Britain back in 1956, when he familiarized scientists of many countries with the work of Soviet scientists.

The Tokamak international pilot thermonuclear reactor project has been under way in Vienna since 1978 on the initiative of the Soviet Union, with the participation of scientists from a number of Western European countries as well as from the United States and Japan.

Already it can be said that such a reactor is technically feasible, and specialists believe it can be built in the relatively near future, in any case, before the year 2000.

During the recent visit to Paris we expressed the appropriate considerations to French President François Mitterrand. He received our proposal positively. We deem it important, moreover, necessary, to pool the efforts of all states concerned in the implementation of thermonuclear synthesis, which will make it possible to solve one of the most acute global problems, the energy problem.

There are a lot of pressing tasks in the world today that require coordination and cooperation. I would like to emphasize again that the Soviet Union is firmly and consistently in favor of the broadest cooperation, of pooling the efforts of states in using the achievements of scientific and technical progress exclusively for peaceful purposes and humankind's progress. I can assure you that the Soviet Union does not lack the readiness or goodwill for this cooperation.

I wish you success in your fruitful scientific activity, in the noble field of upholding the cause of a world without arms, a world without wars.

November 13, 1985

23

A MEETING
WITH BERNARD LOWN

MIKHAIL GORBACHEV, General Secretary of the Central Committee of the Communist Party of the Soviet Union, received Professor Bernard Lown, U.S. co-chairman of the International Physicians for the Prevention of Nuclear War (IPPNW), in the Kremlin on December 18, 1985. Academician Yevgeny Chazov, Soviet co-chairman of IPPNW, took part in the meeting.

During the conversation Bernard Lown spoke of the activities of IPPNW, which brings together more than 145,000 physicians and medical workers from more than 50 countries. By studying the possible medical and biological consequences of nuclear war and informing the public, political figures, and governments of the findings, the IPPNW makes a substantial contribution to the cause of preventing nuclear war.

The program being put forward by the IPPNW envisages a freeze, reduction and elimination of nuclear arms, prohibition of nuclear tests, renunciation of a first use of nuclear weapons, nonproliferation of the arms race to outer space and broad international peaceful cooperation.

Bernard Lown emphasized the exceptional importance of drawing broad masses of people into a discussion of the problems of ending the arms race and removing the threat of nuclear war. He said that the voice of the peoples of the world should be heard and should have an effect on governments' decisions.

Mr. Lown highly valued the USSR's peace initiatives, in particular the moratorium on all nuclear explosions, which was put into effect on August 6 of this year. The call to announce such a moratorium was contained in the message of the Fifth International Congress of the IPPNW addressed to Mikhail Gorbachev and to President Ronald Reagan of the United States in the summer of this year. Mr. Lown said that termination of nuclear testing meets the aspirations of all the world's peoples.

Mikhail Gorbachev congratulated Professor Bernard Lown

and Academician Yevgeny Chazov for the award of the Nobel Peace Prize for 1985 to International Physicians for the Prevention of Nuclear War. He said that there exists in the Soviet Union great respect and sympathy for the activities of this movement and for its socially significant life-defending mission. The IPPNW rightfully holds an authoritative place in the world antiwar movement. Doctors reveal the grim truth which people need to know so they can protect that which is irreparable. In this sense the Hippocratic Oath, which obliges physicians to protect their patients against everything that might threaten their lives, assumes a truly new dimension in the nuclear age.

The appeal of the Fifth Congress of this international movement of physicians to the General Secretary of the CPSU Central Committee and to the President of the United States is imbued with the ardent wish to protect all people of Earth against the disastrous consequences of nuclear catastrophe.

Human thought is not always capable of grasping changes of historic scope in time. This is a serious failing, particularly dangerous now that nuclear holocaust directly threatens every home and every family. So the voice of the peoples of the world and of their public organizations in defense of peace is all the more important now. This is a kind of expression of the instinct of humankind's self-preservation.

Peace based on deterrence by means of nuclear weapons is a precarious one. It is impossible to consolidate peace through an arms buildup and space arms. No one has yet invented a more reliable and effective model of relations among states than détente and cooperation under conditions of peace and mutual security. The lowering of the level of military confrontation among them would consolidate the framework of these relations, making them stable and reliable.

Proceeding from these factors, we agreed to a meeting between the Soviet and American leaders in Geneva, said Mikhail Gorbachev. In the course of the meeting an important beginning was made in the normalization of Soviet-American relations and preconditions were created for the improvement of the international situation as a whole.

However, we see another thing as well: Reactionary, aggression-minded circles in the U.S., which some time ago tried hard to disrupt the Geneva meeting, are now attacking its results. A broad campaign has been launched against the normalization of relations with the USSR and against the consolidation of mutual trust in Soviet-American relations to which the sides agreed in Geneva. Propaganda in the press, television and cinema are being actively used for fanning mistrust and hostility toward the USSR and the Soviet people. The impression is that there are people in the U.S. for whom the desire to improve mutual understanding between our peoples as expressed in Geneva is very much in the way. By all appearances, the notorious "hawks" have set themselves the task of preventing the implementation of the Geneva Accords and of disrupting or at least lessening the importance of another Soviet-American summit meeting. Unfortunately, the latest statements of U.S. statesmen as well are at variance with the "spirit of Geneva."

As for the Soviet Union, its policy is clear and consistent. The Soviet Union is prepared to go its part of the road toward the construction of a structure of durable mutual security and peaceful cooperation with the United States. But we expect the same from the U.S. leadership. We extended a hand to the United States in Geneva. We are prepared to pass from competition in armaments to disarmament, from confrontation to cooperation. "Cooperation, not confrontation" was the slogan of the recent International Congress of the Physicians for the Prevention of Nuclear War. One cannot but agree with this. Cooperation is nowadays the indispensable condition for both the progress of our civilization and of our common survival.

The Soviet Union will go as far as is needed toward the complete elimination of nuclear weapons and toward the ultimate removal of the threat of war with their use. We are in favor of really ensuring humanity's primary right, the right to live. We are for the immediate freezing of nuclear arms, for a complete ban of nuclear tests without time-limit, for the most effective control of these weapons. Reciprocity is our only condition.

As a real major step on the way to universal nuclear disarmament we proposed to the United States a radical fifty per cent reduction of strategic nuclear arsenals with, of course, a complete ban on space strike arms. This means the renunciation of the "Star Wars" program, a program which can only destroy all efforts at the elimination of nuclear arms and whip up the arms race to unprecedented proportions. As it is justly noted in the appeal of the physicians' movement, the threat of global nuclear conflict would increase sharply as a result of "Star Wars."

Actually, this is understood now by the whole world. As many as 151 states, in fact all the United Nations member countries except for the United States, just voted for the resolution of the United Nations General Assembly on the prevention of the arms race in outer space.

Mikhail Gorbachev especially touched upon the question of ending the tests of nuclear weapons, called for persistently by the IPPNW, which substantiates its call with convincing reasons. The moratorium on all nuclear explosions, announced by the Soviet Union as of August 6 of this year, has been highly appreciated in the world. "Making this step, we proceeded from a sincere desire to break the vicious circle: To stop the endless sophistication of nuclear weapons and steer matters to an actual immobilization of their stocks. I told this to President Reagan in Geneva," Mikhail Gorbachev said. "To our profound regret, the United States has not up to now followed our example."

In reply to Bernard Lown, Mikhail Gorbachev said: "We are ready to extend the USSR-introduced moratorium on nuclear explosions if the United States reciprocates. We are urging the U.S. Administration to do that. A unique chance is still there to make the moratorium mutual and to extend it beyond January 1. To miss this chance, which paves the way to a final ban in treaty form on all tests of nuclear weapons would be unreasonable, to say the least. A solution to this question is in the hands of the U.S. Government.

"Professor Lown is right: The people of the world are waiting for the termination and prohibition of the tests of nuclear weapons without delay. This is also indicated by a resolution to that effect, which was recently passed, practically unanimously, by the UN General Assembly (with three negative votes—those of the United States, Great Britain, and France)."

In conclusion, Mikhail Gorbachev wished his interlocutors and all the members of International Physicians for the Prevention of Nuclear War new successes in their highly necessary and lofty activities.

24

A MESSAGE
TO THE PARTICIPANTS
IN THE CONGRESS FOR
A PEACEFUL FUTURE
OF THE PLANET

I GREET the participants in the Congress of Scientists and Prominent Figures in Culture for a Peaceful Future of the Planet.

Your Congress opens the calendar of tangible actions which will certainly abound in 1986, which has been declared by the United Nations Organization the International Year of Peace. It is significant that you have gathered in Warsaw, a city whose past reminds one of the horrors of the last war and whose present-day appearance symbolizes humanity's irresistible will for constructive endeavor and peace.

Humanity today is facing quite a few complex and difficult problems at national, regional and global levels. But there is not one more urgent among them than the task of removing the nuclear threat—stopping the arms race on Earth and preventing it from spreading to outer space—and preserving civilization.

The Soviet-U.S. meeting in Geneva has kindled hope for improvements in the international situation and stronger mutual security. To have this hope materialized, it is essential that both sides fulfill the accords reached in good faith. The Geneva process should be carried on and determine the further course of events in the world. This is demanded by the peoples and is really necessary.

I can assure the delegates to the Congress that the Soviet Union will continue to do its best to curb the arms race, to terminate it on Earth and prevent it in outer space. This is what our far-reaching steps, plans and proposals are aimed at, coming into line with the interests of further progress of all humankind. Our choice is not military competition, but comprehensive international cooperation in all spheres, including the sphere of science and culture.

In a bid to assist to a maximum degree a radical improvement of the international situation and the ridding of the human race, once and for all, of the fear of the possibility of a nuclear holocaust or use of other barbaric weapons of mass annihilation, the Soviet Union has just advanced a peace initiative of historic significance addressed to the United States of America, the other nuclear powers and to all governments and nations of the world.

We propose reaching agreement on the adoption of a program for the complete elimination of nuclear weapons the world over within the next fifteen years, before the end of the twentieth century. We put forward a concrete plan of step-by-step measures leading toward that goal and provide for strict international verification of their implementation. We are convinced that this is a realistic prospect, naturally on the condition that the development of space strike weapons is renounced. The atom only for peace, outer space only for peace—this is our program.

We also propose to eliminate, as early as in this century, chemical weapons, their stockpiles and the industrial base for their manufacture—also under strict verification, including international on-site inspections.

We suggest banning the development of non-nuclear arms based on new physical principles and approaching nuclear and other weapons of mass destruction in their hitting power.

We also consider it possible to reach, at long last, meaningful accords on mutual troop and arms reductions in the center of Europe at the Vienna talks and on non-use of force and strengthening mutual confidence at the conference in Stockholm.

As one more confirmation of the seriousness and sincerity of its intentions and of its readiness to go over as soon as possible to practical actions for strengthening peace and ridding mankind of the threat of nuclear war, the Soviet Union has decided to prolong for another three months the moratorium it declared on any nuclear explosions and urges the United States and then other nuclear powers to accede to it.

In short, the Soviet Union comes up with a concrete program for achieving the aim to which your Congress is devoted, the aim of safeguarding a peaceful future for this planet. And we appeal to the peace forces throughout the world to support this program.

We are convinced that mankind's intellectual potential

should be used for amplifying its material and cultural riches and not for developing new types of deadly weapons of global destruction. Peaceful cooperation of states and peoples, and not preparation for "Star Wars"—such is the way we understand humanity's approach to the question of space. Peaceful space is an important precondition for banishing the danger of war from the lives of people.

The great power of the struggle for peace lies in words of truth, truth about the terrible consequences of a nuclear conflict unless it is averted. The participants at your Congress—influential representatives of scientific and cultural communities—can play a significant role in disseminating this truth and making broad public circles aware of their humane duty to take an active part in efforts for a really lasting peace.

I wish your Congress success in its work toward the common aim which is the main one for all—the triumph of a durable peace on Earth.

Mikhail Gorbachev
January 17, 1986

25

BUILDING UP
FOOD RESOURCES

This speech was made at the Conference of Leading Party Workers and Managerial Staffs in Tselinograd in the Kazakh Soviet Republic (Central Asia).

W<small>E HAVE</small> invited leaders of the Party and local government bodies of the regions of Kazakhstan and the territories and regions of Siberia and the Urals, a large group of secretaries of rural district Party committees, chairmen of collective farms and state farm managers as well as agrarian scientists to attend this meeting in Tselinograd in order that we may discuss Party and economic affairs.

The April 1985 Plenary Meeting of the Central Committee was followed by direct preparation for the Twenty-seventh CPSU Congress. Intense activity is under way in the country. It involves all work collectives and all spheres of Soviet society. We have to handle many important and complex current and future problems simultaneously.

The review and election campaign in the Party organizations is gathering momentum. Always a major event in the life of the CPSU, especially now, in view of new tasks and the forthcoming Congress, the significance of this campaign increases immeasurably. It is important to conduct reviews and elections in keeping with Party principles, in an atmosphere of constructive criticism and self-criticism, and with the Communists' high sense of responsibility to the people being maintained.

The CPSU Central Committee expects the Party organizations to emerge from this review and election campaign organizationally and ideologically stronger. They have to discard all that hampers their full-scale activity and become capable of inspiring, organizing and leading work collectives to fulfill the tasks now facing the country. Success here will largely depend on those people whom Communists elect to lead Party organizations, particularly on secretaries of primary organizations and Party committees.

The Twenty-seventh CPSU Congress is to adopt a revised edition of the Party program and Guidelines for National Economic and Social Development during the Twelfth Five-Year Plan up to the Period ending in the Year 2000. The drafting of these documents is soon to be completed and, after consideration by a Plenary Meeting of the CPSU Central Committee they will be presented for public discussion. Such a method of drafting documents that involves not only the leading bodies of the Party and the State but all Communists and working people will make it possible, we believe, to bring to the Congress scientifically based proposals enriched by the experience of the entire Party and the entire society.

I would like, however, to make one suggestion. There is no point at all in just waiting for the program and the Guidelines to be adopted by the Congress. The spirit of the times calls for an immediate full-scale effort. The major goals have been established, and we should persistently move ahead, braving all difficulties and checking our actual performance against the Guidelines of the April Plenary Meeting and the subsequent resolutions of the Central Committee. The times we are living in, and the tasks we are facing, compel us to be firm, determined and wise in pursuing the policy we have charted.

One of the major imperatives for us is successfully to combine long-range decision-making with the carrying out of the tasks at hand. Long-range planning and setting of priorities for social and economic development are matters of immense importance. But, at the same time, one should clearly realize that even the most breathtaking plans and finest prospects are worthless unless followed up by an actual effort and by a quest for effective solutions. To do otherwise is day-dreaming. . . .

I would like to emphasize the great significance of the work being done today to achieve the targets of the last year of the Eleventh Five-Year Plan. These are important for creating a reserve for the future and for ensuring a good start of the new five-year plan period which we intend to make a turning point in accelerating our economic and social development.

Every work collective well knows its reserves and what it must do in order to meet the plan targets of this year. A great deal must be done in industry, capital construction, transport, services and trade. Special mention should be made of the tasks facing agriculture. For all our difficulties, we can now count on harvesting more grain than we did last year and on an increase in the output of other farming produce, in particular fodder. There are realistic opportunities for meeting the plan targets in livestock production.

We have now come to a decisive stage in the harvesting campaign. Our ability to fulfill the requirements of the national economy for food and fodder grain depends, to a great extent, on the contribution made by Kazakhstan and the territories and regions of Siberia and the Urals. Aware of this, the Government and the Central Committee of the CPSU have rendered them a lot of help. Now it is your turn to act, Comrades. We hope the Party organizations and working people of Kazakhstan and the regions of Siberia and the Urals will display maximum energy and ability in gathering the harvest and will contribute substantially to the country's grain resources.

It seems symbolic that we are discussing food problems soon after we have discussed in Tyumen the fuel and energy situation. Both are indispensable for building an efficient economy, improving the living standard of the people and building up the country's economic and defense potential.

The creation of a dependable foodstuff base is a matter of the entire Party and the whole nation. The April Plenary Meeting of the CPSU Central Committee firmly pronounced the implementation of the Food Program an urgent task requiring special attention.

I think the May 1982 Plenary Meeting of the Central Committee can be considered a point of reference for analyzing the state of agriculture and the entire agroindustrial complex. A little more than three years have passed since then. The time has shown that we were correct in adopting the Food Program and a set of important decisions aimed at solving crucial problems of the development of the agroindustrial complex. Work is in full swing to carry out the Party's measures. The agricultural machine-building industry is undergoing serious modernization. The targets for the production of mineral fertilizer are close to being met. The area of reclaimed lands has increased considerably.

I would like to make special mention of the large-scale work being done to change the social conditions in the countryside. The construction of housing, service and cultural facilities, and of roads has intensified. All this created favorable conditions for encouraging specialists to stay in the countryside. The implementation of important measures to improve the economic situation at collective and state farms through an increase in purchase prices and bonuses has enhanced their economic position and improved economic performance. The introduction of the cost accounting and team contract methods has favorably influenced people's attitude to work and the results of their work.

Summing up the results of our work since the May 1983 Plenary Meeting, we can say that we have chosen the correct path, learned a great deal, and accomplished a lot.

It is highly significant that there has been a nationwide change of attitude toward the problems related to the development of the agroindustrial complex. The development of agriculture and related industries is now considered a national concern. The demands, needs, and requirements of the countryside are in the focus of attention and are being met promptly.

A legitimate question arises. How has all this affected the performance of collective and state farms and other agroindustrial enterprises and organizations? What has society as a whole gained?

As for the overall agricultural output, the figures for 1983-84 show that the profit increased by 22 billion roubles, or that the output grew by nine per cent as compared to the previous two years of the five-year plan. The output of grain, potatoes, sugar beets, vegetables and fruits also rose. During this same period the average annual production of meat increased by nine per cent, of milk by eight per cent, and of eggs by six per cent. Provided the plan for the current year is fulfilled, state purchases of livestock products will exceed the respective figures for 1982 as follows: meat (live weight) by 2.5 million tons, milk by 9.2 million tons, and eggs by 3.5 billion.

In those years the number of farms working at a loss considerably decreased, and the level of profitability in collective and state farm production on the whole rose. In 1983, the net profit of collective and state farms reached just under 24 billion roubles, and the profitability level equaled nearly twenty-two per cent. In 1984, which was more difficult because of weather conditions, profit stood at 20 billion roubles, and the profitability level at eighteen per cent.

The growth of agricultural output also affected the per capita consumption of foodstuffs. This year the per capita consumption of meat and fish will total 78 kilograms (with fish accounting for 17.7 kilograms), milk 318 kilograms, eggs 260, bread 134 kilograms, potatoes 110 kilograms, vegetables and melons 106 kilograms, fruit and berries 46 kilograms, and sugar nearly 45 kilograms.

What does all this mean? As far as the overall calorific value of our diet is concerned, we are on a level with the world's most developed countries. For the time being, our per capita consumption of meat and fruit is lower than in some countries and is somewhat below the established rational norms of nutrition. From this point of view, meat production is the most important element in the fulfillment of the Food Program. We are lagging behind in this field.

As for other products—milk, eggs, fish, sugar, vegetables and potatoes—the level of their per capita consumption is not lower, and in the case of some products is even higher than in many countries. It corresponds, or is close to, the Food Program targets. The population's requirements for bread and baked products are satisfied with a wide assortment.

Nevertheless, the problem of providing the population with foodstuffs has not yet been fully resolved. For some products demand exceeds supply. The reason for this is that cash incomes have grown faster in our country than the output of foodstuffs. At the same time, state prices of the staple foodstuffs have in effect remained stable for two decades, though their prime cost has been growing. For instance, our shops sell meat at prices which make up one-third or half of its prime cost. At present this difference is made up by a state subsidy which, in the case of meat, amounts to an impressive 20 billion roubles annually.

The fact that in the USSR staple foodstuffs are accessible to all groups of the population is a great achievement. But while noting this, we cannot ignore the issues that worry many Soviet people. Working people address to the Central Committee an increasing number of letters in which they deplore a disrespectful attitude on the part of some people to the work of those who produce grain and other farm products.

"Bread is life," write Comrades Ivanov and Mangalov from the township Magansk in the Krasnoyarsk Territory (Siberia). "It is the wealth, strength and might of our homeland. But what a barbaric attitude to bread one can often see! It is high time this problem is attended to in earnest."

Or here's another letter. "We have nobody starving," says Comrade Sukhanova from Moscow. "One can find loaves of white bread in garbage cans, and the food wastes of canteens are enough to overfeed all livestock."

There are many such letters. Apparently, this subject must be given careful attention both in the work collectives and in the central bodies of government—in fact, in every family too. It is our common task to radically change the attitude to bread and to other foodstuffs.

It is quite obvious, however, that the food problem can be settled largely through persistent work by the Party and by the entire society to develop our agriculture and the agroindustrial complex in general.

In the meantime there are quite a few examples of the increased material, technical and economic opportunities in many regions, territories and republics still being underused. Some managers continue to try and find sources of additional income not in large harvests, higher livestock productivity or thrifty management, but in receiving extra budget allocations and bank credits.

Drawbacks and mistakes have seriously hindered the implementation of the measures designed to impart greater stability to agriculture and, primarily, to crop farming. I should like to stress once more that we won't be able to remake our weather. So in concrete and often difficult conditions the only viable approach is to look for the most effective ways and methods of securing large harvests.

This is the key task of our work in the agroindustrial complex. Its solution is of paramount importance for the regions and territories of Siberia, the Urals and Kazakhstan. Instability in crop farming badly tells on the performance of local collective and state farms. During the four years of the current five-year plan, the targets for most agricultural products in Kazakhstan remained unfulfilled. The republic has a great debt in grain sales to the state. There has been a drop in a number of qualitative indices, and in several districts both field and livestock productivity has declined.

In the past few years, plans for the production and sale of grain to the state have also systematically remained unfulfilled in many Ural and Siberian regions of the Russian Federation. Over the last four years a large debt has accrued in grain sales to the state in many collective and state farms of the Altai and Krasnoyarsk territories and of the Novosibirsk, Orenburg, Kurgan and Chelyabinsk regions. They have also undersupplied large quantities of milk and meat.

Failures in meeting the plan targets for the production and purchase of grain put stress on the satisfaction of the country's needs. This forces us to import grain and thus spend sizable amounts of hard currency. We have set the task of further increasing grain production so as to fully satisfy domestic needs in grain. This is the premise from which the collective and state farms, Party, local government and economic management bodies in the grain-producing republics, territories and regions of the country must proceed in their work.

What does this mean in practical terms? If we single out the main targets, it means that no matter how unfavorable the weather conditions may be, the country has to harvest no less than 200 million tons of grain annually, while a good year should net 250 million or even more. This is what I see as the strategic task of our crop farming for the immediate future!

But the solution of the grain problem does not come down to simply growing more grain. It also includes its rational use.

We cannot compensate for shortcomings in fodder production by the use of large amounts of grain as fodder. This is an inadmissible practice which should not be tolerated. However, it has taken root in many areas. Realizing the great importance of the problem, we should seek a solution to it. Certain lessons on this score have already brought results. In the period from 1983 to 1984 the plans for the procurement of coarse and succulent fodder were not only fulfilled, but overfulfilled. This provided conditions for achieving higher results in the output of livestock products with a lower volume of concentrated fodder. That is why collective and state farms should pay the same attention to fodder production as to grain production. Not less and not worse —these are the two sides of the coin, so to speak. It is necessary to ensure a bumper harvest of fodder crops and a better quality of fodder on the basis of using the modern achievements of science and the experience accumulated at collective and state farms.

I would even say that at present the problem of quality should be given top priority. Control surveys show that due to the low quality of fodder, twenty to thirty per cent of nutrient substances are lost in many regions of the USSR. The excessive consumption of fodder grain is also caused by inadequate measures being taken in some places to eliminate the shortage of fodder protein. On many farms this has already been recognized and vigorous measures taken to solve the protein problem. Some farms, though, rely on the help of state resources. We should support the former and strongly denounce the parasitical attitudes of the latter.

Now that the plans for the next five-year period are being shaped it is very important that at every collective or state farm, in all districts, regions, territories and republics, the problems connected with the increasing of meat resources be thoroughly considered. This is a top priority task. In the final year of the Eleventh Five-Year Plan meat output is expected to increase by two million tons (slaughter weight) as compared with 1980. In order to meet the targets of the Food Program we must double this figure during the Twelfth Five-Year Plan.

On the whole, the targets set for the output of grain, fodder, meat, milk and other agricultural produce show that intensive work lies ahead in the next five-year plan. This should be completely understood by all workers of the agroindustrial complex and, above all, by our leading cadres.

These questions arise: How can we reach such targets and do we have all the necessary conditions for this? It is not rhetoric, but an earnest answer to say definitely on behalf of the Central Committee of the Party that today we have such possibilities and such conditions. This is evidenced by the work done by thousands of collective and state farms in a number of territories and regions since the May 1982 Plenary Meeting of the CPSU Central Committee.

At present a task of top priority is to ensure high returns in agriculture and the agroindustrial complex as a whole. The level of returns per unit of assets in the countryside remains low so far. In the two years following the May 1982 Plenary Meeting of the Central Committee, the production assets of collective farms and state farms in the Kurgan Region have increased by almost thirteen per cent, while gross agricultural output has fallen there by twelve per cent. A similar picture obtains in the Kustanai Region, where the increment in basic production assets during the same period was up fourteen per cent, while the output of products diminished. A decline in agricultural production, despite a noticeable increase in fixed assets per worker, has taken place in a number of other regions of the Russian Federation, the Ukraine, Kazakhstan and Uzbekistan.

The basic link which we must mend in order to fulfill the whole range of practical tasks facing us in the countryside is the proper organization of production and labor at collective and state farms, and all enterprises of the agroindustrial complex. Wide use must be made of the available experience of highly productive, efficient work. Everything depends here on the activity of leading cadres, Party, government and economic bodies, and not on additional capital investments.

I would like to dwell on a few of the practical matters in greater detail.

First, what is needed is more boldness in going over to new and advanced technologies, to more effective forms of using material resources and then to concentrate them primarily in those areas where they can yield the highest returns. It is essential for us during the next five-year period to give the utmost importance to growing grain crops with the application of intensive methods.

About 17 million hectares of wheat and nearly all grain corn is being cultivated according to intensive methods this year. Despite erratic weather, the yield gain is quite impressive. As the data of the Ministry of Agriculture and the USSR Academy of Agricultural Sciences show, farms obtain from four to five tons of grain per hectare in many areas, or 1.5 to 2 tons more than with the usual technology.

The new methods are gaining ever firmer ground. Following proposals from the localities, grain crops will be sown according to intensive methods on an area of over 31 million hectares for the 1986 harvest. Of this area, almost 4 million hectares will be sown in corn. In the near future, given good preceding years, we can extend the use of intensive methods to an area of not less than 60 million hectares. It is here that fertilizers, machinery and other resources should be primarily concentrated, so as to guarantee high yields and impart the necessary stability to grain production.

But there is more to it than that. We have had a brief meeting with scientists today. The results of this discussion may be summed up as follows: The paramount issue at this stage is the observance of technological standards in the fields. In agriculture the same kind of technological discipline is required as, for example, in the smelting of steel or iron. A slight error, and the metal will be of a different quality. This is the stage of work in the fields that we have approached. In order to obtain the maximum effect through the use of intensive methods, skilled personnel is indispensable. But we have not everywhere achieved an adequate level of professional training.

Many of our farmers are used to working in the following way: They do the sowing and then harvest what has grown. Just that and nothing more. With intensive methods you can't work that way. Using these methods, the cultivation of crops requires much skill and experience of a farmer. This is why personnel should be properly trained, for without thorough knowledge the situation won't improve. This, Comrades, is the reliable way of obtaining high and stable yields. The time of general instructions and slogans is gone. Party committees must keep this enormously important matter under their daily control and promote in every way the use of intensive methods, relying on science and advanced experience.

Secondly, the potential of scientifically-based crop-farming systems is still being inadequately used in many places. Such systems have been worked out for every zone, and, in fact, for every farm. This is an important means of raising soil fertility. Also, one must remember that the neglect of any of the elements of the crop-farming system disrupts the entire cycle in the battle for a good harvest and may bring the expenditure of labor and money to naught. I would like to make special mention of fallow land. Or, to be more precise, of the attitude toward it. Remember the hot debates that went on just a few years ago about whether or not to maintain fallow land. Science and the point of view based on the data of science won in the end. Now we have about 22 million hectares lying fallow. In the main grain-producing regions of Kazakhstan, Siberia and the Urals they occupy 15-20 per cent of plowland.

Terentii Maltsev, who is present here, used every occasion to remind me of this method saying that the matter should be brought to its logical conclusion. If the land lying fallow in Siberia and in the upturned virgin land areas of Kazakhstan makes up less than twenty per cent, we'd rather have none at all.

We have now either attained or come near to attaining this level. But the results are quite varied and have to be analyzed thoroughly. There is plenty of evidence to show that in arid years well-prepared and properly cultivated fallow land has produced double or triple the harvest of the land that did not lie fallow. This was particularly noticeable in bad years. The quality of grain has also been far better than in other fields. But that has not been the case everywhere. For example, even in such major grain-producing areas as the Omsk, Saratov, Orenburg and Tselinograd regions, or the Altai Territory, the extension of the land left to lie fallow has not yet ensured a proper growth of gross grain harvests.

What is the matter? It is that some land left to lie fallow has not had proper handling. This is not a new problem. We have spoken about it more than once. In one case the fallow land was not plowed up in good time, in another it was left uncultivated and free to grow over with weeds. Now what about district and regional agroindustrial amalgamations, agricultural specialists, and zonal research institutes? And, above all, Comrades, how can an agronomist look indifferently at all this? The land is a matter of his vital concern, of his honor and conscience as a specialist and lawmaker in the fields!

Next. It is obvious to all of us that in the specific conditions of our country, with its pronounced continental climate and oft-recurring droughts, it is impossible to have stable agricultural production with ameliorated, above all, irrigated lands.

We have accomplished much by carrying out a sweeping program of agricultural land improvement. This work will be further expanded under plans already worked out and adopted. This firm line of ours was reaffirmed at the CPSU Central Committee Plenary Meeting in October 1984.

Yet a top priority of today is not to enlarge the area of ameliorated land but to use it effectively. The harvests obtained so far do not correspond either to the expenses we have incurred or to the actual potentialities of the improved lands. All that the Ministries of Agriculture, Land Reclamation and Water Management and the USSR Academy of Agricultural Sciences have, in fact, been doing so far is to take note of this unsatisfactory state of affairs. There have been enough instructions in this respect, yet the heads of the above-mentioned organizations have failed to show a proper Party sense of responsibility for implementing the decisions of the CPSU Central Committee and the Government.

One can sometimes hear this kind of reasoning: It is enough

to have irrigated lands and good harvests will come automatically. This is something, you know, that reminds me of the reasoning of die-hard partisans of extensive farming. In matters relating to the use of irrigated lands we can least of all afford to wait for something to turn up automatically. In irrigated and ameliorated lands it is a must to get crops cultivated by intensive methods. Furthermore, the measures for a radical improvement of the ameliorated arable land should be taken without any delay. That is where the capital investments on hand must be used, first and foremost. This is the demand of the CPSU Central Committee and the Government, and it must be met unfailingly.

Fourth, the problems of livestock farming. We have to admit that, despite certain effort, scientific and technological progress so far has had little effect on this sector. Some high-ranking officials and experts still try to resolve the problems of boosting the output of meat, milk and other products through the use of extensive development factors.

Several years ago, when we emphasized as the main trend in livestock farming qualitative improvement and higher productivity, rather than growth of livestock population, many showed no support for this idea or were even opposed to it. Practice has shown, however, that our approach is justified. And it cannot be otherwise. This has been proven by the practice on many advanced farms. In the past two or three years, when the number of cows and other livestock in the country did not effectively increase, and the number of cows even decreased, there was a rise, not sharp but nonetheless steady, in the output and state procurement of livestock products.

We must continue to concentrate not on a growth of the livestock population, as this involves great expenditure for the construction of new farms as well as maintenance by the farm personnel, but on the determined introduction of intensive methods of livestock output. It is a fair guess that there will continue to be districts and even regions where livestock population should be increased if the production of fodder develops at a priority rate there. But the chief attention should be given to intensifying livestock farming.

If the delivered weight of each head of cattle is increased by at least fifty kilograms, we shall obtain an additional 1.5 million tons of meat in live weight, with the number of cattle remaining unchanged. This would be far cheaper and economically more efficient than obtaining the same additional amount of meat through a growth of the cattle population which would then have to be increased by nearly five million head.

Our dairy farming also needs a new approach. We must more actively avail ourselves of the opportunities opened up by breeding, by introducing new technologies and balanced-out feeding methods. These are the main prerequisites for high productivity. If today we were to obtain an average of 3,000 kilograms of milk from each cow of the existing number of cows in the country we would not know what to do with the surplus.

The questions of intensifying poultry and livestock farming and raising their productivity are particularly pressing in the regions and territories of Siberia and Kazakhstan and should be given the greatest attention.

The problem of improving storage and processing of farm produce is a most important problem of the Twelfth Five-Year Plan. The central bodies, which are responsible for furnishing the material and technological base for storage and processing, and the local Party and government organizations, which should look for ways of solving this problem, must be criticized. There is a need to ensure faster rates of development of the third sphere of the agroindustrial complex, particularly machine building for the food industry.

Participation of other ministries is indispensable for the solution of this problem. Local Party organizations and government bodies must work harder to carry out this task of major importance for the whole state and determine what exactly must and can be done locally to modernize and retool food, meat and dairy industry enterprises, vegetable storehouses and plants that manufacture and assemble refrigeration equipment.

Comrades, I would like to emphasize that there are problems whose solution entirely depends on you. Is it really a problem for big cities and regional and territorial centers, with their vast industrial potential and dozens of building organizations, to build facilities necessary for storing and marketing fruits and vegetables? I have been told, for example, that the system of delivering fruits and vegetables to shops directly from the fields works well in Tselinograd. It is a very important undertaking. The failure to make such systems work in some places is the result of an irresponsible attitude rather than difficulties. This is the only way of putting it, because this problem affects people's day-to-day needs and dampens the efforts to raise people's standard of living.

Building ministries should not push the construction and modernization of food industry enterprises into the background. I hope the builders will draw appropriate conclusions from this discussion.

There is one more question. The technological and organizational changes under way in agriculture and related industries require new attitudes toward the use of our research institutions' potentialities. It goes without saying that agricultural science has done and continues to do a great deal, of course. This is well known. But we cannot rest on our laurels.

The Central Committee has set the task of intensifying research efforts. Science must become a true catalyst of progress in the countryside. What is needed here is to drastically raise the level and enhance the effectiveness of research.

We are now passing through a stage where more vigorous efforts to promote the key directions of scientific and technological progress and fundamental research toward solving the pressing problems of biology and biotechnology are imperative. The Politburo has recently examined this issue and has passed a detailed resolution on it. The latest findings of scientists, the new achievements in this field, enable us to boost sharply the intensity of the major biological processes.

Progressive directions and modern patterns and methods of research open up vast opportunities for selection. The application of genetic and cell-engineering methods can dramatically speed up the development of new plant varieties in crop farming which are resistant to diseases, droughts and frost and are well adapted to the specific natural conditions of each region. This applies also to the breeding of new, more productive breeds of livestock and poultry.

As the problems of scientific support for agriculture stand now, they require the broad interaction of experts from various fields of knowledge. So here I would like to appeal to the USSR Academy of Sciences to step up its cooperation with the USSR Academy of Agricultural Sciences and with other research institutions of an agroindustrial orientation. Intensive integration of fundamental science with research institutions of the agroindustrial complex is a major source of improving the standards of agricultural science and the effectiveness of its influence on agricultural production.

Greater attention should be paid to the introduction of research findings into practice. This can take various forms. Experience shows, however, that the most rational form of all is that of research and production associations. This has been tested and borne out by many years of practice. . . .

We are unanimous in understanding the need for the earliest possible accomplishment of the tasks facing the agroindustrial complex. I have no doubt that we all agree that this requires a great amount of organizational and political work. The answer to the question of how to do this work more efficiently can be found in the decisions of the April 1985 Plenary Meeting, in the materials of the conference in the CPSU Central Committee on the problems of scientific and technological progress and in other Party documents. It is our duty to put into effect the ideas, instructions and conclusions outlined in these documents, resolutely and consistently.

What is needed is an enterprising effort in the nation's agrarian sector. This applies to all cadres—Party, government, managerial and trade union. This applies to Party organizations at all levels.

Resourceful, well-thought-out work of Party organizations will enable us to tap deep-lying reserves of production and secure high returns on the productive, economic and manpower potential that has been created in the countryside. That is exactly what now has to be regarded as a matter of top priority. I would like to refer in this context to the role of our rural district Party committees. Currently there are 3,200 of them. They are in charge of over 49,000 collective farm and state farm Party organizations. There are 6,500,000 Communists in the countryside, which is over one-third of our entire Party membership. This is a force, a vanguard that can do really great things, both in production and in social development. The CPSU Central Committee highly appreciates the activities of this large contingent of our Party and the contribution the Party committees make toward carrying out the Party's political strategy and the Food Program in particular.

There is, however, something I have to criticize. An inquiry by the corresponding Central Committee departments into the operation of a number of regional Party organizations has shown that many district Party Committees are slow in reorganizing their work and sometimes forget that a Party committee is a body of political leadership.

Some district committees veer off the correct path. It is difficult at times to distinguish the forms and methods of the work of a Party committee from those of an economic governmental body. Not all committees give proper attention to upgrading ideological work.

Work with personnel is of immense importance to a rural district committee. Collective farm and state farm managers are indeed our gold mine. We must highly value and raise the prestige of the difficult jobs of chairmen and managers in farms, so as to have a stable and capable staff of economic leaders in each district, region, territory and republic. . . .

This conference and counsel, preceding the forthcoming Party Congress and the beginning of the next five-year plan, are of particular significance not only to this major agricultural region but to all of our country and to our entire society. Kazakhstan, Siberia, and the Urals have the necessary conditions for implementing grain procurement plans successfully and making a tangible contribution to the nation's food resources. That will be a good present for the Twenty-seventh Congress.

September 7, 1985

BOOK THREE

TOWARD A BETTER WORLD

26

TO THE AMERICAN READER

Before you, respected reader, is the third collection of my speeches published in the United States. It is a continuation, as it were, of the dialogue begun between us a year ago, a dialogue at the center of which stand the most urgent problems of world politics, namely international security and Soviet-American relations. These are problems shared by both of us. And we should think about them together and agree on how best to solve them to our mutual benefit.

The works included in this collection (covering the period February–December 1986) concern various subjects and fields, from the most specific to the very broad, both domestic and worldwide. And still, it is my firm conviction that they are born of one idea: we can no longer live and think as we have in the past. Attempts to push tomorrow back to yesterday are too dangerous, especially in our day and age, and especially as they concern military affairs, where the price of a single error is irreversible catastrophe.

Each century, while giving birth to new ideas, gains new perceptions. Indeed, each and every one of us looks at the world differently than our fathers, grandfathers, and great-grandfathers did. Likewise, our children, not to mention our grandchildren, won't be able to understand many of today's cares and concerns. Such is the way things are.

The 20th century, however, is unique: it has witnessed the appearance of a range of new factors that compel us to perceive differently the effect that decisions taken by individual governments would have on the future of civilization, the relationship between the extension of our knowledge and the way we use it, and time and space themselves. Power politics that does not go beyond the use of gunpowder is one thing, and power politics based on a potential capable of making the myth about the world's end come true in a matter of minutes is quite another. Or, say, it is one thing when a handful of workshops emit smoke into the air, and quite another when we have overall air pollution threatening the world with an ecological disaster. Life itself demands that each national economy, and the world economy as a whole, be restructured, whether we like it or not.

In short, the time has come to ask ourselves and one another many questions, including unpleasant ones, for not all of them fit in with our customary notions of things that are so readily presented as "axioms" or "age-old truths." But it is quite unnecessary for anyone to abandon his own faith and to adopt one that is alien to him. Let each live by his own convictions and worship his own God. We must calmly sum up the collective experience of humankind, and draw objective conclusions from objective premises.

There is no reason why anyone should assume the role of an omniscient, implacable oracle. There is no state that has nothing to learn from others. We are all teachers and pupils in one way or another. But reality often has a way of becoming distorted in the human consciousness.

Innumerable are the times when domestic crises have given rise to international and even world crises; how often have people vented their anger on others when they are beset by internal difficulties. They have learned to drape even the most blatant, vulgar greediness in national colors, wrap it in high-flown rhetoric. Is it not self-evident that justice, social and ethnic justice in particular, lies at the foundation of democracy in any country. It is the cornerstone of harmonious inter-state relations—not superficial or elitist justice but that which embraces each and every one.

Consider the underlying ideological and moral conception of our 27th Party Congress, and of the new edition of the Party Program adopted at the Congress. In our view the competition between the two systems takes place simultaneously with a growing tendency toward the interdependence of states in the world community; herein lies the dialectics of the development of the modern world. A contradictory, but interdependent and in many ways integral, world is emerging in which the struggle between capitalism and socialism should take the form only of peaceful competition and peaceful rivalry. In this world, the guarantee of security is increasingly becoming a political rather than a military task.

Security, if we speak of the USSR and the U.S.A., can only be mutual, or, if we take international relations as a whole, only universal.

There will always be disputes over the nature of freedom, just as there will always be debates over the question of what is love. Each person, and even more so each generation, has its own standards of measurement and its own perceptions of these and similar matters. They depend on many circumstances, both transient and permanent, on one's temperament and state of health, on whether one is rich or poor. We have an old saying: A sated man does not understand a hungry one. Soviet people find it difficult to accept the idea that one man is destined to be sated, while the lot of another is to live hand-to-mouth. Americans probably have their own parable about the fat man and the thin one, their own disputes denying infallibility.

But one thing is certain: peace and life are inseparably linked. Only in conditions of peace can people take part in heated discussions about rights and freedoms, preferences and biases. Owing to the logic of historical development, a yearning for peace has come to occupy the highest position in the hierarchy of human values and political priorities. For the vast majority of people today, peace has become the criterion for judging what is permissible and what is not, what is lawful and what is not. In a nuclear age one's rights are not determined by what one "wants," since power permits one to "want," but by humanity's obligation to the present and future inhabitants of our planet. All can and must act together following this approach—in my view the only correct, moral, and forward-looking approach—to the problem of war and peace. This means everyone—people of all countries and nationalities, people with different world outlooks and convictions, people of different religious faiths and social status.

The United Nations proclaimed 1986 the Year of Peace. The Soviet Union sincerely supported this decision, supported it in deed and in action. Throughout this year silence has reigned at our nuclear testing sites. And we are not testing strike systems or their components in outer space. The USSR has put forward a whole range of businesslike proposals for bringing about a fundamental improvement in the world situation.

Almost all of our initiatives are outlined in this book. At this point I will mention only the most important among them:

—on January 15, 1986, we put forward a proposal on the step-by-step, strictly controlled elimination of nuclear arms by the year 2000;

—in late February we formulated the basic principles of an all-embracing system of international security that covers the military, political, economic, and humanitarian fields;

—at the Soviet-American negotiations we presented a package of detailed and balanced proposals on nuclear and space weapons;

—jointly with its Warsaw Treaty allies, the USSR has advanced a program to reduce armed forces and conventional armaments in Europe;

—the Soviet Union has outlined a wide-ranging plan before the countries of the Asia-Pacific region aimed at ensuring peace and cooperation in that part of the world;

—throughout the year, the task of ending experimental nuclear explosions under strict international control has not been removed from the agenda. In an effort to solve the problem, the USSR has extended its unilateral moratorium four times.

It's easy to brand our initiatives as "propaganda" without taking the trouble to consider them carefully. It's the easiest thing to do, especially when one doesn't really want to solve the problems. But let us ask ourselves, without prejudice, what it is that we are "propagandizing"?:

An end to nuclear tests. The elimination of nuclear weapons under effective control in any form. The dismantlement of military bases outside a country's national frontiers. The reduction of conventional armaments and, eventually, complete disarmament. A halt to propaganda of hate toward other peoples. The building of good-neighborly relations and cooperation between all countries in the name of life itself.

Is that so bad? Why is it that some prefer to advertise violence and cruelty, idolize weapons, turn diplomacy into an instrument of power politics and interstate relations into confrontation bristling with arms? Some people are trying to prove that military technology is the answer to the eternal question of "to be or not to be." Those who call for the use of force believe that "one nail drives out another." But that is suicidal self-deception. It is an ill-intentioned attempt to clothe vice as virtue so as to *prevent* people from recognizing (instead of helping them to recognize) an elementary truth: if there is to be life, weapons must cease to be.

It is not easy for adults to relearn. That is so. But nothing can be done about it; this is the demand of the times. The no-to-weapons signal will be flashed more and more often before the world's nations and their leaders. And no one should regard this objective necessity as an encroachment on national sovereignty and prestige or national pride, especially when they are intricately connected with force.

Is it right to deride common sense continually, to test people's nerves and keep them in a constant state of fear?

Is it permissible to take the planet's resources without moderation, to pollute its atmosphere and bodies of water, to destroy nature, and to overstrain ecological systems?

Is it a responsible thing to do to put national egoism before everything else, an egoism that knows no restrictions or even self-restrictions, be it under the flag of consumerism or "supreme interests"?

What must be done to make our common home on earth a safe one for all nations, and not just a well-appointed dwelling for one or two of them who happen to be luckier? The Soviet Union thinks that we should answer the challenges of our time together. And "together" does not mean doing things at the expense or to the detriment of one another. It means to try to see, first of all, what unites us and makes each of us part of one whole, not what divides us and puts us at opposite poles.

Who has thought up the stereotype, the idea that the USSR is America's enemy? How long has it been sowing confusion in people's minds? It would be interesting to know. Russia didn't meddle in the American revolution; in fact, it helped it in some way. Russia's "attentive neutrality" was beneficial to the struggle of the North American colonies for their liberation. The United States, as is known, "greeted" our revolution in October 1917 quite differently. When the American interventionists, along with others, had to withdraw from Soviet territory, those who stood at the helm in the United States were deeply offended; so much so that they did not recognize the USSR for sixteen years.

In general, I would like to note the following. Whenever one reads books on American history, one begins to wonder: where has the old, virtuous America gone? Where has the reverse come from—the idea of "not recognizing" another country, of "punishing" it, even with hunger; of deciding arbitrarily what is "good" and what is "bad," and of wishing others ill. It is indeed true that people hate those whom they have wronged.

I'm not trying to reproach anyone. Nothing could be further from my mind. Even in family relations reproaches are harmful, let alone in relations between states. I'm only calling for reflection without prejudice, setting aside timeworn myths and falsehoods.

I'm moved by different considerations. Why, for instance, does the development of Soviet-American relations nearly always lag behind world development? Why are we roused to constructive joint action mainly by terrible and dangerous events and not by normal realistic thinking? Why do peals of thunder prove more convincing than arguments prompted by common sense?

Yes, we have a socialist system, and our people prefer this system to any other—a system they have won through revolution and have defended in wars against interventionist forces and fascists, through the sacrifice of scores of millions of lives. We do not believe that our present system is perfect in every respect and are making a big effort to make our life better, brighter, and richer, both spiritually and materially. All right, we are different. But is this reason for enmity, for trying to impose on others one's own system, one's own way of life, one's own yardstick for measuring freedom? And why such an arrogant claim to being "perfect"? It is a dangerous, very dangerous claim, I would say.

Today we again have a common enemy. This enemy is more terrible than German fascism or Japanese militarism during the Second World War, when our two countries fought side by side. This enemy is nuclear war. In fighting against it the USSR and the U.S.A. must be on the same side, unconditionally. In an alliance formed to combat the threat of nuclear catastrophe, no one should have to sacrifice his cherished ideals, let alone his interests. Nuclear weapons are essentially immoral and inhuman. Their existence can find no justification in any religion or theory or in life itself. What can be proved by nuclear might? Only one thing: that man is foolish and imperfect, that he has deeply ingrained atavistic instincts. However, if the worst should happen, there would be no one left to prove this to. After such a war there will be no preachers or believers; neither rural Russian homes nor New York skyscrapers, neither the Kremlin nor the White House; neither man nor beast will survive. There will be no living thing left!

Soviet society is ready for peaceful competition with the capitalist system. We do not fear such competition. Nothing in our philosophy prevents the conclusion of the most radical agreements on disarmament, including complete demilitarization of the world under international control. Call it historical optimism or anything you like, but the fact remains that in all our creative undertakings peace is our chief ally and helper. I say this loud and clear, without reservations. The arms race, the military confrontation, the muscle-flexing— none of these is our choice, our kind of policy. It may be recalled that right after the revolution we did not even have an army and were not going to set one up. It came into being only when our land had been invaded.

How do we start ridding the earth of the scourge of militarism? It would be most practical, in our view, to begin from the beginning—by ending nuclear tests. After that, military arsenals should be reduced. At the same time, confidence between states should be built up and civilized relations cultivated. All that can be achieved only if we realize that in a nuclear age an essentially new approach to the question of war is needed. Psychologically, the possession of nuclear power gives rise to and sustains the hope of achieving world domination, of making other countries live according to the laws of those who wield a nuclear sword. This is, of course, an illusion, for nuclear war will inevitably destroy the very notion of "domination," together with those aspiring to it. But this is something that still needs to be understood. And policies must be shaped patiently and purposefully in quite a different direction than the one in which they are being formed today.

In order that people should have things under control, the Soviet Union has persistently been urging governments to set a limit to the militarization of science, to curtail work on the development of new military technologies and, as a first step, to stop nuclear testing. In August 1985 the USSR announced a unilateral moratorium on all nuclear explosions. Quiet has reigned at our test sites, although Western powers have continued to explode one charge after another.

In introducing the moratorium we were aware that Washington might start maneuvering, referring to "verification difficulties" and "a lack of confidence," and then, when the propaganda impact of such arguments has been spent, sweep aside all excuses and pretexts and say: "We must do what we must do in the interest of national security, and that's that!" Such a possibility existed from the outset. Still, one liked to think that common sense would prevail. After all, for the moratorium to become bilateral and then universal, no material outlays or special efforts were needed. In fact, nothing was needed except political will and a sense of responsibility for the present state and future of humanity. Between the ending of tests and the drafting of an agreement there was only half a step, for the document would only have formalized the actual state of affairs.

Thus, not only weapons and the latest technological ideas are being tested in Nevada. It is a test primarily of the policies of states, of how serious are their declarations renouncing nuclear war and promising a nuclear-free world, a test of their historical maturity. There is no need to be cunning here—to try to develop *postnuclear* weapons while testing nuclear ones. It is all rather obvious.

In this context it seems pertinent to recall something from the past, both recent and not so recent. How did the present vicious circle of an arms race come about? Over 25 types of the most horrible weapons—nuclear arms and munitions, strategic bombers, atomic submarines, multiple-warhead missiles, the neutron bomb, etc.—have been created since 1945 and introduced into world politics by the United States. The Soviet Union has been forced to catch up with the United States, to bridge gaps, while putting off many of its urgent tasks until later.

But such "militarist success" has cost the United States itself dearly. Economically, according to official statistics, total U.S. military spending in the years 1946–1986 came close to 3,400,000 million dollars. Surely this amount of money could have been spent in ways that would have benefitted the American people. The cost was also high, extremely high, militarily and politically, from the point of view of that country's effective security.

Each new weapon system added to the U.S. arsenal has increased the risk- and fear-factor. As a result the United States has ceased to be invulnerable, and the oceans around it no longer serve as its "guardian angels." To have created such a situation U.S. militarism has inflicted the greatest blow to the interests of the American people as well.

If one doesn't stop, this will go on and on. Action will produce counteraction. Let's say the USSR makes a first move; you will at once try to catch up. If the Americans start a new round of the arms race, we will find an antidote for it. But when will it stop? How long must this tug-of-war go on before common sense takes the upper hand, thus preventing the irreparable from happening? A peculiar feature of the present situation is that the Soviet Union possesses a wide range of responsive measures. Duplication of U.S. achievements—something that suited the United States very well—is now ruled out. This is both better and worse. Better, because it will mean less expenditure for us. Worse, because the technological incompatibility this leads to will further complicate arms control or will even make the problem insoluble from a technical point of view.

And now the main question: what have we got to quarrel over? Why should we be enemies—do we have anything to divide between us? We do not compete on the world market. Our interests do not conflict geographically. There are no Soviet bases close to your borders. We have many ideological and political differences, but they should not be a reason for mutual destruction. Why then seek trouble?

I read American newspapers and magazines regularly and listen to the radio, and so receive a mass of information. And I never cease wondering: why this hostility, this hatred toward us? What is the cause of it, what motives lie behind it? Can it be that jingoism—that refuge of ignorance—has become a mass ideology? For when one talks with Americans (and I have had many such talks) one usually feels nothing of the kind—neither hatred, nor bloodthirsty aggressiveness. One feels a desire for cooperation, peace, and good-neighborliness. So what is happening? Apparently someone wants us to be enemies. But who?

Some people say that the Soviet Union cannot be trusted. If there are people in the United States who really believe that, let's sort things out together. Why cannot the Soviet Union be trusted? What is the basis for such mistrust? Let us calmly, without unnecessary polemics and without giving in to emotions that drown out the voice of reason, recall the history of our countries, the history of our relations, and clear up the perplexities and misunderstandings—since they exist. Let us also find out if a mountain is not really a molehill. And if that is the case (and we believe it is exactly so), who needs this and why? And what can and must be done to stop this unwise practice?

I want to make this quite clear: in the Soviet Union, too, many are troubled by the problem of trust. They say quite frankly that the United States is not to be trusted. And they back up their position by referring to facts. For sixteen years the Soviet Union was not recognized by the United States. It is the Soviet Union, not the United States, that has been encircled with war bases. We were not the first to develop new means of warfare. It was against us that definite dates for a preemptive nuclear attack were set; it was our country that was divided on the map into occupation zones, and even the kind of state system it should have was predetermined. Documents of the National Security Council relating to this subject have been declassified. One can now read them. We were subjected to all sorts of insults, and "punished." It has been suggested that we be relegated to the scrap heap of history. And so on and so forth. I shall not go on with the list of facts that nourish our profound mistrust. But at times I ask myself: how would matters stand if we, and not the United States, were guilty of all the things mentioned and much else? How would you, esteemed Americans, feel about it? What would your reaction be?

The Soviet leadership believes that ruthlessness has no future in foreign policy (although certain U.S. circles have a thirst for it), and that confrontation is of no use economically, ideologically, or militarily. But sometimes a really dead-end situation develops, and one asks oneself: What more can one do when all one hears is the same stereotyped, cheerless "No."

My frankness might be surprising and perplexing. Nothing has apparently happened to warrant such a candid discussion. Perhaps the motive is the obvious disappointment in the course of events since the Geneva summit meeting. Although in words we came closer together after Geneva, the division in actions and in positions has grown wider. Thus far no new agreements have been reached, while there is a rush to bury previous agreements. The U.S.A. has announced plans to abandon the SALT-I Agreement and the SALT-II Treaty. The public is being prepared for a cancellation of the treaty, which has no time limit, on ballistic missile systems (ABM). The Star Wars program is being carried out at an accelerated pace. Work outside the laboratory has begun on the anti-satellite system ASAT. Judging by certain facts, the U.S.A. is testing in Nevada nuclear devices of third generation and fundamentally new strike systems using the energy of nuclear explosions. It follows from several highly authoritative statements that the United States is developing an entire set of technology for an actual, full-scale nuclear war.

Generally speaking, there are sufficient grounds for disappointment. Another matter for thought is the purpose which the American political lexicon serves—is it to express certain ideas or to cover up those ideas? No less disturbing is the unwillingness of Western politicians to look facts in the face, as well as their attempts to draw people's attention away from these facts with various ruses, rhetoric, and demagogy. Peace-loving verbiage doesn't at all inhibit the preaching of force or the singing of praises to nuclear weapons as a basis for a "deterrence strategy." Some people say that all of this is for domestic consumption. I will not make any judgments as to the morality of such an attitude, but it is high time to realize that today the entire world is being drawn into a discussion on life and death, and attitudes differ.

The radiation from an explosion of the smallest charge is more than three times as great as that of the Chernobyl accident. The use of even a small portion of the existing nuclear weapons—and over fifty thousand units of such weapons have been stockpiled to date—will be tantamount to catastrophe. I often recall the cruel saying of the ancients—you can take everything away from a man except death. He who strikes first will destroy himself. He will die even without a retaliatory blow, as a consequence of the explosion of the very warheads which he himself has detonated. I wish to thank the doctors, both American and Soviet, for disclosing that truth, for having calculated, using mathematical models, the outcome of a nuclear war. It was the politicians' turn to say this.

And during my meeting with U.S. President Ronald Reagan in Reykjavik on October 11 and 12, 1986, the Soviet Union stated that truth. But unfortunately, the United States did not share that view, and so we could not work toward a common goal. And it was not our fault. A turning-point in world history did not take place, even though it could have and we were as close to it as we have ever been before. A unique, historical opportunity has perhaps passed us by. Regrettably, there was a definite lack of a new approach on the part of the Americans.

We brought to Reykjavik a whole package of concrete proposals. Acceptance of these proposals could have become a driving force for the establishment of a nuclear-free world. What did the USSR propose to the U.S.A.?

1. To reduce strategic defensive arms by 50 percent on both sides in the coming five years, by the end of 1991. To eliminate the remaining 50 percent during the next five years, by the end of 1996.

2. To eliminate completely Soviet and American medium-range missiles in Europe. Furthermore, in contrast to our previous proposals, we did not insist this time that the powerful nuclear potential of Great Britain and France be included in the general count.

3. To establish three-way control—with national means, international methods and on-site inspection—over the process of eliminating nuclear weapons and over the strict observance by both sides of the agreements reached.

4. We proposed that in the course of the next ten years the USSR and the U.S.A. undertake to refrain from using their right to withdraw from the ABM Treaty, which is of unlimited duration, and to observe strictly all of its provisions; to refrain from testing space elements of antimissile defense systems in outer space, and to keep all testing and research within the boundaries of the laboratory.

5. To begin without delay talks with the aim of completely banning nuclear testing.

We offered the most large-scale compromises which, in the event of their being accepted, would have placed Soviet-American relations on a stable foundation. But these compromises also have their limits. If we disarm on earth, we cannot at the same time arm in outer space.

If SDI, as the American side has declared several times, is to render nuclear weapons useless, the question arises as to what will be rendered useless if, under three-way control, nuclear warheads and carriers are to be destroyed. A convincing answer to this question has not been given. Have the people obsessed with SDI worked out a postulate that domination in outer space implies domination on earth? Whatever the case may be, we naturally could not agree to the ABM Treaty being dropped from the set of disarmament accords. And indeed we had no right to act otherwise: the Soviet people would never agree to this.

And thus SDI—a program for achieving military superiority through militarization of outer space—wrecked actual agreements. We have been convinced again and again that SDI is not a defense system. Rather it is an attempt to replace or to supplement nuclear arms with even more destructive and insidious weapons. It is a new technological wrapping for the same old claims on world leadership and hegemony.

On the advertising boards SDI is depicted as all but an "insurance policy" for the American people. Appropriations for the SDI program are in fact expenditures on the universal funeral of all humanity. It sounds harsh, but truth doesn't always sound pretty.

SDI does not frighten us in military terms. The USSR can develop an anti-SDI program that will not be a duplication of the U.S.A.'s program, and not as expensive. Furthermore we can develop it sooner than the American Star Wars program will be carried out. But we don't want to do this. SDI and anti-SDI will mean an endless arms race that can get out of control.

What is to be done then? The would-be experts on international affairs, primitive enough to examine everything through a prism of anti-Sovietism, are ready to light the fireworks because in Reykjavik we didn't manage to reach an agreement. They cling to the lack of success and talk about Reykjavik as a failure.

I categorically reject this interpretation that turns the facts inside out. Reykjavik was an important and significant event. The meeting was useful in many ways. Ideas were reevaluated. Issues were discussed on a qualitatively new level. It was found that all the material means for building an enduring peace, a peace that is worthy of mankind, are available and that the most dangerous weapon systems can be scrapped.

At the same time, the American Administration's obstinacy shed new light on declarations and statements that the U.S.A. is supposedly no longer striving for superiority, on the worth of its declarations that no one can win a nuclear war, that reasonable compromises should not be rejected out of hand, etc. But, it turned out that the U.S.A. is still dreaming of superiority and cherishing the hope of victory in Star Wars and in a war on earth. And by compromise it has in mind mainly concessions by others. There is an absolute polarity between their words and actions.

The world must definitely change if civilization is to continue to exist. People are tired of words. They want action—constructive action. Action that will take into consideration equally the legitimate interests of each and all. This is the aim of Soviet policy, a policy of peace and disarmament. We stand for the continuation of the Geneva and Reykjavik dialogues—in Washington, Moscow, or any other place in the world.

We have reached a crossroads. For us to go to war—that is out of the question. The USSR and the U.S.A., every government and every nation, remaining as they are, must conduct their affairs in the international arena prudently and properly, and must live in a civilized manner. There is still time to choose the direction we will take. But time is not an inexhaustible resource. It is being depleted constantly. It shrinks before our very eyes. We must not lose this time. Political activity must proceed more quickly in order to reach at last the level scientific thought has attained and to outstrip the technical development of the arms race as much as possible.

We take matches away from children so they won't burn down the house or burn themselves. Today we must take nuclear weapons away from the adults so they won't burn down the universal home—earth—and so that they won't murder mankind.

A most important task is to work out a new mode of political thought and probably a new international law. A new way of thinking must develop that is characterized by respect for people and nations whose social coloring and social beliefs are different from ours. International law must be purged of double standards and categorically condemn aggressive wars and all other forms of international violence. In a future world community that will be different from the one we have today we will have to work together again to find ways of distributing wealth among all the countries of the world.

I have in mind especially the developing countries with a total population of more than two billion. Here we have a whole region of poverty. The national income of the former mother countries is eleven times higher than that of the former colonies. This gap is not narrowing but widening. It is a most acute problem. Its solution calls for constructive and creative cooperation between governments and nations on a world scale.

In the old days corporals warned young recruits that once a year guns fire by themselves. Today, when we rely heavily on computers, generals and politicians assure us that the opposite is true. So are we to wait for an accident to happen? And meanwhile are we to continue to pile up huge mountains of weapons on earth and prepare for their deployment in outer space? And then, if we can manage it, are we to establish military bases on the Moon and force Mars to justify its name as the God of War? In the meantime, the earth will be left to rot. And indeed why should we worry about what happens to the earth if politicians have acknowledged their inability to forestall the worst, thus condemning the planet to extinction?

And can we really continue to live like this?

Today it is not man who is asking nature to show mercy, rather nature is appealing to man to be merciful. Everyone is indebted to nature, you as well as we. But you are the more indebted: producing 53 percent of all goods manufactured in the world, developed capitalism accounts for 63 percent of all ecological refuse.

These figures can only roughly or theoretically be translated into rubles or dollars. For how can we calculate that which is priceless? For example, how can we estimate the price of the death of animals and vegetation? Valuable genetic stock is being depleted, many types of flora and fauna have become extinct, and the delicate balance of nature has been upset.

We may recall the plight of modern agriculture from which a hundred states are suffering. The Sahara, overrunning traditional farming lands, is moving headlong southward. It is possible to stop the spread of deserts, which have already taken over five billion hectares of land—one hectare for every inhabitant of the planet. According to specialists, to do this seventy billion dollars must be spent before the end of the century. In the next 15 years, if nothing changes, 15,000 billion dollars will be spent on the arms race. If military allocations were reduced only by a fraction, it would be possible to attack this threatening malady that is spreading like wildfire.

The world economy annually discharges into the atmosphere 200 million tons of carbon monoxide, more than 50 million tons of different hydrocarbons, 120 million tons of cinder and 150 million tons of sulphur dioxide that turns into "acid rain." Acid rain is quickly turning Europe into a "balding continent." Coniferous trees are dying out from the Mediterranean to the Baltic Sea. We are distressed by this calamity, which has also hit our own northern forest tracts.

The pollution level of the westerly winds in the European part of the USSR is about ten times higher than that of the easterly winds. But we are not condemning anyone. We propose cooperation. And that is why we are saddened when our tragedy—the accident at the Chernobyl nuclear power plant—has brought out in certain people in the West a malicious delight in the misfortune of others, an enthusiasm for everything anti-Soviet and a spate of primitive passions.

Man rose above all other living creatures on earth on the wings of humanism. Today five billion people living on this planet need humanism more than anything else. They need it for establishing good-neighborly relations between individuals and states. The fostering of a new way of thinking is, in my opinion, instrumental in bringing about a radical turn in the life of the world community. Revolutions always begin in the mind. The way to save civilization and life itself does not lie in thinking up new technologies for ever more accurate and lethal weapon systems, but rather in liberating the mind from prejudices—political and social, national and racial—from arrogance, self-conceit and the cult of force and violence.

In conclusion I would like to say that our era is marked by sharp changes. So many events and transformations are taking place within a very short period of time in our country, in your country and in the world as a whole. It is true that "time is money." But above all time is life—in the literal sense, and today in the political sense as well. We must make haste to remove the fears and threats looming over us, our children and our descendants. We in our country are changing and altering our mode of political thought and are adapting to the present realities, the realities of the nuclear age, the space age, and the computer age. We are waiting for this from everyone else; from you, the American people.

Let me say this: we have no evil or secret designs against your country; we are not hostile to the American people. And if anyone asserts otherwise, he is simply acting with bad intentions. We regard the people of the United States with respect.

I would like to use this opportunity to wish each of my readers, his near ones, and the great American people happiness and prosperity.

Mikhail Gorbachev

27

PRESS CONFERENCE

Reykjavik, Iceland, October 12, 1986

Good evening, ladies and gentlemen, comrades, greetings to you all.

Our meeting with the U.S. President, Mr. Reagan, ended about an hour ago. It had lasted a little longer than we had planned. This was made necessary by business in hand. So I want to make my apologies to you for not being able to come for the press conference at the appointed time.

You already know that the meeting took place on the initiative of the Soviet leadership. But, naturally, there would have been no meeting if Mr. Reagan had not agreed to it. That is why, I would say, it was our joint decision to have that meeting in Reykjavik.

Now it is over. It is sometimes said that when you talk to someone face to face, you can't see his face. I've just emerged from a meeting which, especially in its closing stage, passed in heated debates. And I am still under the impression of those debates. Nevertheless, I will try now not only to share my impressions but also to sort out what took place. Yet it will be the first impressions and evaluations, the first analysis. The meeting as a whole is yet to be evaluated more thoroughly.

It was an important meeting and you yourselves will realize this when I describe its contents, the problems which were the subject of a very broad, very intensive, and very serious discussion.

The atmosphere at the meeting was friendly. We had an opportunity to present our views freely and without restrictions. This enabled us to deepen our understanding concerning many major problems of world politics, bilateral relations, primarily those questions which are in the focus of world attention, problems of war and peace and the ending of the nuclear arms race, in short, the entire complex of questions coming under that subject.

I am a regular reader of the world press and I've seen in the last few days what a broad response the news of the meeting has evoked. A good deal was said in this connection both about the General Secretary of the CPSU Central Committee and about the U.S. President. The question was asked whether they had not been too hasty, whether there was any need for such a meeting, who made concessions to whom, who out-played whom, and so on. But you know, the reason why we made our proposal to the U.S. President to have a meeting without delay and his decision to respond to our invitation positively were very important.

I would now like to recall Geneva where we met for the first time. That was a major dialogue and now, after quite some time, we continue to regard the Geneva meeting that way.

At that time, if you remember, we recognized the special responsibility of the USSR and the United States of America for safeguarding peace, and declared jointly that nuclear war should never be unleashed and that there could be no winners in it. That was a statement of immense importance. We also declared that neither side would seek military superiority. That was also a very important statement.

Almost a year has passed since Geneva. The Soviet leadership has remained loyal to the commitments it assumed there. Having returned from Geneva, we extended our mor-atorium: it was to remain in effect till January 1 this year. Silence has reigned at our test sites for 14 months now—is this not evidence of our commitment to the Geneva accords and of our sense of responsibility for the destinies of peace? Those were not easy decisions to make since tests in Nevada continued at that time and are going on now. On January 15 we made a major statement in which a program for the elimination of nuclear weapons by the end of this century was set forth.

Last June the Warsaw Treaty countries put forward a major comprehensive program for large-scale reductions in con-ventional armaments and armed forces in Europe. That was also a major step in view of the concern voiced by the West Europeans and the United States.

Drawing the lesson of the Chernobyl tragedy, we proposed the convening of an emergency session of the IAEA General Conference in Vienna. It took place and you know about its results—they are very promising. Now we have an international mechanism which makes it possible to resolve many important questions concerning the safety of nuclear power engineering.

In other words, in the period under review—and I don't think I am exaggerating in making such an evaluation of our policy since what I speak of is facts, not mere intentions—we have been doing everything possible to help bring about a new way of thinking in this nuclear age. It gives us pleasure to note that the shoots of this new thinking are sprouting, especially on European soil. This was evidenced, among other things, by the success of the Stockholm meeting.

Now I'll probably conclude the list of the concrete actions that we have taken, guided by the letter and spirit of the Geneva accords with President Reagan. The facts themselves, I think, enable you to form your own judgments as to the seriousness of our attitude to these accords.

Still, why was the Reykjavik meeting necessary, what were the motives for our initiative?

The fact is that the hopes for major changes in the world situation, which we all entertained, began to evaporate shortly after the Geneva meeting, and, in my opinion, not without cause.

Much has been said, perhaps too much, at the Soviet-U.S. talks; between fifty and one hundred variants of proposals have been afloat, as I told the President yesterday. This fact alone raises doubts as to the fruitfulness of the discussions under way there. If there were one or two, even three variants, which would make it possible to narrow somehow the scope of discussions and concentrate the search on some major directions, one could then expect that the search would lead to concrete agreements and proposals to the governments. But nothing of this kind is taking place at Geneva, although the discussion there is concerned with key issues of world politics.

Frankly speaking, these negotiations have recently been marking time, in fact, they are practically deadlocked. The arms race has not been stopped, and it is becoming increasingly clear that developments are approaching a point where a new spiral of the arms race becomes inevitable, with unpredictable political and military consequences.

Our major initiatives, which I have already mentioned, have evoked a broad response from the world public. But they have not met with due understanding on the part of the U.S. Administration.

The situation has worsened; once again there is growing anxiety around the world. I think it's no exaggeration to say—you yourselves are witnesses to it—that the world is in a state of turmoil. The world is in a state of turmoil, and it demands that the leaders of all countries, above all the major powers, primarily the Soviet Union and the United States, display political will and determination so that the dangerous trends can be halted.

So, something had to be done in order to overcome such a course of developments. We came to the conclusion that a new impetus was necessary, a powerful impetus to turning the process in the required direction. Such impetuses could be provided only by the leaders of the USSR and the United States of America. That is why, in replying to President Reagan's letter of July 25, I decided to invite him to a meeting to be held immediately. I wrote: The situation is such that we ought to put aside all affairs for a couple of days and meet without delay.

The letter was handed to the President by Comrade Shevardnadze.

Now, this extremely important meeting has been held. We believed that many things would depend on its outcome. And, naturally, we did not come to the meeting empty-handed.

What have we brought to Reykjavik? We have brought a whole package of major proposals which, if accepted, could within a brief period really bring about, I would say, a breakthrough in all directions of the struggle for limiting nuclear weapons and really eliminate the threat of nuclear war, and would make it possible to start moving toward a nuclear-free world.

I suggested to the President that we, right here in Reykjavik, give binding instructions to our foreign ministers and the departments concerned *to have three agreements drafted,* which the President and I could sign later during my visit to the United States of America.

The first concerned strategic arms; it should stipulate a 50 percent reduction of these arms, and no less, with a view to fully eliminating these deadliest of weapons already by the end of the century.

We acted on the belief that the world is waiting for really major steps, substantial reductions rather than some cosmetic steps intended merely to calm public opinion for a while. Really bold, responsible actions are now needed in the interests of the entire world, including the peoples of the Soviet Union and the United States of America.

Naturally, the Soviet and the U.S. delegations that would be assigned the job of drafting the agreement on strategic arms should work out a balanced reduction of their historically formed structure honestly and with care.

The point at issue is the very triad that was recognized way back when SALT-II was being drafted. But when I raised this question with the President, in response everything that features at the Geneva talks was brought up once again—levels and sublevels, in short, much arithmetic, and everything meant to confuse the essence of the matter. We then proposed the following for the sake of being more precise: that each component of the strategic offensive armaments—land-based strategic missiles, submarine-launched strategic missiles, and strategic bombers—be reduced by half.

The U.S. delegation agreed to that. Thus, we reached agreement on a very important issue.

I would like to draw your attention to the fact that we made substantial concessions here. You will remember, too, that when we made our 50-percent-cut proposal at Geneva, we counted medium-range missiles as strategic weapons since our territory is within their reach. Now we have dropped that demand, along with the question of forward-based systems. Agreement was thus reached in Reykjavik on cuts in strategic weapons thanks to these major concessions.

Our next proposal concerned medium-range missiles. We proposed that instructions be given to draw up an accord on weapons of that type too; the idea was to give up all the options, temporary or interim, that had been discussed so far, and to go back to the earlier American proposal on the total elimination of American and Soviet medium-range missiles in Europe. And what makes our new proposal different from our Geneva proposals is that we now left completely aside the nuclear potentials of France and Britain. You understand, of course, that this was a very large concession on our part. Indeed, those two countries are allies of the U.S.A. and they have nuclear potentials which continue to be built up and upgraded. And all of their military activities are closely coordinated within NATO. We know this for certain. Nevertheless, we removed that obstacle to agreement.

There was also concern about Asia. We offered a compromise there as well: let us sit down and start negotiations right away, air our complaints, and find a solution. We understood that the question of missiles with a range of less than 1,000 kilometers was bound to come up. So we made a proposal regarding that question: a freeze on those missiles and the holding of talks to decide what to do with them.

These are the large-scale measures we wanted to see carried out. I think that the Americans had not expected this from us, but they entered into the discussion and said frankly that they were not willing to remove their missiles from Europe. They again asked us to accept their interim option. We, however, insisted on completely ridding Europe of both Soviet and American medium-range missiles.

During the discussion on that question we called the U.S. President's attention to the fact that he seemed to be abandoning his brainchild, the "zero option," which at one time he was offering us with such insistence, even though we had now decided to take it up.

The discussion, and very heated discussion, continued into today. And we decided to make yet another constructive move: we said that if the American and Soviet missiles in Europe were eliminated we would agree to have 100 warheads left on our medium-range missiles in Asia while the Americans would have as many on theirs on U.S. territory. Eventually we reached an agreement on that type of nuclear weapons too, although, as I've already said, it was also a major concession on our part.

After all, a start has to be made somehow. I have pointed this out on more than one occasion. Bold, innovative solutions are needed! If we always turn to the past for advice and make use of what belongs to very different times, without considering where we are today and where we will be tomorrow, and that there may be no tomorrow at all if we act in this way, there will be no dialogue whatsoever. There must be some way of making a start. So we decided to take this step, although, I repeat, this was not easy for us.

In view of our readiness to make deep cuts in nuclear weapons, we put the question as follows: as soon as we enter the concrete phase of the elimination of nuclear weapons, we must be absolutely clear on the question of verification. Verification must now become stricter. The Soviet Union stands for triple verification, which would enable each side to feel perfectly confident that it would not be led into a trap. We reaffirmed our readiness for any form of verification. That question was solved, too, because of this stand of ours.

If we set about the practical abolition of nuclear weapons, another problem will arise: each side should have guarantees that during that time the other side will not be seeking military superiority. I think this is a perfectly fair and legitimate requirement both from a political and a military point of view.

Politically—if we were to begin reductions, we should see to it that all existing brakes on the development of new types of weapons are not only preserved, but also strengthened.

Militarily—steps should indeed be taken to preclude the following situation: both sides have been reducing their nuclear potentials, and while the reduction process is under way one of the sides secretly makes the necessary preparations and captures the initiative and attains military superiority. This is inadmissible. I apply this to the Soviet Union. And we have every right to demand the same of the American side.

That is why we raised this question: if we should enter the stage of a real, deep reduction, within ten years—and that's how things looked to us at the meeting—the nuclear potentials of the Soviet Union and the United States would have been eliminated; in that case, it would be necessary to ensure that during this period the mechanisms restraining the arms race, such as the ABM Treaty above all, are not weakened, but strengthened. Our proposal was thus reduced to the following: the sides should strengthen the ABM Treaty, a treaty of unlimited duration, by assuming equal commitments not to use the right to pull out of this Treaty within the ten-year period, the period during which the nuclear potentials would be reduced.

Is this proposition a correct one, is it logical? It is logical. Is it serious? It is serious. Does it meet the interests of both sides? It meets the interests of both sides. We also pointed out that all obligations under the ABM Treaty should be strictly fulfilled within these ten years, that only ABM research and testing in laboratory conditions should be allowed.

What did we mean by this? We realize the commitment of the U.S. Administration and the U.S. President to SDI. Our consent to the continuation of laboratory tests apparently grants the President the opportunity to perfect his ideas and eventually to clarify exactly what SDI is. But for many people, ourselves included, it is already clear as to what SDI is all about.

And it was at that point that a true battle began between two differing approaches to issues in world politics, including those of the termination of the arms race and a ban on nuclear weapons. The President insisted to the bitter end that America should have the right to conduct research and testing on every aspect of SDI both in and outside the laboratory, including in outer space. But who will agree to this?

We were on the verge of taking major and historic decisions, because until now the central issue in previous treaties—ABM, SALT-I, SALT-II—has always been arms limitations only, while today it has become considerable reductions. We have now been convinced one more time that the U.S. Administration, confident in American technological superiority, is hoping to obtain military superiority through SDI. And so it has gone so far as to bury the accords which had almost been achieved and on which we had already reached agreement. The instructions were to be given for drawing up the treaties, and the procedures were to be worked out for their actual implementation. They could be signed during my visit to Washington. But the American side torpedoed all of this.

I told the President that we were missing a historic chance. Our positions had never been so close. When saying goodbye, the President told me that he was disappointed and that I had arrived unwilling to reach agreements and accords. Why, he asked, do you, because of the one word SDI, display such a rigid approach to this issue and to that of testing? And I answered that it is not a matter of words, but rather of substance.

Herein lies the key to understanding what the U.S. Administration has in mind—the same thing as the U.S. military-industrial complex has in mind. The U.S. Administration is being held captive by this complex and thus the President is not free to take such a decision.

We took breaks, resumed debates and I noticed that the President was not supported. And that was why our meeting failed even though we were already near to producing historic results. That was the dramatic situation that developed at the meeting in Reykjavik. In spite of the very substantial concessions our side had made, we failed to reach an accord.

Although it was fraught with difficulties, our dialogue with the U.S.A. continued after Geneva. I expressed my opinion to the President as to what our meeting during my visit to the United States should be like. This is not a condition; it is my understanding of our responsibility, both my own and the President's. This responsibility requires precisely this approach to a future meeting in Washington.

We need a productive meeting. It should lead to tangible results and cardinal changes, especially on such vital issues as those of controlling nuclear arms, ending the arms race, and eliminating nuclear weapons. I told the President in my letters to him and again in person during our meeting: Mr. President, you and I must not allow our meeting in Washington to fail. That is why I called for a meeting without delay, which was held here in Reykjavik. We have constructive contributions to make so as to reach agreement in Washington; these are serious proposals and serious draft decisions.

I cannot allow myself even for a minute to consider the possibility of a meeting in Washington failing. What then, generally speaking, would people think in the Soviet Union, in the U.S.A. and all over the world? What sort of politicians are heading those two huge nations on which the fate of the entire world greatly depends? They meet with one another, exchange letters, and have already held their third meeting, but they cannot agree on anything. I think this would be simply a scandalous outcome with unpredictable consequences.

We just cannot allow this to happen. It would be disappointing not only for our own countries, but for the entire world. This is in fact an outline of a Washington meeting as it should be held and the results we should achieve. That was what prompted us to propose a working meeting here, in Reykjavik, so as to sort out everything in a businesslike manner, to listen to each other attentively and to try to find points of contact and common approaches that would meet the interests of our two countries, the interests of our allies and the interests of the peoples of all countries.

Regrettably, the Americans came to this meeting empty-handed, with the same old moth-eaten trash from which the Geneva talks are already choking. We tabled the proposals, which I have already spoken about, in order to overturn the situation developing, to clear the path, to bring negotiations up to a new level, and to make real decisions. And now you also know what happened.

What is to be done? The reality is that both the United States and the Soviet Union remain. A character in a novel by one of our Russian writers had planned "to close out" America. We are free of such syndromes. America is a reality. But it is not just the Soviet Union and the United States; the entire world is a reality, and today one cannot obtain authority or, what is more important, resolve any problems if one does not reckon with the realities of the modern world.

We felt that there was a definite lack of a new way of thinking at this meeting. And the ghost of pursuit for military superiority reemerged. This summer I met with Mr. Nixon, and he said to me then: I have grounds to say, on the basis of my vast political and life experience, that the search for that ghost of superiority has taken us too far. Now we do not know how to break away from the mounted stockpiles of nuclear weapons. All this is complicating and poisoning the situation in the world.

I think, nevertheless, that the entire meeting here was of major significance. We did, after all, come close to reaching agreements; only they have yet to be endorsed. We put our proposals forward in a package. I think you understand why this was done. The very path that we have traversed in reaching these agreements here in Iceland on major cuts in nuclear weapons has given us substantial experience and we have made considerable gains.

I think that both we and the U.S. President should reflect

upon the entire situation that ultimately arose here at this meeting, return once again to the issues under discussion, and try to step over the obstacles dividing us. We have agreed on many things already and have traversed a long path. The President most likely needs to consult with Congress, with political circles and with the American public.

Let America ponder all this. We will be waiting and will not withdraw the proposals we have made public. In fact, we have come near to reaching an agreement on these proposals. This is the first point.

Second, I think that all the realistic forces in the world must act now. All of us—those in the socialist world, in the capitalist world, and in the developing world—now have a unique chance: to really start, at last, work toward ending the arms race, banning nuclear weapons, eliminating these weapons, and removing the nuclear threat from mankind. In connection with this we submitted the following proposal to the U.S. President: let us agree that our representatives start talks on banning nuclear explosions immediately after the conclusion of our meeting in Reykjavik. Furthermore, we displayed a flexible approach and said that we regard this as a process during which we would also examine at some stage, perhaps even on a top-priority basis, the issue of ceilings on nuclear explosion yields, the issue of the number of nuclear explosions per year, and the fate of the 1974 and 1976 treaties. We would thus move further toward the elaboration of a comprehensive treaty banning all nuclear explosions.

We were close to establishing a formula on this issue as well. We told the American side that we do not demand that they introduce a moratorium. That is up to you. You will report to your Congress and to your people as to whether you will continue nuclear explosions or whether you will join our moratorium after the talks have started. That is up to you. But let us begin full-scale talks to work out an agreement that would ban nuclear explosions completely and finally.

Thus the positions drew closer together here. But the search was ended and all discussions halted when talks broke down on the issue of the ABM Treaty and we ended the meeting.

I think that we and the Americans should think about all of this, and that the world public should reflect upon the situation that has evolved in the world in regard to the principal issues of concern to the peoples of all countries—those of war and peace and of the nuclear threat. I do not think it is any exaggeration to say that everything we proposed to the President meets the interests of the American people and the peoples of all countries. If someone thinks that is not true, he should listen to the demands of the American people, the Soviet people, and the peoples of all countries.

Arriving here for this meeting, I said that it was time for action. The time to act really has arrived, and we must not waste it. And we will act. We will not give up our peace policy, our policy of fighting against the arms race and for the banning of nuclear weapons, our policy for eliminating nuclear weapons and the threat posed to the entire planet. And I am positive that we are not alone in this struggle.

This is what I wanted to tell you right now, immediately after the conclusion of the meeting. Perhaps I could say more if I had had more time to ponder everything that happened. It seems to me, however, that I expressed myself clearly and definitely on all issues.

We touched also on many other issues in the course of the meeting with the President. We discussed humanitarian issues and dealt with specific problems in that sphere. Two groups of experts were at work. You probably already know about that. One of them was headed from our side by Akhromeyev, Marshal of the Soviet Union and Chief of the General Staff, while the American side was headed by Paul Nitze. They worked practically the entire night.

The group on humanitarian issues was headed from our side by Bessmertnykh, Deputy Foreign Minister, and from the American side by Ms. Ridgway, Assistant Secretary of State.

There was an interesting exchange of opinions there as well, and certain aspects of the understandings reached could have become a component part of the final document. But because the meeting as a whole collapsed, the entire process came to a standstill.

As you see, this was an interesting, important, and promising meeting on the whole. But for the time being it has ended this way.

But let us not despair. I think that with this meeting we

have reached the very important stage of understanding where we are. And it has been shown that accords are possible. I am sure of this.

Thank you.

Do you really have questions after such a detailed speech? Well, let's have them. We will be here until dawn.

Question *(Czechoslovak Television):* Mikhail Sergeyevich, you said that a historic chance has been missed here, in Reykjavik. When, do you think, will a new chance emerge?

Answer: You know I would answer optimistically. Because much was accomplished before the meeting and at the meeting itself. If we think everything over again and if realism and responsibility reign—in the United States, in the White House, and in our Soviet leadership—then the chance will not be lost to resolve these issues.

Question *(The Japan Broadcasting Corporation):* Does this mean that the dialogue with the U.S.A. and with the Reagan Administration is continuing? Or you think that the possibilities for a productive dialogue with President Reagan are very slim?

Answer: I think that the need for dialogue at present is even greater, no matter how fraught with difficulties it might be.

Question *(the Soviet newspaper Pravda):* Mikhail Sergeyevich, why do you think the U.S. Administration decided to wreck the negotiations, to act so irresponsibly, and to ignore world public opinion?

Answer: It seems to me that America has yet to make up its mind. I don't think it has done this yet. This, we felt, reflected on the President's stand.

Question *(the Australian Radio Broadcasting Corporation):* You said that President Reagan is being held captive by the military-industrial complex. Does this mean that no progress will be made at all over the next two years? Do you have hopes that the next U.S. President will not be held captive by this complex?

Answer: Irrespective of what the military-industrial complex is at present and irrespective of the weight it carries in present-day America, let us not overestimate its potential. In any country the final say is with the people, and this includes the American people.

Question *(Icelandic Radio and Television):* After the meeting's poor outcome will the Soviet Union counter in some way the American SDI program and will it launch its space-arms program full blast?

Answer: I think that you have understood the essence of the Soviet position. If we have now approached a stage at which we will start cutting drastically nuclear weapons, both strategic and medium-range missiles (we have already come close to reaching an understanding with the Americans to do this within the next ten years), then we have the right to demand the guarantee that nothing unexpected and unforeseen will take place during this period. This also includes spheres such as that of the ABM system, and especially its space-based element.

I told the President that SDI does not worry us in military terms. In my opinion, there are only a few people even in America who believe that such a system can be created. Furthermore, if in the end America decides to do this, our reply will not be symmetrical. It's true, Mr. President, I told him, that I am allegedly your ally on the issue of SDI. He was surprised by this. And I told him it turns out that because I so sharply criticize SDI, you are supplied with a convincing argument that SDI is necessary. You put it simply: if Gorbachev is against it, then that means it's a good thing. And thus you earn applause and financing. True, cynics and skeptics have appeared who say: what if this is Gorbachev's crafty design—to stay out of SDI and thus ruin America. So you figure this one out yourself. But at any rate SDI does not scare us. I say this with confidence, for it is irresponsible to bluff in such matters. There will be a reply to the Strategic Defense Initiative. There will be one, though it will be asymmetrical. And it will not cost us much at that.

But what is the danger involved in SDI? For one thing, there is a political danger. Right away a situation is created which lends itself to uncertainty and stirs up mistrust and suspicion of one another. Then the reduction of nuclear weapons will be put aside. In short, a quite different situation is needed for us to seriously consider the question of reducing nuclear weapons. Second, we must not forget about the military side of the issue. SDI can lead to the appearance of new types of weapons. This we also can say with competence. It can bring about an entirely new stage of the arms race that can have very serious consequences.

It works out that, on the one hand, we agree to start reducing nuclear weapons—at present the most dangerous and dreadful—and, on the other, we are supposed to agree to research, and even carry it out to space, with the intention of creating novel weapons. This does not correspond to logic.

Question *(The Washington Post):* You have just held another meeting with President Reagan after two days of sessions. What is your impression of the President as a political figure? Do you believe that he shares your sense of responsibility for the destinies of the world?

Answer: My impression is that Mr. Reagan and I can continue the dialogue and search for ways to resolve major pressing problems, including those I have spoken about.

Question *(The Danish Broadcasting Corporation):* Do the unsatisfactory results of the meeting mean that no progress will be achieved on the banning of nuclear tests and on other problems which were discussed yesterday and today? Is this problem—the banning of nuclear tests—linked with other problems discussed at the sessions?

Answer: I have already answered this question. We do not believe that our contacts with Americans and with the President, much less international relations, have been severed as a result of the latest developments. The quest is under way, and it will be continued. All the more so, for the developments that took place here, in Iceland, make all people realize that they should join the common struggle for the normalization of the international situation, the quest for resolutions to dead-end situations, including those which were discussed in Reykjavik. In fact, one such dead-end situation arose here. However, I am an optimist.

Question *(GDR Television):* You said that the meeting had brought no results. Does this mean that it was useless? What do you think: has peace become more reliable since the Reykjavik meetings?

Answer: I believe you have thought your question out thoroughly. One thing I always like about our German friends is their concise manner of expression including the expression of thoughts. The fact that we concluded our meeting without having reached agreement on the problems to which we seemed to have found approaches —this, of course, is sad and disappointing. Nonetheless, I would not say the meeting was useless. On the contrary, it is a new stage in a complicated and difficult dialogue in the search for solutions. After all, these are difficult solutions to complex issues. Therefore, let us not spread panic throughout the world. But at the same time, the world should know all that is going on, and it should not feel like a passive bystander. The time has come for vigorous action from all quarters.

Question *(the American TV company ABC):* Mr. General Secretary, I do not understand why, when given an opportunity to achieve agreement with President Reagan on cuts in nuclear weapons, the Soviet side did not agree to SDI research. You yourself said in Geneva that you were willing to pay a high price for nuclear arms cuts. And now, when such an opportunity appeared, you dismissed it.

Answer: Your question contains an element of criticism, so I will answer it in some detail.

First, the U. S. President came to Reykjavik empty-handed. The American delegation, I would say, brought us trash from the Geneva talks. It was only thanks to the far-reaching proposals of the Soviet side that we came close to reaching some very major agreements (though they were not in fact formalized) on cuts in strategic offensive weapons and on medium-range missiles. We naturally hoped in that situation— and I think this is perfectly clear to a politician, a military man, and any normal person in general—that since we were signing such major agreements, we should make sure that nothing would happen that might thwart that difficult process toward which we had been moving for decades. I have already said what is meant here. I will add: the American side has long been burrowing under the ABM Treaty. It has already called into question SALT-II and would like now in Reykjavik to stage a funeral for the ABM Treaty, and with the participation of the Soviet Union and Gorbachev at that. This will not do. The whole world would fail to understand us. I am convinced in this.

If we begin to attack the ABM Treaty, too, the last mechanism which has contributed so much to constraining, in spite of everything, the process of the arms race, we are worthless politicians. But it is not enough to simply preserve it at a time when deep cuts in nuclear weapons are being initiated; it must be strengthened. And we have proposed a mechanism for strengthening it—not to use the right to pull out of the ABM Treaty for the ten years it will take to totally reduce and destroy the nuclear potentials of our countries.

At the same time, in order to ensure that neither the Soviet Union nor the United States seeks to overtake the other in space research and thus achieve military superiority, we said: we are for laboratory research and testing but against taking that research and the testing of components of space-based ABM defenses into outer space. Such is our demand. Thus, our demand, in this case also, was constructive and took into consideration our partner's positions. If it were to agree, the U. S. Administration would gain an opportunity to resolve its problems within the framework of continued laboratory research but without attempts to develop space ABM defenses. That's "an iron" logic, as children say, and sometimes we should take our lessons from them.

Now let us give the women the floor.

Question *(The Guardian):* Is the Soviet Union planning any new initiatives for Western Europe after what happened in Reykjavik?

Answer: I think Western Europe hears what I am saying and if it thinks our proposals over and studies them closely, it will find that they meet its interests. We are far from being indifferent to the interests of Western Europe, in whose soil the shoots of new thinking are taking root and where responsibility for the preservation and strengthening of our common European home is growing.

Question *(Newsweek):* What are your plans concerning a visit to Washington? You said that an agreement or two must be achieved before such a visit. Can such agreements be achieved before you come to Washington?

Answer: I think that in spite of the dramatic developments of today, we are not farther from Washington but closer to it. If the President and the U. S. Administration will listen to my proposal to continue reviewing everything we discussed here in Reykjavik and consult those circles whose counsel they deem essential, I do not think everything will be lost. There are opportunities, relying on what we had here in Reykjavik, to reach agreements that would make a meeting in Washington a real possibility which could produce results.

Question *(CNN):* Mr. Gorbachev, you said in your speech that President Reagan should think the situation over and keep counsel with Congress and the American people. Do you think that American public opinion will back the Soviet approach?

Answer: We will wait and see.

Question *(Rude Pravo):* I would like to ask you as a politician and a lawyer: How do you view human rights priorities in the nuclear-missile age and what role can the human factor play in resolving questions of war and peace?

Answer: You are a philosopher. I once studied philosophy myself and have now turned to it again. I think that when we discuss human rights, we should remember that today the question of safeguarding peace and freeing man from the nuclear threat is the main priority. If there is peace, there will be life—and we will sort out our problems one way or another. The number of educated people and educated nations in the world is constantly growing. Nations will sort things out. That is why in discussing human rights I would attach priority to man's right to live. This is first.

Second—as to the human factor—I believe that in the nuclear age (and I consider this a manifestation of a new way of thinking) the threat of nuclear war gives a new dimension to the role of the human factor in preventing this war. A nuclear war will affect everyone regardless of where it breaks out. It is only ill-wishers who see the hand of Moscow behind all anti-war movements, behind all those who work for peace. Today women, children, and men of all ages are rising up, joining hands, and demanding an end to the dangerous trend leading the world toward nuclear war. The role of the human factor in these conditions is growing immensely.

Queston *(Izvestia):* There has been much and frequent talk in the White House to the effect that Soviet ICBMs pose the main danger to America. We proposed in Reykjavik that this main danger to America be eliminated within ten years. What do you think? Why did the other side prove unwilling to eliminate this main danger, avert it from its country?

Answer: You are right to pose this question. For many years the following argument was used: the Soviet Union, they alleged, is not serious about disarmament and ending the arms race, inasmuch as it disregards America's concerns.

As you see, we proposed radical reductions. And we put the question very pointedly, at that. There is a triad of strategic weapons recognized by both us and the Americans. We suggested that the whole triad of strategic armed forces be cut by 50 percent over the first five years. This was a major step.

At the same time, however, we told the Americans that we had a concern of our own. A large part of the United States' strategic forces is deployed on submarines. This is close to 700 missiles with a total of nearly 6,000 independently targetable multiple warheads. And these submarines are known to be circulating in the seas and oceans around the Soviet Union. Where will they strike? This is no less dangerous than heavy land-based missiles.

In short, when they do not want to deal with certain questions, they look for problems and raise artificial obstacles. Here, however, in Reykjavik, we excluded the possibility of such fabricated obstacles. This is what's important. We undertook a very important step in removing stipulations with regard to medium-range missiles, which we consider to be strategic weapons. We also struck forward-based systems from the list. All this is a demonstration of our good will. Nevertheless, the Americans made no effort to meet us halfway.

The Americans think that they will achieve military superiority over us via outer space and thus realize the idea of one of their presidents, who said: he who will dominate outer space will dominate earth. This shows that we are forced to deal with imperial ambitions.

The world today is not what it once was, however. It does not want to be, and will not be, the private domain of either the United States of America or the Soviet Union. Every country has the right to choose, the right to its own ideology, to its own values. If we fail to recognize this, there will be no international relations. There will be only chaos and the law of the jungle. We will never agree to this.

America must long for the "good ole days," when it was strong and militarily superior to us, since we had emerged from the war economically weakened.

Apparently there is nostalgia for the past in America. Yet we would wish for our American partners to come to grips with today's realities. It is essential that they do so. Otherwise, that is if the Americans do not start thinking in today's terms and proceeding from today's realities, we all will not make progress in our search for the right solutions.

Question *(Bulgarian television):* I take it that the Geneva talks will not be stopped, and that the Soviet leadership will give instructions to the Soviet delegation to search for ways to resolve the problems which are yet unresolved.

Answer: You are correct.

Question: Do you think that after the Reykjavik meeting similar instructions will be given to the American delegation?

Answer: I hope so.

Question *(the Czechoslovak ČTK news agency):* In your opinion, how will the outcome of the Reykjavik meeting influence the all-European process?

Answer: I think that at this moment of responsibility the politicians and the peoples of Europe will measure up to the situation. Time requires actions, not just eloquent statements that are not followed up by anything concrete. The world is tired, fed up with empty talk; it needs real progress in the sphere of disarmament and the elimination of nuclear weapons. I believe that this trend will gain prominence. I am pinning particular hope on the wisdom and sense of responsibility of the politicians and peoples of Europe.

Question *(the American television company NBC):* As I understand, you are directly calling on other members of the world community to act as a kind of a lobby in order to influence the United States and make it change its mind?

Answer: We know how developed lobbyism is in your country, how the political process goes in America. Perhaps that is why it was difficult for the President to make a decision at this meeting. But when the matter at hand deals with consolidating peace and undertaking real steps to this end, when concerted efforts are needed—this concerns all, not just the United States and the Soviet Union—then, I think, one should speak not about lobbyism, but about the sense of responsibility, the common sense of peoples, about the appreciation of today's peace and the need to protect it. Therefore, it is insulting to accuse peoples or movements campaigning for peace of being lobbyists for the Soviet Union. The point is that people uphold their political and civic positions.

Question *(the Icelandic newspaper Morgunbladid):* I work as a newspaper publisher in Iceland. Was it difficult for you to decide to come to Reykjavik? After all, Iceland is a member of NATO. At the same time, as you know, our government proposed that the North be made a nuclear-free zone, and I would like to know your attitude toward this.

Answer: I wanted to conclude with this topic and will gladly take advantage of this question put by a representative of the Icelandic press to do so. I would like to remind everyone that it was the USSR who suggested Iceland as a possible venue for the meeting. That is why we had no difficulties whatsoever in deciding to come here.

I want to thank the government of Iceland and the people of Iceland for employing their entire potential—human, organizational, and material—toward resolving all problems involved in arranging this important meeting. We are grateful for this, and we have felt at ease here. I received much interesting information from Raisa Maximovna, who had many meetings in Iceland. They were all very interesting. We are pleased with the friendly atmosphere here and the great interest shown to our country. We thank Iceland and the Icelandic government for what they have done. We wish your people prosperity.

As to the latter part of your question concerning the intention of your country's government to make the North a nuclear-free zone—we welcome this.

Dear friends, thank you for your attention. I think that we have spent this time together usefully. I wish you all the best.

28

TELEVISED SPEECH

Report on the Meeting in Iceland with President Reagan

Moscow, October 14, 1986

Good evening, dear comrades.

As you know, my meeting in Iceland with the President of the United States, Ronald Reagan, concluded the day before yesterday, on Sunday. A press conference on its results has been televised. The text of my statement and my replies to journalists have been published.

Having returned home, I consider it my duty to tell you how the meeting went and how we assess what took place in Reykjavik.

The results of the meeting in the capital of Iceland have just been discussed at a meeting of the Politburo of the CPSU Central Committee. A report will be published tomorrow outlining the opinion our Party's leadership has formed about this major political event, the consequences of which, we are convinced, will be felt in international relations for a long time to come.

Before Reykjavik much was said and written about the forthcoming meeting. As is usually the case in such situations, there was a myriad of conjectures and views. This is normal. And in this case there was speculation as well.

Now that the meeting is over its results are in the center of attention of the world public. Everybody wants to know: What happened? What results did it produce? What will the world be like after it?

We strove to give the main questions of world politics—ending the arms race and nuclear disarmament—top priority at the meeting in Reykjavik. And that is how it was.

What are the motives for our persistence in this matter? One often hears conjectures abroad that the reason lies in our domestic difficulties. There is a thesis in Western calculations that the Soviet Union will ultimately be unable to endure the arms race economically, that it will break down and bow to the West. One need only squeeze the Soviet Union harder and step up the position of strength. Incidentally, the U.S. President made a remark to this effect in an address after our meeting.

I have said repeatedly that such plans are not only built on air; they are dangerous as they may result in fatal political decisions. We know our own problems better than anyone else. We do have problems which we openly discuss and resolve. We have our own plans and approaches on this score, and there is a common will of the Party and the people. In general, I would have to say that the Soviet Union's strength today lies in its unity, dynamism, and the political activity of its people. I think that these trends and, consequently, the strength of our society will be growing. The Soviet Union has the capacity to respond to any challenge, should the need arise. The Soviet people know this; the whole world should know this, too. But we are opposed to playing power games, for this is an extremely dangerous thing in the nuclear-missile age.

We are firmly convinced that the protracted feverish state of international relations harbors the threat of a sudden and fatal crisis. We must take practical steps away from the nuclear abyss. We need joint Soviet-American efforts, efforts on the part of the entire international community in order to radically improve international relations.

For the sake of these goals we, the Soviet leadership, carried out extensive preparatory work on the eve of the meeting, even before we received President Reagan's consent to attend it. Taking part in this work, in addition to the Politburo and the Secretariat of the CPSU Central Committee, were the Ministry of Foreign Affairs and the Defense Ministry, plus some other departments, representatives of science, military experts, and specialists from various branches of industry. The positions we worked out for the Reykjavik meeting were the result of wide-scale, repeated discussion with our friends, with the leadership of the socialist community countries. We sought to make the content of the meeting as meaningful as possible, putting forth far-reaching proposals.

Now about the meeting itself, how events developed there. This should be discussed not only in order to affirm the truth, which is already being distorted by our partners in the Reykjavik talks, but, more importantly, to inform you of what we plan to do next.

The first conversation with President Reagan started on Saturday, at 10:30 A.M. After the greetings necessary on such occasions and a brief conference with journalists, the two of us remained alone; only our interpreters were present. We exchanged views on the general situation, on the way the dialogue between our two countries was developing, and outlined the problems to be discussed.

Then I asked the President to listen to our concrete proposals on the main questions which prompted our meeting. I already spoke at length about them during the press conference. Still, I will recall them here in brief.

A whole *set of major measures* was submitted to the talks. These measures, if accepted, would usher in a new era in the life of mankind—a nuclear-free era. Herein lies the essence of the radical change in the world situation, the possibility of which was obvious and realistic. The talk was no longer about limiting nuclear arms, as was the case with the SALT-I, SALT-II and other treaties, but about the elimination of nuclear weapons within a comparatively short period of time.

The first proposal concerned strategic offensive weapons. I expressed our readiness to reduce them by 50 percent within the next five years. The strategic weapons on land, water, and in the air would be halved. In order to make it easier to reach accord, we agreed to a major concession by revoking our previous demand that the strategic equation include American medium-range missiles reaching our territory and American forward-based systems. We were also ready to take into account the U.S. concern over our heavy missiles. We regarded the proposal on strategic arms in the context of their total elimination, as we had suggested on January 15 this year.

Our second proposal concerned medium-range missiles. I suggested to the President that both Soviet and American missiles of this class in Europe be completely eliminated. Here, too, we were willing to make a substantial concession: we stated that, contrary to our previous stand, the nuclear-missile weapons of Britain and France need not be taken into account. We proceeded from the necessity to pave the way to detente in Europe, to free the European nations of the fear of a nuclear catastrophe, and then to move further—toward the elimination of all nuclear weapons. You will agree that this was another bold step on our part.

Anticipating the possible objections, we said we would agree to freeze missiles with a range of under 1,000 kilometers and immediately begin talks on what is to be done with them in the future. As for the medium-range missiles in the Asian part of our country—this issue was invariably present in President Reagan's "global version"—we suggested that talks be started immediately on this subject as well. As you see, here, too, our proposals were serious and far-reaching, facilitating a radical solution of this problem as well.

The third question I raised during my first talk with the President, one that formed an integral part of our proposal package, was the existing *Anti-Ballistic Missile (ABM) Treaty and the Nuclear Test Ban Treaty*. Our approach is as follows: Since we are entering a totally new situation which will witness the beginning of substantial reductions in nuclear weapons and their complete elimination in the foreseeable future, it is necessary to protect oneself from any unexpected developments. We are speaking of weapons which to this day make up the core of this country's defenses. Therefore it is necessary to exclude everything that could undermine equality in the process of disarmament, to preclude any chance of developing weapons of a new type that would ensure military superiority. We regard this stance as perfectly legitimate and logical.

This being the case, we have firmly stated the need for strict observance of the 1972 ABM Treaty of unlimited duration. Moreover, in order to consolidate its regime, we proposed to the President that a mutual pledge be taken by the U.S. and the Soviet Union to refrain from pulling out of the treaty for at least ten years, during which time strategic weapons would be abolished.

Taking into account the particular difficulties the Administration created for itself on this problem when the President personally committed himself to space weapons, to the so-called SDI, we did not demand termination of work in this field. The implication was, however, that all provisions of the ABM Treaty would be fully honored—that is, research and testing in this sphere would not go beyond laboratories. This restriction applies equally to the U.S.A. and to the USSR.

Listening to us, the President made remarks, asked for clarification on certain points. During the conversation, we presented the question of verification firmly and with resolve, linking it with the postnuclear situation. This situation demands special responsibility. I told the President that if both countries embark on nuclear disarmament, the Soviet Union will make its position on verification stricter. Verification must be plausible, comprehensive, and indisputable. It must create full confidence in reliable compliance with the agreement and include the right to on-site inspection.

I must tell you, comrades, that the President's initial reaction was not entirely negative. He even said: "What you have just stated is reassuring." But it did not escape our attention that our American interlocutors (George Shultz as well as Comrade Shevardnadze had joined the conversation on these issues by then) appeared to be somewhat confused. At the same time, immediate doubts and objections cropped up in their separate remarks. Straight away, the President and the Secretary of State started talking about divergencies and disagreement. In their words we clearly discerned the familiar old tones we had heard at the Geneva negotiations for many months: we were reminded of all sorts of sublevels on strategic nuclear armaments, the "interim proposal" on missiles in Europe, and that we, the Soviet Union, should join the SDI and should replace the existing ABM Treaty with some new agreement, and many other things in the same vein.

I expressed my surprise. How can this be? We propose to accept the American "zero option" in Europe and take up negotiations on medium-range missiles in Asia while you, Mr. President, are abandoning your previous stand. This is incomprehensible.

As for ABM, we propose to preserve and strengthen this fundamentally important agreement, and you want to give it up and even propose to replace it with some new treaty, and thereby—following renunciation of SALT-II—to wreck this mechanism standing guard over strategic stability. This, too, is incomprehensible.

We grasped the essence of the SDI plans as well, I said. If the United States creates a three-tiered ABM system in outer space, we shall respond to it. However, we are concerned about another problem: SDI would mean the transfer of weapons to a new medium, which would destabilize the strategic situation, make it even worse than it is today. If this is the United States' purpose, this should be stated plainly. But if you really want reliable security for your people and for the world in general, then the American stand is totally ungrounded.

I told the President directly: We have put forward major new proposals. However, what we are hearing from you now is precisely what everybody is fed up with and what can lead us nowhere. Mr. President, please, reexamine our proposals carefully and give us an answer point by point. I gave him an English translation of a draft of possible instructions that had been drawn up in Moscow and which, in the event that agreement is reached in principle, could be given to the Foreign Ministers and other departments to draw up *three draft agreements*. They could be signed later during my visit to the U.S.A.

In the afternoon we met again. The President announced the stand that had been drawn up during the break. As soon as he uttered the first phrases, it became clear that they were offering us the same old moth-eaten trash, as I put it at the press conference, from which the Geneva talks are already choking: all sorts of intermediate versions, figures, levels, sublevels, and so on. There was not a single new thought, fresh approach, or idea which would contain even a hint of a solution, of advance.

It was becoming clear, comrades, that the Americans had come to Reykjavik with nothing at all to offer. The impression was that they had come there empty-handed to gather fruits in their basket.

The situation was taking a dramatic turn.

The American President was not ready to take any radical decisions on questions of principle, to meet the Soviet side halfway so as to give a real impetus to productive and encouraging negotiations. This is precisely what I impressed upon the President in my letter, in which I put forward the idea that an urgent meeting be held in order to give a powerful impetus at the level of the top leaders of the two countries—an impetus to negotiations on nuclear disarmament.

Confident that our proposals were well-balanced and took

the partner's interests into account, we decided not to abandon our efforts to bring about a breakthrough at the meeting. A ray of hope on strategic armaments appeared, following many clarifying questions. Clinging to this we took one more great step in search of a compromise. I told the President: We both recognize that there is a triad of strategic offensive armaments—ground-based missiles, strategic submarines and strategic bombers. So let us make a 50-percent reduction in each part of the triad. And then there will be no need for all sorts of levels and sublevels, for all sorts of calculations.

After lengthy debate, we managed to reach mutual understanding on that issue.

Then the discussion turned to the problem of medium-range missiles. The Americans stubbornly stuck to the so-called interim proposal which provides for the preservation of a part of their missiles, including Pershing-2 missiles, in Europe, and, naturally, of our corresponding SS-20 missiles. We categorically opposed this, for reasons I have already described. Europe deserves to be free of nuclear weapons, to stop being held nuclear hostage. As for the President, it was difficult for him to fight his own "zero option," which he had promoted for so long. And still, we sensed the Americans' intention to thwart agreement under the guise of special concern for their allies in Asia.

The American side said much that was ungrounded. It is embarrassing to repeat it here. The talks began to move forward only when on this issue, too, we took one more step to meet the American side and agreed to the following formula: zero missiles in Europe, 100 warheads on medium-range missiles in the eastern part of our country and, accordingly, 100 warheads on medium-range missiles on U.S. territory. Most importantly, we managed to agree on eliminating nuclear weapons on the European continent.

Thus, accord was reached on the problem of medium-range missiles, too, and a major breakthrough was made in this direction of nuclear disarmament. The American Administration failed to hold out against our insistent striving to achieve positive results.

However, there still remained the ABM issue and the ban on nuclear explosions.

Two groups of experts, one from each side, worked through

the night before we met on Sunday for our third talk, which was scheduled to be the concluding one. They thoroughly analyzed what had been discussed at the two previous meetings with the President and reported the results of their night-time debates respectively to the President and myself.

The result? *A possibility arose of undertaking to work out agreements on strategic offensive armaments and on medium-range missiles.*

The ABM Treaty in this situation acquired key significance; its role was becoming even more important. Could one destroy, I asked, what has made it possible so far to somehow restrain the arms race? If we now begin reducing strategic and medium-range nuclear weapons, both sides should be confident that during that time nobody will develop new systems that would undermine stability and parity. Therefore, in my view, it would be perfectly logical to fix the time-frame—the Americans mentioned seven years, and we proposed ten years—within which nuclear weapons must be eliminated. We proposed ten years during which neither the Soviet nor the American side may avail itself of the right—and they have such a right—to withdraw from the ABM Treaty, and during which research and tests may be conducted in laboratories only.

Thus, I think, you understand why we chose exactly ten years? This was no random choice. The logic is plain and fair. Fifty percent of strategic armaments is to be reduced in the first five years, the other half in the next five years. This makes ten years.

In connection with this I proposed that our high-ranking representatives be instructed to start full-scale talks on the discontinuation of nuclear explosions and thus in the end an agreement could at last be worked out completely banning explosions. In the course of working out the agreement—and here again we displayed flexibility and assumed a constructive stand—specific issues connected with nuclear explosions could be resolved.

The reasoning President Reagan used in his response is a familiar one to us in that we have come across it earlier both in Geneva and in his public statements; SDI is a defense system. If we begin eliminating nuclear weapons, how will we protect ourselves from some madman who might get hold of them? And Reagan is ready to share with us the results obtained within the research done on SDI. In answering this last remark, I said: Mr. President, I do not take this idea seriously, your idea about sharing with us the results of research on SDI. You do not even want to share with us oil equipment or equipment for the dairy industry, and still you expect us to believe your promise to share the research developments in the SDI project. That would be something like a "Second American Revolution," and revolutions do not occur that often. I told President Reagan that we should be realists and pragmatists. This is a more reliable approach, for the issues at hand are very serious.

By the way, when trying to justify his position on SDI yesterday, the President said that he needed this program to ensure that America and its allies remain invulnerable to a Soviet missile attack. As you see, he did not even make any mention of madmen. And the "Soviet threat" was again brought to light.

But this is nothing but a trick. We proposed that not only strategic armanents, but also all the nuclear armaments in the possession of the U.S. and the USSR, be eliminated under strict control.

How can there be a need to protect the "freedom of America" and its friends from Soviet nuclear missiles if these missiles no longer exist?

If there are no nuclear weapons, why should we need to protect ourselves from them? Thus the entire Star Wars undertaking is purely militaristic in nature and is directed at obtaining military superiority over the Soviet Union.

Let us return, however, to the talks. Although an agreement on strategic arms and medium-range missiles had been reached, it was premature to believe that everything had been completely settled as a result of the two first sessions. An entire day was ahead, nearly eight hours of nonstop and intense discussions in which these issues, which seemed to have been agreed upon already, were to be raised again and again.

The President sought to touch upon ideological issues as well in these discussions and in this way demonstrated, to put it mildly, total ignorance and the inability to understand both the socialist world and what is happening there. I rejected the attempts to link ideological differences to issues of ending the arms race. I persistently drew the President and the Secretary of State back to the subject that had brought us to Reykjavik. It was necessary to remind our interlocutors repeatedly about the third element of our package of proposals, without which it would be impossible to reach accord on the whole. I have in mind the need to comply strictly with the ABM Treaty, to consolidate the regime of this major treaty and to ban nuclear tests.

We had to draw attention again and again to things that seemed to be perfectly clear: having agreed to major reductions in nuclear arms, attempts—both in deed and in thought—to shake strategic stability and to circumvent the agreements should be made to be impossible. That is why we should have confidence in the preservation of the ABM Treaty, which has no time limit. You, Mr. President, I said, ought to agree that if we are beginning to reduce nuclear weapons, there should be the full assurance that the U.S. will not do anything behind the back of the USSR, while the Soviet Union will also not do anything to jeopardize U.S. security, to disvalue the agreement or to create difficulties.

Hence the key task to strengthen the ABM regime: to keep the results of the research under this program in the laboratory and prevent them from being applied in outer space. It is necessary that the right to pull out of the ABM Treaty is not used for ten years in order to create the confidence that in settling the issue of arms reduction at the same time we are ensuring security for both sides and for the world as a whole.

But the Americans obviously had other intentions. We saw that the U.S. actually wants to defeat the ABM Treaty, to revise it so as to develop a large-scale space-based ABM system for its own conceited ends. It would simply be irresponsible of me to agree to this.

As far as nuclear testing is concerned, it was perfectly clear here as well why the American side does not want to conduct serious talks on this issue. It would have preferred to carry these talks on endlessly and thus postpone the settlement of the issue of banning nuclear tests for decades. And once again we had to reject attempts to use the talks as a cover and to get a free hand in the field of nuclear explosions. I said bluntly that I was having doubts about the honesty of the U.S. position and questioned whether there wasn't something in it damaging for the Soviet Union. How can an agreement on the elimination of nuclear arms be reached if the United States continues to perfect these weapons? Still we were under the impression that SDI was the main snag. If it could have been removed it would have been possible to reach an accord on banning nuclear explosions as well.

At a certain point in the talks, when it became absolutely clear that to continue the discussion would be a waste of time, I reminded the other side that we had proposed a definite package of measures and asked them to consider it as such. If we have worked out a common position on the possibility of making major reductions in nuclear arms and at the same time have failed to reach agreement on the issue of ABM and nuclear testing, then everything we have tried to create here falls apart, I said.

The President and the Secretary of State reacted poorly to our firm position, but I could not pose the question in any other way. This is a matter concerning the security of our country, the security of the entire world, all peoples and all continents.

Our proposals were major, truly large-scale and clearly in the nature of compromise. We made concessions. But we did not see even the slightest desire on the American side to respond in kind or to meet us halfway. We were deadlocked. We began thinking about how to conclude the meeting. And nevertheless we continued our efforts to engage our partners in constructive dialogue.

During the conversation that was supposed to be the concluding one we ran out of time. Instead of going our separate ways—we to Moscow and they to Washington—yet another break was announced to allow the sides to think everything over and meet one more time after dinner. On returning to the house of the city's mayor after the break, we made yet another attempt to end the meeting successfully. We proposed the following text as the basis for summing up the positive results.

Here is the text:

"The Soviet Union and the United States will oblige themselves not to use their right to withdraw from the ABM Treaty, which has no time limit, for a period of ten years and during this period to ensure strict observance of all of its provisions. All testing on the space elements of the ABM defense in outer space will be prohibited excluding research and testing conducted in laboratories.

"In the first five years of this decade (until 1991 inclusive) the strategic offensive arms of both sides will be reduced by 50 percent.

"In the next five years of this period the remaining 50 percent of the strategic offensive arms of both sides will be eliminated.

"Thus, the strategic offensive arms of the USSR and the U.S.A. will be completely eliminated by the end of the year 1996."

Commenting on this text, I made an important addition in reference to the document which had been given to the President at the end of our first conversation. This document is basically a proposal to hold special negotiations after the ten years are up and nuclear weapons no longer exist in order to work out mutually acceptable decisions as to what should be done next.

But this time, too, our attempts to reach an agreement were to no avail. For four hours we again tried to make our interlocutors understand that our approach was well founded, that it was not at all threatening, and did not affect the interests of the genuine security of the United States. But with every hour it became more obvious that the Americans would not agree to keep SDI research and testing in the laboratories. They are bent on going into outer space with weapons.

I said firmly that we would never agree to help undermine the ABM Treaty with our own hands. We consider this an issue of principle, as well as a national security issue.

We were thus literally two or three steps from making possibly historic decisions for the entire nuclear-space era, but we were unable to make those last steps. A turning point in the world's history did not take place, even though, I will say again with full confidence, it could have.

Our conscience is clear, however, and we cannot be reproached. We did everything we could.

The scope of our partners' approach was not broad enough. They did not grasp the uniqueness of the moment and, ultimately, they did not have enough courage, sense of responsibility, or political resolve which are all so needed to settle key and pressing issues in world politics. They stuck to old positions which had already eroded with time and did not correspond to the realities of today.

Foreigners in Iceland, and my comrades here have asked me what, in my opinion, were the main reasons for the attitude of the American delegation at the Reykjavik meeting? There are a number of reasons, both subjective and objective, but the main one is that the leadership of that great country relies too heavily on the military-industrial complex, on the monopolistic groups which have turned the nuclear and other arms races into a business, into a way of making money, into the object of their existence and the meaning of their activities.

In my opinion, the Americans are making two serious mistakes in their assessment of the situation.

The first is a tactical mistake. They believe that sooner or later the Soviet Union will reconcile itself to the fact that the U.S. is attempting to revive its strategic diktat, that it will agree to the limitation and reduction of only Soviet weapons. It will do so because, so they think, the USSR is more interested in disarmament agreements than the U.S.A. But this is a grave delusion. The sooner the U.S. Administration overcomes it—I repeat perhaps for the hundredth time—the better it will be for them, for our relations and for the world situation in general.

The other mistake is a strategic one. The United States seeks to exhaust the Soviet Union economically with a buildup of sophisticated and costly space arms. It wants to impose hardships of all kinds on the Soviet leadership, to foil its plans, including those in the social sphere and those for improving our people's living standards, and thus spread among the people discontent in regard to their leaders and the country's leadership. Another aim is to restrict the Soviet Union's potential in its economic ties with developing countries which, in such a situation, would all be compelled to bow down before the United States. These are far-reaching designs. The strategic course of the current U.S. Administration also rests on delusions. Washington, it seems, does not wish to burden itself with a thorough analysis of the changes taking place in our country, does not wish to draw the appropriate practical conclusions for itself and for its course, but is rather busy with wishful thinking. It is building its policy toward the USSR on the basis of this delusion. It is, of course, difficult to predict all the long-term consequences of such a policy. One thing is clear to us already now: it will not and it cannot benefit anyone, including the United States.

Before addressing you, I read through the U.S. President's statement on Reykjavik. I noticed that the President gives himself all the credit for all the proposals discussed. Well, it seems as though these proposals are so attractive to the Americans and the peoples throughout the world that it's possible to resort to such a ruse. We are not consumed by vanity, but it is important that people get the true picture of what happened in Reykjavik.

So what is next? I already said at the press conference that the work done before the meeting and that done in Reykjavik was not in vain. We ourselves did a lot of thinking in connection with the meeting and reexamined a great deal. We have now better cleared the way to continue the fight for peace and disarmament. We freed ourselves from obstructions that had developed, from insignificant issues, and from stereotypes which hindered new approaches in the important area of our policies.

We know where we stand and see the possibilities available to us more clearly. The preparations for the Reykjavik meeting helped us to formulate a platform—a new, bold platform which promises greater chances for ultimate success. It meets the interests of our people and society at this new stage of socialist development. This platform also meets the interests of other countries and nations and thereby merits trust. We are confident that it will be received with understanding in many countries of the world and in the most differing political and public circles.

I think that many people around the world, including leaders vested with power, can and must draw weighty conclusions from the Reykjavik meeting. Everyone will have to think again and again about the essence of the matter, and about why such persistent efforts to achieve a breakthrough and start advancing toward a nonnuclear world and toward universal security have thus far failed to produce the needed result.

I would like to hope that the President also has a better insight now into our analysis, the intentions of the Soviet Union, and into the possibilities and limits for adjusting the Soviet stand. And I hope Mr. Reagan understands our analysis more fully and more precisely since receiving firsthand explanations of our constructive measures for stabilizing and improving the international situation.

The American leadership will obviously need some time. We are realists and we clearly understand that the issues that have remained unsettled for many years and even decades can hardly be settled at a single sitting. We have a great deal of experience in doing business with the United States. And we are aware that the domestic political climate can change there quickly and that the opponents of peace across the ocean are strong and influential. There is nothing new here for us.

If we do not despair, if we do not slam the door and give vent to our emotions—although there is more than enough reason for this—it is because we are sincerely convinced that new efforts are needed aimed at building normal interstate relations in the nuclear epoch. There is no other alternative.

And another thing: after Reykjavik, the infamous SDI became even more conspicuous as an epitome of obstructing peace, as a strong expression of militaristic designs, and an unwillingness to get rid of the nuclear threat looming over mankind. It is impossible to perceive this program in any other way. This is the most important lesson of the Reykjavik meeting.

In summing up these eventful days, I would like to say the following. The meeting was a major event. A reappraisal was made. A qualitatively new situation developed in that no one can continue to act as he acted before. The meeting was useful. It paved the way for a possible step forward, for a real positive shift, should the U.S.A. finally adopt realistic positions and abandon delusion in its appraisals.

The meeting has convinced us that the path we have chosen is correct and that a new mode of political thinking in the nuclear age is necessary and constructive.

We are energetic and determined. Having embarked on a program of reorganization, the country has already traversed a certain path. We have just started this process, but changes have already been made. Growth in industrial production over the past nine months reached 5.2 percent, labor productivity grew by 4.8 percent. National production income rose 4.3 percent as compared to the previous year.

This all is the strongest support for the Party's policies on the part of the people, for this is support by deed.

This shows that under new conditions the people's efforts are helping to accelerate the growth of the country's economic potential and are thus consolidating its defense capabilities.

The Soviet people and the Soviet leadership have unanimously agreed that the policy of socialism can and must be a policy of peace and disarmament. We shall not swerve from the course of the 27th CPSU Congress.

29

TELEVISED SPEECH

The Impact of the Meeting in Iceland with President Reagan

Moscow, October 22, 1986

Good evening, dear comrades.

I speak with you again, and the subject is again the same—Reykjavik. This is a very serious issue. The outcome of the meeting with the U.S. President has stirred the entire world. A great deal of new data have come out over the past few days demanding assessments which I would like to share with you today.

You will remember that I said at the press conference in Reykjavik that we shall return again and again to this meeting between the leaders of the USSR and the U.S.

I am convinced that we have not yet realized the full significance of what happened. But we will reach this realization; if not today, then tomorrow. We will grasp the full significance of Reykjavik and will do justice to the accomplishments and gains, as well as to the missed opportunities and losses.

Dramatic as the course of the talks and their results were, the Reykjavik meeting greatly facilitated, perhaps for the first time in many decades, our search for a way to achieve nuclear disarmament.

I believe that as a result of the meeting we have now reached a higher level, not only in analyzing the situation, but also in determining the objectives and the framework of possible accords on nuclear disarmament.

Having found ourselves a few steps from an actual agreement on such a difficult and vitally important issue, we all grew to understand more fully the danger facing the world and the need for immediate solutions. And what is most important, we now know that it is both realistic and possible to avert the nuclear threat.

I would like to point out here that the Soviet program for eliminating nuclear arms by the year 2000 was until recently described by many "experts" in world politics as illusory and an unrealizable dream.

This is indeed the case when past experience is neither wealth nor counsel, but a burden that makes the search for solutions all the more difficult.

Reykjavik generated more than just hopes. Reykjavik also highlighted the difficulties encountered on the way to a nuclear-free world.

If this fact is not understood, it is impossible to assess correctly the results of the Icelandic meeting.

The forces opposed to disarmament are great. We felt that during the meeting and we feel this today. Reykjavik is being talked about a great deal.

Those who look realistically at the facts assess the meeting in Iceland as a major political event.

They welcome the fact that as a result of this meeting progress was made toward new qualitative levels in the fight against nuclear weapons. The results of Reykjavik, as they are viewed by the Soviet leadership, are encouraging to all who seek a change for the better.

Interesting assessments are being made in many countries at the state level, in public circles and in the scientific community. The opportunities that have been opened up are being characterized as corresponding to the aspirations of all mankind.

It is a common view that the meeting has raised both the Soviet-American dialogue and the East-West dialogue as a whole to a new level.

For the dialogue has been taken out of the plane of technical estimates and numerical comparisons and has been placed onto one with new parameters and dimensions.

From this height new prospects can be seen for the settlement of today's urgent issues. I am referring to security, nuclear disarmament, the prevention of new spirals in the arms race, and a new understanding of the opportunities that have opened up before humanity.

One could say that the debate over the results of the meeting has only just begun. I believe, I am even confident, that this debate will grow. And, we believe, the joint efforts of the people, of political figures and of public organizations will grow as well in an endeavor to take advantage of the opportunities that opened up in Reykjavik.

A course was outlined there for settling vitally important issues on which the very fate of humanity depends.

In the time that has passed since Reykjavik, however, something else has become clear.

Those groups linked with militarism and making profits from the arms race are obviously scared. They are doing their utmost to cope with the new situation and, coordinating their actions, are trying in every way possible to mislead the people, to control the sentiment of broad sections of the world public, to suppress the people's quest for peace, and to impede governments from taking a clear-cut position at this decisive moment in history.

These groups have at their disposal political power, economic leverage, and the powerful mass media. Of course, one should not overestimate their strength, but one should not underestimate it either. All indications are that the battle will be a difficult one.

Forces are being regrouped in the camp of the enemies of detente and disarmament. Feverish efforts are being made to create obstacles in order to stem the process started in Reykjavik.

Under these circumstances, I consider it necessary to return to the urgent issues which arose in connection with the meeting in Iceland.

Our point of view, which I made public one hour after the meeting, has not changed. I consider it necessary to state this not only in order to reiterate the appraisals made earlier.

I am doing this to draw your attention to the juggling with words and dissonance which we are observing. This might be the result of confusion or perplexity, but this also might be a preplanned campaign to fool the people.

The aims which were set before the meeting are explained differently. The initial negative reports of the Reykjavik meeting have quickly and concertedly become words of praise.

A hectic campaign has been started to misappropriate the other side's proposals.

The greatest efforts are being made to defend SDI, a project that was shown to be worthy of shame in Reykjavik. Generally speaking, Washington is now experiencing some hectic times.

But what is this? A preelection game that needs to depict Reykjavik as a success? Or are we dealing with a policy that will be unpredictable for years to come?

This needs to be studied carefully.

It certainly did catch our attention as to how and where certain political groupings are trying to steer the discussion of the results of the meeting.

The key elements of this campaign are worth mentioning. Efforts are being made in a bid to whitewash the destructive position of the U.S. Administration, which came to the meeting unprepared. They came, I would say one more time, with the same old baggage. But when the situation demanded definite answers, the U.S. side wrecked the chances for concluding the meeting with an accord.

A new situation has developed since Reykjavik, and meanwhile efforts are being made to force the USSR to return to the old approaches, to the unproductive numbers debates, and to walking in circles in a deadlock situation.

Evidently there are a great number of politicians in the West for whom the Geneva talks serve as a screen, and not as a forum for seeking accords.

What was once disguised thoroughly is now being disclosed: there are powerful forces in the ruling circles of the U.S. and Western Europe which are seeking to frustrate the process of nuclear disarmament. Certain people are once again beginning to claim that nuclear weapons are even a good thing.

A half-truth is the most dangerous lie, as a saying goes. It is extremely disquieting that not only have the mass media, leaning toward the right, taken such a stand, but so have leading figures in the U.S. Administration. And at times this stand is even one of downright deception.

I have already had the opportunity to report how things went in Reykjavik. We arrived at the meeting with constructive and the most radical arms-reduction proposals in the entire history of Soviet-U.S. negotiations. These proposals take into account the interests of both sides.

Upon arrival in Iceland, I spoke about this on the eve of the meeting in a conversation with the leaders of that country. The proposals had already been handed over to the President of the United States by the middle of my first conversation with him.

Far-reaching and interconnected, these proposals form *an integrated package* and are based on the program made public on January 15 for the elimination of nuclear weapons by the year 2000.

The *first* proposal is to reduce by half all strategic arms with no exceptions.

The *second* proposal is to eliminate completely Soviet and U.S. medium-range missiles in Europe and to start talks immediately on missiles of this type in Asia, as well as on missiles with a range of less than one thousand kilometers. We suggested that the number of such missiles be frozen immediately.

The *third* proposal is to consolidate the regime of the ABM Treaty and to start full-scale talks on a total nuclear test ban.

The discussions in Reykjavik, which I described in detail in my previous speeches, opened with the Soviet proposals.

Tremendous efforts and intense arguments resulted in the positions of the two sides drawing reassuringly closer together in two of the three areas.

The talks enabled the two sides to establish specific periods for the elimination of strategic offensive arms. We came to the agreement with President Ronald Reagan that the arms of this type belonging to the USSR and the U.S.A. can and must be completely eliminated by the year 1996.

An accord was also reached on the complete elimination of U.S. and Soviet medium-range missiles in Europe and on a radical cut in missiles of this type in Asia.

We attach great importance to these accords between the USSR and the United States: they prove that nuclear disarmament is possible.

This is the first half of the truth about the Reykjavik meeting. But there is still the other half and this is, as I have already said, that the U.S. side frustrated an agreement which, it seemed, was quite near at hand.

The U.S. Administration is now trying in every way possible to convince the people that the possibility of a major success in reaching definite agreements was not realized due to the Soviet Union's unyielding position on the issue of the so-called Strategic Defense Initiative (SDI).

It is even being asserted that we allegedly lured the President into a trap by putting forward "breathtaking" proposals on the reduction of strategic offensive arms and medium-range missiles and that later we ostensibly demanded, in the form of an ultimatum, that SDI be renounced.

But the essence of our position and proposals is as follows: we stand for the reduction and the eventual complete elimination of nuclear weapons and are absolutely against a new stage in the arms race and against its transfer to outer space.

Hence we are against SDI and for the consolidation of the ABM Treaty.

It is clear to every sober-minded person that if we start the process of radically cutting and then completely eliminating nuclear weapons, it is essential to rule out any possibility of either the Soviet or U.S. side gaining a unilateral military superiority.

It is precisely the extension of the arms race to a new sphere and the attempts to take offensive arms into outer space in order to achieve military superiority, that we perceive as the main danger of SDI.

SDI has become a barrier to ending the arms race, to getting rid of nuclear weapons, the main obstacle to a nuclear-free world.

When Mr. Shultz, U.S. Secretary of State, tells the American people that SDI is a sort of "insurance policy" for America, this, to say the least, is an attempt to mislead the American people.

In fact, SDI does not strengthen America's security but, by opening up a new stage of the arms race, destabilizes the military-political situation and thereby weakens both U.S. and universal security.

The Americans should know this.

They should also know that the U.S. stand on SDI announced in Reykjavik basically contradicts the ABM Treaty. Article XV of the Treaty does allow a party to withdraw from the Treaty, but only under certain circumstances, namely, "if it decides that extraordinary events related to the subject matter of this Treaty have jeopardized its (that party's) supreme interests." There have not been and are no such extraordinary events. It is clear that the elimination of nuclear weapons, if begun, would make the emergence of such extraordinary events even less likely. This is only logical.

Article XIII of the ABM Treaty, however, stipulates that the sides should "consider, as appropriate, possible proposals for further increasing the viability of this Treaty." The U.S., on the contrary, is seeking to depreciate the Treaty and deprive it of its meaning.

Each of these quotations is from the Treaty signed by the top representative of the United States.

Many stories have been invented to raise the prestige of SDI. One of them is that the Russians are terribly afraid of it. Another has it that SDI brought the Russians to the talks in Geneva and then to Reykjavik. A third is that only SDI will save America from the "Soviet threat." The fourth says that SDI will give the United States a great technological lead over the Soviet Union and other countries, and so on and so forth.

Understanding the problem, I can say now only one thing: continuing the SDI program will push the world into a new stage of the arms race and destabilize the strategic situation.

Everything else ascribed to SDI is in many respects rather dubious and is done in order to sell this suspicious and dangerous commodity in an attractive wrapping.

In upholding his position that prevented an agreement being reached in Reykjavik, the President asks the rhetorical questions: "Why are the Soviets so adamant that America remain forever vulnerable to Soviet rocket attack? Why does the Soviet Union insist that we remain defenseless forever?"

I must say I'm surprised by such questions. They give the impression that the American President has the opportunity of making his country invulnerable, of giving it secure protection against a nuclear strike.

As long as nuclear weapons exist and the arms race continues he has no such opportunity. Naturally, this also applies to ourselves.

If the President counts on SDI in this respect, it is futile. The system would be effective only if all missiles were eliminated. But then, one might ask, why an antimissile defense at all? Why build it? I won't even mention the money wasted, the system's cost, which, according to some estimates, will run into several trillion dollars.

So far, we have been trying to persuade America to give up this dangerous undertaking. We urge the American Administration to look for invulnerability and protection elsewhere—by totally eliminating nuclear weapons and establishing a comprehensive system of international security that would preclude all wars, nuclear or conventional.

The SDI program still remains an integral part of U.S. military doctrine.

The Fiscal 1984–1988 Defense Guidance now in force which the Pentagon produced at the beginning of Reagan's term in office, directly provides for the "prototype development of space-based weapons systems" including weapons to destroy Soviet satellites and accelerate the development of the system of the antimissile defense of U.S. territory with the possible U.S. pullout from the ABM Treaty.

The document says that the United States should develop weapons that "are difficult for the Soviets to counter, impose disproportionate costs, open up new areas of major military competition and obsolesce previous Soviet investment." Once again, as you can see, there is, as former President Nixon put it, a chase of the ghost; once again, there are plans to wear out the Soviet Union.

It is hard for the current administration to learn lessons.

Is this not the reason why its commitment to SDI is so stubborn? The plans for Star Wars have become the chief obstacle to an agreement on removing the nuclear threat. Washington's claim that we are now moving toward an agreement is of no use.

To eliminate nuclear weapons as a means of deterring American aggression, and, in return, be threatened from outer space can only be accepted by those who are politically naive. There are no such people in the Soviet leadership.

It is hard to reconcile oneself to the loss of the unique chance of saving mankind from the nuclear threat. With precisely this in mind, I said at the press conference in Reykjavik that we did not regard the dialogue as closed and hoped that President Reagan, on returning home, would consult the U.S. Congress and the American people, and adopt decisions logically necessitated by what had been achieved in Reykjavik.

Quite a different thing has happened. Aside from distorting the entire picture of the negotiations in Reykjavik—about which I will speak later—in recent days they have taken actions that, following such an important meeting between the two countries' top leaders, appear as simply wild to any normal point of view.

I am referring to the expulsion of another fifty-five Soviet Embassy and consular staff from the United States. We will, of course, take measures in response, very tough measures on an equal footing, so to speak. We are not going to put up with such outrageous practices. But now, I have this to say.

What kind of government is this, what can one expect from it in other affairs in the international arena? To what limits does the unpredictability of its actions go?

It turns out that it has no constructive proposals on key disarmament issues and that it does not even have a desire to maintain the kind of atmosphere essential for a normal continuation of the dialogue. It seems that Washington is not prepared for any of this.

The conclusion is obvious. It is confirmed by the considerable experience which has been accumulated. Every time a gleam of hope appears in the approaches to the major issues in Soviet-American relations and to a solution of questions involving the interests of the whole of mankind, a provocative action is immediately staged with the aim of frustrating the possibility of a positive outcome and poisoning the atmosphere.

Which is the real face of the U.S. Administration then? Is it looking for answers and solutions or does it want to finally destroy everything that may serve as a basis for headway and deliberately rule out any normalization?

Quite an unattractive portrait is emerging of the Administration of that great country—an Administration quick to take disruptive actions. Either the President is unable to cope with the entourage literally breathing hatred for the Soviet Union and for everything that may lead international affairs into calm waters or he himself is this way. In any event, there is no restraining the "hawks" in the White House, and this is very dangerous.

As for informing the American people about the meeting in

Reykjavik, the following has taken place, which is entirely in the spirit of what I have already mentioned: facts have been concealed from them. They were told the half-truth of which I spoke earlier. Things were portrayed so as to show that the United States, acting from a position of strength, virtually wrested consent from the Soviet Union to reach agreement on U.S. terms.

And the day is not far off when the United States will ostensibly attain its goal: it is essential, they say, not to slacken the pace of military preparations, to speed up the Star Wars program and to increase pressure in all directions.

These days have witnessed the drowning of a great cause in petty politicking and the sacrificing of the vital interests of the American people, allies, and international security as a whole to the arms manufacturers.

A good deal has been said about the openness of American society, about the freedom of information, the pluralism of opinions, and the fact that everyone there can see and hear what he pleases.

In Reykjavik, when pointing out the differences between our two systems, the President told me, and I quote: "We recognize freedom of the press and the right to hear any point of view." But how do things stand in reality?

Here is the latest fact.

It has been brought to my attention that a public organization of ours, the Novosti Press Agency, has published in English the text of my press conference in Reykjavik and of my speech on Soviet television and sent them out to many countries, including the United States.

Well, the fact is that the pamphlets with these texts have been detained at the U.S. customshouse for several days now. They are being prevented from reaching the American reader. There's the "right to hear any point of view" for you!

Or take, for example, the cinema. As I told the President when we were discussing humanitarian affairs, a great number of American films are shown on the Soviet screen. They give Soviet people an opportunity to become acquainted with both Americans' way of life and their way of thinking.

In "free America," on the other hand, Soviet films are practically not shown. The President avoided making any reply and, as usual in such cases, fell back on free enterprise, which lets everyone do whatever he wants.

I also told him about the publication of American books in this country as compared to that of our books in the United States: the ratio is approximately twenty to one.

I put the question of radio information before the President as well. I said that in this field, too, we are on an unequal footing. You have surrounded the Soviet Union with a network of radio transmitters and broadcast around the clock everything you like in many languages of the Soviet Union from the territories of other countries. America, availing itself of the fact that we are not its close neighbor, has isolated itself from our radio information by using the medium wave band—receivers in America are only of that kind. The President had nothing to say to that either.

Then I suggested to him that we take the following approach: we stop jamming the "Voice of America" broadcasts and you give us an opportunity to conduct radio broadcasts directed at the United States on your territory or somewhere nearby so that the broadcasts might reach the population of your country. The President promised to think about it.

It appears that the United States is becoming an increasingly closed society. People there are being isolated from objective information in a cunning and effective way. This is a dangerous process.

The American people should know the truth about what is going on in the Soviet Union, about the true content of Soviet foreign policy, about our real intentions, as well as the truth about the state of affairs in the world as a whole.

At the present stage, I would say, this is becoming extremely important.

Now a few words about how the outcome of the Reykjavik meeting is being portrayed in the United States. It took only several hours, or days at most, for everything discussed at Reykjavik to begin dispersing in the fog of inventions and fantasies. Attempts are being made to destroy the seedlings of trust before they take root.

The President stated recently that the only object of agreement had been ballistic missiles, and his assistants said plainly that bombers and all cruise missiles remained untouched.

The Secretary of State presented another version—that our accord dealt with all strategic arms. By the way, the latter was present during my talks with the President, as was our Minister of Foreign Affairs Eduard Shevardnadze.

Mr. Speakes, the White House spokesman, stated that possibly Mr. Reagan had been misunderstood and had actually never agreed to the elimination of all nuclear weapons.

Things got to the point of outright misrepresentation.

It is alleged, for example, that during the past meeting the U.S. President did not agree to the Soviet proposal on a *complete* elimination of *all* strategic offensive arms of the USSR and the U.S.A. by 1996, and that a common point of view on our proposal was never reached.

With all the responsibility of a participant in the talks I state: the President did, albeit without particular enthusiasm, consent to the elimination of all—I emphasize—not just certain individual ones, but all strategic offensive arms. And these are to be eliminated precisely within ten years, in two stages.

The interpretations of the discussion of the nuclear testing issue are a far cry from the truth, too. The United States' unilateral approach to this issue is pictured in such a way as to lead one to believe that the Soviet Union has given its full consent. This is not the case, nor could it be.

The issue of the elimination of medium-range missiles in Europe is also being presented in a distorted fashion, to say nothing of the fact that it is being withdrawn from the package proposed by the Soviet side.

But our consent to freeze the number of missiles with a range of under 1,000 kilometers is also being portrayed as the Soviet Union's "recognition" of the United States' "right" to deploy American missiles of the same class in Western Europe.

With such interpretations I myself will soon be in doubt as to what we really spoke about at Reykjavik: about removing the nuclear threat, reducing and eliminating nuclear arms? Or about how to keep this threat growing, how to diversify the nuclear arsenals and turn not just this entire planet, but outer space, the universe, too, into an arena of military confrontation? For this, comrades, is what is happening.

The prospects of reaching a mutual understanding between the Soviet and American sides so frightened certain people that they began erecting inconceivable obstacles ahead of time and inventing "preconditions."

An assistant to the President went so far as to say that before embarking on nuclear disarmament the U.S.A. must see some changes in the political climate in the Soviet Union.

All this is just not serious, not serious at all.

When similar claims were made seventy or forty years ago it was still possible to regard them as an inability to think things through, or as historical blindness. Nowadays they can only be the demonstration of a complete lack of understanding of reality.

The issue of conventional arms is also mentioned as one of the "preconditions." In and of itself it is serious enough.

To this day there is a well-worn thesis in the West concerning the "superiority" of the Soviet Union and other Warsaw Treaty states in conventional arms. It is this that is allegedly compelling NATO to continue building up its nuclear potential.

Of course, there is in fact no disbalance whatsoever. After Reykjavik this fact was publicly recognized for the first time by Mr. Shultz and Mr. Reagan. But the crux of the matter does not lie in the maintenance of parity. We do not want the arms race to move from the sphere of nuclear arms to the sphere of conventional ones.

Let me remind you that our January proposal on the elimination of nuclear weapons before the end of the century included also the provisions on the elimination of chemical weapons and on radical reductions in conventional armaments.

We have returned to that issue more than once since January. The proposals of the Warsaw Treaty countries were presented in greatest detail last summer in Budapest. We sent them to the other side, that is, the NATO countries.

So far we have received no answer.

Every day that has passed since Reykjavik has made it more

clear that the meeting in Iceland was that touchstone which determines the true value of the words and declarations of political figures.

So much has been said of the need to be free of the nuclear nightmare, of how we will be able to breathe more easily in a nuclear-free world. Let the USSR and the U.S.A. get things in motion.

But no sooner had a ray of hope appeared when many of those who had just been cursing nuclear weapons and pledging their allegiance to the idea of a nuclear-free world went back on their word.

Certain quarters in Western Europe even voiced their feeling that it was difficult to part with American nuclear weapons, with American missiles.

Evidently, the point is that the policy-makers in the West are thinking of nuclear weapons not in the terms of defense at all. Otherwise it would be difficult to explain why pretexts are now being sought for keeping the missiles in place or why support for the SDI program is being expressed at the government level.

Here is something for both us and the West European public to ponder.

In addition to direct attacks, subtle maneuvers are being made. Is it not possible to take from the negotiating table what is most advantageous, while ignoring that which is not to one's taste for one reason or another?

They say that difficulties at Reykjavik arose because we, the Soviet side, put forward our cardinal proposals in a package. But the package contains a balance of interests and concessions, a balance of withdrawn concerns and the interdependence of security interests. Here everything is as if on scales; the two pans must be balanced.

That is why, evidently, those in the West want to shatter this logically substantiated and just variant of an overall accord into pieces, doing nothing to restore the balance of compromises.

All the proposals we made at Reykjavik are objectively connected with central strategic-weapons systems. Our concessions are also a part of the package. No package, no concessions.

This is a reality of our national security. But such an approach ensures the security of the U.S.A. and all other countries as well.

That is why we attach such significance to strengthening the ABM Treaty. We are not endangering it in any way. On the contrary, we are opposed to having it revised, supplemented, or what not, and we are even more opposed to having it replaced with something else, as the President suggested at Reykjavik. Or maybe this was just a slip of the tongue.

Let me put it frankly: I was very much surprised when during the meeting he began persuading the Soviet side and me personally not to regard the ABM Treaty as gospel. What, then, should one's attitude to treaties be like? Should they be treated as mere slips of paper?

Without strict observance of the treaties, and especially such a fundamental one as this, it is impossible to ensure international order and basic stability. Otherwise the world would be subject to arbitrary rule and chaos.

Let me say once again: when SDI is given preference over nuclear disarmament, only one conclusion can be made—with the help of that military program efforts are being made to disprove the axiom of international relations of our epoch, an axiom laid out in simple, clear-cut words signed by the U.S. President and myself last year. These words read: nuclear war must not be fought and cannot be won.

Let me say in conclusion that the Soviet Union has put the maximum of goodwill into its proposals. We are not withdrawing these proposals; they still stand! Everything that has been said by way of their substantiation and development remains in force.

Good night, comrades. All the best.

30

TELEVISED SPEECH

On the Resumption of U.S. Nuclear Testing

Moscow, March 29, 1986

Good evening, dear comrades!

At our meeting tonight I would like to share my views with you on the situation that has emerged around the Soviet Union's moratorium on nuclear tests.

Several days ago the United States carried out yet another nuclear explosion. It is clear to us all that the timing was not chosen at random. The blast was staged just before the end of the Soviet Union's unilaterally declared moratorium. Yesterday it was learned that in the coming days, in the near future, the United States intends to set off yet another nuclear device.

Soviet people, like people of good will in all countries, are incensed by these actions of the United States. They write about this in their letters to the Party's Central Committee and request that an assessment be made of the resulting situation. They ask how this should all be understood, what conclusions should be drawn, why the United States has taken such a step, and how our country's leadership intends to act in these conditions.

We consider it our duty to respond to these questions, and this, in effect, is the reason for our meeting tonight.

I must tell you frankly that we regard the present actions of the American administration, which is continuing nuclear tests despite the pressing demands of the peoples, as a pointed challenge to the Soviet Union, and not only to the Soviet Union but to the whole world, to all peoples, including the American people.

The question of ending nuclear tests has acquired tremendous importance now that whole mountains of inflammable nuclear material have been stockpiled in the world. This much is clear.

Firstly, the ending of nuclear tests is the most realistic way of achieving an end to the arms race. Without such tests it is impossible to either perfect or develop new types of nuclear arms. In short, if together with the United States and other nuclear powers we were to reach an accord on ending nuclear explosions, it would be possible to get the entire process of nuclear disarmament out of the deadlock.

Further, continued testing inflicts a tremendous and perhaps not yet fully understood harm on the environment, on the natural surroundings in which we all live. Do we not feel obliged to show concern for our own home? And not only for ourselves, but for our children and grandchildren as well.

And finally, in this difficult endeavor we need not start from scratch, so to speak. A definite road has already been traversed and joint experience acquired: that is, tests in the atmosphere, in water and on land have not been conducted for many years now; nor have there been explosions in outer space.

It was with due account precisely for these circumstances that, after thoroughly weighing all the pros and cons, eight months ago, on the day of the 40th anniversary of the tragedy of Hiroshima and Nagasaki, the Soviet Union put forward an initiative of extraordinary importance—to stop all nuclear explosions both for military and peaceful purposes. And it called on the United States of America and other nuclear states to follow its example—to start an advance along the road of nuclear disarmament.

I have already had an opportunity to say that in conditions of unabating tension in the international situation this was not an easy decision for us to make. If you like, this step required both an awareness of the responsibility resting on the governments of nuclear powers, and the necessary political will. In acting as it did the Soviet leadership had the mandate of its people, which knows the price of peace and sincerely strives for its preservation and consolidation, for cooperation with all peoples.

Acting in this way, we proceeded from the deep conviction that the world in its development has entered a stage which calls for new approaches to international security matters. Today, in the nuclear and space era, one cannot think in the categories of the past. All must ultimately come to realize that everything has radically changed. The question now is not only of the preservation of peace but of the survival of humanity as well.

These are the motives behind our decision to announce the unilateral moratorium on nuclear tests.

The good initiative of the Soviet Union—and I am immensely pleased to say this—has been regarded with understanding and general approval in the world. Our action has been highly appreciated by the working people of all countries: Communists and Social Democrats, liberals and conservatives, Christians and Moslems, a multitude of public organizations, prominent political figures, scientists and cultural figures, and millions of ordinary people.

How did the other side conduct itself? That is, the U.S. Administration.

In words, it stands for the elimination of nuclear weapons. It has made a good number of statements on that score. But in actuality, a gap between words and practical policy has again manifested itself. The U.S. government has continued to conduct nuclear tests despite the Soviet Union's call and example, despite persistent demands on the part of the American people and the peoples of the whole world.

We set certain hopes on the Geneva meeting with the President of the United States of America and expected to reach an agreement with him on this matter as well. As you remember, encouraging statements were made there by both sides as well as jointly, statements to the effect that nuclear war is inadmissible, that such a war cannot be won, that neither side would seek nuclear superiority.

The results of the Geneva meeting prompted us to take yet another step of good will: to extend the moratorium until March 31 of this year. We thereby confirmed in deed our responsible attitude toward the dialogue between the leaders of the two powers, and we hoped, of course, for reciprocal steps on the part of the U.S. Administration.

I think you will agree that our Statement of January 15 of this year, which set forth a concrete and realistic program for the elimination of nuclear arms, is yet another illustration of our true intentions—to put an end to nuclear confrontation. In taking this step, we thought least of all of how to gain extra "propaganda points," as journalists say in such cases, of how to outsmart or outdo the other side. We consider such an approach to the burning problems of present-day politics inadmissible. Our actions were motivated by our responsibility both to the Soviet people and to other peoples, the responsibility for the removal of the nuclear threat, for the preservation and strengthening of peace.

In February the leaders of six nonaligned states, expressing the prevailing sentiments in world public opinion, urged the leaders of the Soviet Union and the United States to refrain from nuclear explosions until a new Soviet-American meeting. We consented to this.

It would have seemed natural for the U.S. Administration to support the Soviet Union's initiative with practical actions and to respond to the expectations of the peoples. And, at any rate, to confirm precisely through deeds its own statements made in Geneva. But that did not happen.

Everything indicates that the ruling circles of the United States have placed the narrow selfish interests of the military-industrial complex above the interests of the whole of humanity and the American people itself. The manner in which this is done is also quite significant: it is demonstrative, arrogant, disregarding the opinion of the world community. There is neither a sense of realism nor of responsibility.

It is becoming increasingly obvious that the U.S. ruling circles continue to lay emphasis on the pursuance of a militaristic line, to bank on force so as to dictate their will to other countries and peoples. Statements are openly made that it is precisely in this way that they will also influence the policy of the Soviet Union.

What can be said about that? These are ill-fated attempts. Nobody has ever succeeded in using the methods of power-politics against our state, while now they are simply preposterous. The peoples of other countries are also ever more vigorously rejecting the outdated policy of diktat in international relations.

The Soviet political leadership is now faced with the difficult question of how to react to this behavior of the United States.

Our position is clear. We believe that the world has now entered a period when responsible decisions must be taken. Yes, precisely a period when they are absolutely necessary. We will not deviate from the policy of preserving and strengthening peace, which was most definitely confirmed by the 27th Congress of the CPSU. Fulfilling the wish of its people, the

USSR will further step up its efforts to ensure universal security, and will do so in cooperation with all countries and their peoples.

As for our unilateral moratorium, I can say that it continues to remain in effect till March 31, 1986. But even after that date, as was announced, we will not conduct nuclear explosions if the United States acts likewise. We are again giving the U.S. Administration a chance to take a responsible decision—to end nuclear explosions.

Otherwise, the Soviet Union will resume testing. This must be made absolutely clear. We regret it, but our own security and that of our allies will force us to do so. I am saying all this in order that there be nothing left unsaid on that issue.

At the same time I cannot stress enough that our main intention is to stop the nuclear arms race. The simplest, most explicit and effective step in that direction would be to put an end to nuclear explosions.

We have proposed that talks be started immediately on a total ban on nuclear weapons testing, covering issues of verification. All variants are acceptable to the Soviet Union—bilateral Soviet-American talks, tripartite talks with the participation of Great Britain, or multilateral ones within the framework of the Geneva Disarmament Conference.

We have come to the conclusion that the situation requires immediate action. It is not yet too late to halt the nuclear arms race. The first major stride in that direction is needed. Putting an end to nuclear testing by everyone concerned—first of all by the Soviet Union and the United States, as well as by the other nuclear powers—could become such a step. We attach tremendous significance to the solution of this task which concerns the fate of all nations.

I am ready to meet with President Reagan as soon as possible in London, Rome, or in any other European capital that will agree to receive us, in order to reach agreement on this question. And I do not feel that there are political, technical, or any other insurmountable obstacles to this. What is needed is the necessary political will and understanding of our mutual responsibility. We propose to meet, exchange views on this crucial problem and issue instructions to draft an appropriate agreement.

We hope that this proposal of the Soviet Union will be duly

appraised and correctly understood by the President of the United States of America, and by the governments of the countries of Europe, Asia, Africa, and Latin America, of the whole world.

Time is running out. On behalf of the Soviet people we call on the American people and its government, on the peoples and governments of all countries to work vigorously, by practical actions, for the ban on nuclear explosions to become a fact, an immutable norm of interstate relations.

Mankind is standing on a line that requires the utmost responsibility. The consequences of the nuclear arms race can become dangerously unpredictable. We must act together. This matter is of concern to everyone.

This is what I wanted to tell you, dear comrades, at our meeting tonight. Goodbye.

31

TELEVISED SPEECH

On the Reactor Accident at Chernobyl

Moscow, May 14, 1986

Good evening, comrades,

As you all know, a misfortune has befallen us—the accident at the Chernobyl nuclear power plant. It has painfully affected Soviet people and has caused anxiety in the international public. For the first time ever, we have had to deal in practice with a force as sinister as nuclear energy, which has escaped control.

Considering the extraordinary and dangerous nature of what has happened at Chernobyl, the Politburo has taken into its hands the entire organization of work aimed at ensuring the speediest cleanup of the accident and minimizing its consequences.

A government commission was formed and immediately left for the scene of the accident, while at the Politburo a group was formed under Nikolai Ivanovich Ryzhkov to solve urgent problems.

All work is actually proceeding on a round-the-clock basis. The scientific, technical, and economic potentials of the entire country have been put to use. Operating in the area of the accident are organizations of many Union ministries and agencies that are under the guidance of ministers, as well as prominent scientists and specialists, units of the Soviet Army and the Ministry of Internal Affairs.

A huge share of the work and responsibility has been taken on by the Party, government, and economic bodies of the Ukraine and Byelorussia. The operating staff of the Chernobyl nuclear power plant are working selflessly and courageously.

So, what happened?

According to specialists, the reactor's capacity suddenly increased during a scheduled shutdown of the fourth unit. The considerable emission of steam and the subsequent reaction led to the formation of hydrogen, an explosion, damage to the reactor, and the resulting radioactive discharge.

It is still too early to pass final judgment on the causes of the accident. All aspects of the problem—design, construction, technical, and operational—are under the close scrutiny of the government commission. It goes without saying that once the investigation of the causes of the accident is completed, all necessary conclusions will be drawn and measures will be taken to rule out a repetition of anything of the sort.

As I have said already, this is the first time that we have encountered such an emergency, when it was necessary quickly to curb the dangerous force of the atom, which had escaped from control, and to keep the scale of the accident to a minimum.

The seriousness of the situation was obvious. It was necessary to evaluate it quickly and competently. And as soon as we received reliable initial information, it was made available to Soviet people and sent through diplomatic channels to the governments of other countries.

On the basis of this information practical work was begun to clean up the accident and minimize its grave consequences.

In the resulting situation we considered it our top priority duty, a duty of special importance, to ensure the safety of the population and to provide effective assistance to those who had been affected by the accident. The inhabitants of the settlement near the station were evacuated within a matter of hours and then, when it became clear that there was a potential threat to the health of people in the adjoining zone, they too were moved to safe areas. All of this complex work required the utmost speed, organization, and precision.

Nevertheless, the measures that were taken failed to protect many people. Two of them died at the moment of the accident—Vladimir Nikolayevich Shashenok, an adjuster of automatic systems, and Valery Ivanovich Khodemchuk, an operator in the nuclear power station. As of today, 299 people have been hospitalized, diagnosed as having radiation sickness of a varying degree of gravity. Seven of them have died. Every possible form of treatment is being given to the others. The best scientific and medical specialists of the country, specialized clinics in Moscow and other cities are taking part.

They have the most modern means of medicine at their disposal.

On behalf of the CPSU Central Committee and the Soviet Government, I express our profound condolences to the families and relatives of the deceased, to the work collectives, to all who have suffered from this misfortune, who have been struck by personal loss. The Soviet government will take care of the families of those who died and other victims of the accident.

The inhabitants of the areas that heartily welcomed the evacuees deserve the highest praise. They responded to the misfortune of their neighbors as if it were their own and, in the best traditions of our people, showed consideration, responsiveness, and attention.

The CPSU Central Committee and the Soviet Government are receiving thousands upon thousands of letters and telegrams from Soviet people and also from foreign citizens expressing sympathy and support for the victims. Many Soviet families are prepared to take children into their homes for the summer and are offering material help. There are numerous requests from people asking to be sent to work in the area of the accident.

These demonstrations of humaneness, genuine humanism, and high moral standards cannot but move every one of us.

I repeat, assistance to people remains our top priority task.

At the same time intensive work is under way at the station itself and in the adjacent territory to minimize the scale of the accident. Under the most difficult conditions the fire was extinguished and prevented from speading to the other power units. The staff of the station shut down the three other reactors and brought them under control. They are under constant observation.

A stern test has been passed and continues to be passed by all—firemen, transport and building workers, medics, special chemical protection units, helicopter crews, and other detachments of the Ministry of Defense and the Ministry of Internal Affairs.

In these difficult conditions much depended on a correct, scientific evaluation of what was happening, because without such an evaluation it would have been impossible to work out and apply effective measures for coping with the accident and its consequences. Our prominent specialists from the Academy of Sciences, leading specialists from union ministries and agencies as well as in the Ukraine and Byelorussia are successfully dealing with this task.

I must say that people have acted and are continuing to act heroically, selflessly. I believe we shall have an opportunity to name these courageous people and to assess the value of their exploit.

I have every reason to say that despite the full gravity of what has happened, the damage turned out to be limited. To a decisive degree this is due to the courage and skill of our people, their loyalty to duty, the concerted manner in which everybody taking part in eliminating the consequences of the accident is acting.

This task, comrades, is being solved not only in the area of the nuclear power station itself, but also in research institutes, and at many of the enterprises in our country that are supplying everything necessary to those who are directly engaged in the difficult and dangerous struggle to cope with the accident.

Thanks to the effective measures taken, today it is possible to say that the worst is over. The most serious consequences have been averted. Of course, the event is not over yet. We cannot rest content. Extensive and long work still lies ahead. The level of radiation in the station's zone and in the territory in the immediate vicinity still remains dangerous to human health.

As of today, therefore, the top priority task is to eliminate the consequences of the accident. A large-scale program for the decontamination of the territory of the electric power station and the settlement, of buildings and structures, has been drawn up and is being implemented. The necessary manpower, material and technical resources have been concentrated for that purpose. In order to prevent the radioactive contamination of the water basin, measures are being taken at the site of the station and in the adjacent territory.

Organizations of the meteorological service are constantly monitoring the radiation levels on the ground, in the water and atmosphere. They have the necessary technical facilities at their disposal and are using specially equipped planes, helicopters, and monitoring stations.

It is absolutely clear—all these operations will take much time and will require no small efforts. They should be carried out meticulously, in a planned and organized manner. The area must be restored to a condition that is absolutely safe for the health and normal life of people.

I cannot fail to mention one more aspect of the affair. I am referring to the reaction abroad to what happened at Chernobyl. In the world as a whole, and this should be emphasized, the misfortune that befell us and our actions in that complicated situation were treated with understanding.

We are profoundly grateful to our friends in socialist countries who have shown solidarity with the Soviet people at a difficult moment. We are grateful to the political and public figures in other states for their sincere sympathy and support.

We express our kind feelings to those foreign scientists and specialists who showed their readiness to assist us in overcoming the consequences of the accident. I would like to note the participation of the American doctors Robert Gale and Paul Tarasaki in treating affected persons and to express gratitude to the business circles of those countries that promptly reacted to our request for the purchase of certain types of equipment, materials, and medicines.

We are grateful for the objective attitude to the events at the Chernobyl nuclear power plant that was shown by the International Atomic Energy Agency (IAEA) and its Director-General Hans Blix.

In other words, we highly appreciate the sympathy of all those who responded to our misfortune and our problems with an open heart.

But it is impossible to ignore and not to assess politically the way the event at Chernobyl was treated by the governments, political figures, and the mass media in certain NATO countries, especially the U.S.A.

An unrestrained anti-Soviet campaign was launched. It is difficult to imagine what was said and written these days— "thousands of casualties," "mass graves of the dead," "Kiev desolate," and "the entire land of the Ukraine poisoned," and so on and so forth.

Generally speaking, we faced a veritable mountain of lies—most brazen and malicious lies. It is unpleasant to recall all this, but it must be done. The international public should know what we had to face. It must be done to find the answer to the question: what, in fact, was behind this highly immoral campaign? Its organizers, to be sure, were not interested in either true information about the accident or the fate of the people at Chernobyl, in the Ukraine, in Byelorussia, in any other place or country. They were looking for a pretext to exploit in order to try to defame the Soviet Union and its foreign policy, to lessen the impact of Soviet proposals on the termination of nuclear tests and on the elimination of nuclear weapons, and, at the same time, to dampen the growing criticism of the U. S. conduct on the international scene and of its militaristic course.

Bluntly speaking, certain Western politicians were after quite definite aims—to wreck the possibilities for balancing international relations, to sow new seeds of mistrust and suspicion toward the socialist countries.

All this was made completely clear during the meeting of the leaders of "the Seven" held in Tokyo not so long ago. What did they tell the world, what dangers did they warn humanity of? Of Libya, groundlessly accused of terrorism, and of the Soviet Union, which, it turns out, failed to provide them with "full" information about the accident of Chernobyl. But not a word about the most important issue—how to stop the arms race, how to rid the world of the nuclear threat. Not a word in reply to the Soviet initiatives, to our specific proposals on the termination of nuclear tests, on ridding mankind of nuclear and chemical weapons, on reducing conventional arms.

How should all this be interpreted? One involuntarily gets the impression that the leaders of the capitalist powers gathered in Tokyo wanted to use Chernobyl as a pretext for distracting the attention of the world public from all those problems that make them uncomfortable, but are so real and important for the whole world.

The accident at the Chernobyl station and the reaction to it have become a kind of test of political morality. Once again two different approaches, two different lines of conduct were revealed for everyone to see.

The ruling circles of the U. S. A. and their most zealous allies—in particular the FRG—regarded the mishap only as another chance to put up additional obstacles impeding the development and deepening of the current East-West dialogue, progressing slowly as it is, and to justify the nuclear arms race. What is more, an attempt has been made to prove to the world that talks, and, particularly, more agreements with the USSR are impossible, and thereby to give the green light to further military preparations.

Our attitude to this tragedy is absolutely different. We realize that it is another sound of the tocsin, another grim warning that the nuclear era necessitates a new political thinking and a new policy.

This has strengthened our conviction still more that the foreign policy course worked out by the 27th CPSU Congress is correct and that our proposals for the complete elimination of nuclear weapons, the ending of nucler explosions, the creation of an all-embracing system of international security meet those inexorably stringent demands that the nuclear age makes on the political leadership of all countries.

As to the "lack" of information, around which a special campaign with a political content and nature has been launched, in the given case this matter is an invented one. The following facts confirm that this is so. It is well known that it took the U.S. authorities 10 days to inform their own Congress and months to inform the world community about the tragedy that took place at the Three Mile Island atomic power station in 1979.

I have already said how we acted.

All this makes it possible to judge those persons and the way they choose to inform their own people and foreign countries.

But the essence of the matter is different. We hold that the accident at Chernobyl, just as the accidents at U. S., British and other atomic power stations, poses to all states very serious problems which require a responsible attitude.

Over 370 atomic reactors now function in different countries. This is reality. The future of the world economy is virtually unimaginable without the development of atomic power. Altogether 40 reactors with an aggregate capacity of over 28 million kilowatts now operate in our country. As is known, humankind derives a considerable benefit from atoms for peace.

But it stands to reason that we are all obliged to act with even greater caution, and to concentrate the efforts of science and technology to ensure the safe harnessing of the great and formidable powers contained in the atomic nucleus.

To us, the indisputable lesson of Chernobyl is that in the course of the further development of the scientific and technical revolution the question of equipment reliability and safety, the question of discipline, order and organization, assume priority importance. Everywhere and in everything the most stringent demands are needed.

Further, we deem it necessary to support a serious deepening of cooperation in the framework of the International Atomic Energy Agency (IAEA). What steps could be considered in this connection?

First, creating an international system for the safe development of nuclear power based on the close cooperation of all nations dealing with nuclear power engineering. A system of prompt warning and supply of information in the event of accidents or faults at nuclear power stations, specifically when this is accompanied by radioactive emissions, should be established in the structure of this regime. Likewise it is necessary to organize an international mechanism, both on a bilateral and multilateral basis, for the speediest rendering of mutual assistance when dangerous situations emerge.

Second, for the discussion of the entire range of matters it would be justifiable to convene a highly authoritative specialized international conference in Vienna under the IAEA auspices.

Third, in view of the fact that the IAEA was founded back in 1957 and that its resources and staff are not in keeping with the level of the development of present-day nuclear power engineering, it would be expedient to enhance the role and capabilities of that unique international organization. The Soviet Union is ready for this.

Fourth, we believe that the United Nations Organization and its specialized institutions, such as the World Health Organization (WHO) and the United Nations Environment Program (UNEP), should be more actively involved in the effort to ensure safe development of peaceful nuclear activity.

For all this, it should not be forgotten that in our world, where everything is interrelated, alongside the problems of atoms for peace, there also exist the problems of atoms for war. This is the major issue of today. The accident at Chernobyl showed again what an abyss will open if nuclear war befalls mankind. For inherent in the stockpiled nuclear arsenals are thousands upon thousands of disasters far more horrible than the Chernobyl one.

At a time of increased attention to nuclear matters, and after having considered all circumstances connected with the security of its people and all humanity, the Soviet Government has decided to extend its unilateral moratorium on nuclear tests till August 6 of this year, the date on which more than 40 years ago the first atomic bomb was dropped on the Japanese city of Hiroshima, resulting in the death of hundreds of thousands of people.

We again urge the United States to consider most responsibly the measure of danger looming over humanity, and to heed the opinion of the world community. Let the leaders of the United States show their concern for the life and health of people by deeds.

I reiterate my proposal to President Reagan to meet without delay in the capital of any European state that is prepared to accept us or, say, in Hiroshima, in order to reach agreement on a ban on nuclear testing.

The nuclear age forcefully demands a new approach to international relations, the pooling of efforts of states with different social systems for the sake of putting an end to the disastrous arms race and of a radical improvement of the world political climate. Broad horizons will then be cleared for the fruitful cooperation of all countries and peoples. This will benefit all people on earth!

32

THE FIVE-YEAR PLAN: 1986-1990

The Economic and Social Development of the USSR and the Tasks of Party Organizations in Carrying It Out

Moscow, June 16, 1986

Comrades,

Today we will discuss the progress made in carrying out the general policy line determined by the Congress, sum up the preliminary results, draw the lessons from our post-Congress work and define the immediate tasks of the Party.

Little time has passed since the Congress. However, the responsibility of the moment and the scale of the tasks facing society today are so great that we must constantly feel the pulse of changes and check our intentions and plans against the way things are actually going. In other words, we will discuss the most important problems at the moment, how the energy of our plans is being translated into the energy of our actions, what problems and difficulties have arisen and how we should act further.

The 27th Congress of the CPSU set all spheres of Soviet society—political, economic and spiritual—in motion. Social development was given a strong dynamic impetus which stimulated political awareness of the masses. The atmosphere of exactingness and truthfulness which prevailed at the Congress is exerting a mobilizing influence on all practical work. Soviet people meet with enthusiasm and support innovative projects and demand that reorganization should be universal and be carried out in a businesslike manner. All this shows that the ideas of the Congress are becoming firmly implanted in people's minds and are an objective guarantee that the ongoing changes are irreversible.

Today we are even more convinced than before that the decisions we adopted at the Congress are correct and in keeping with the fact that we are living at the critical time. They have a special part to play in the destiny of this country and of socialism in general, and this will have far-reaching consequences for the development of the whole world. We realize better and to a fuller extent the scale and depth of the changes initiated by the Party and all sorts of difficulties we must overcome. We also understand better what our possibilities are today and what possibilities we will have in future.

The interest of other countries in the Congress does not abate. It is especially keen in the socialist countries. The Congress's decisions gave a powerful impetus to the struggle for peace and social progress. Approval and support from our friends convince us that we are going the right way. They also remind us that we have great responsibility for following this course consistently and purposefully.

Sober-minded people in the nonsocialist part of the world could see once again that our extensive plans for social and economic development are inseparably linked with a foreign policy which is aimed at promoting peace and all-round international economic cooperation.

Our plans evoked a different reaction from the militarist and aggressive forces led by U.S. reactionary circles. Their animosity is particularly strong now that they are waging a struggle against the Soviet proposals on ways of improving the international situation and shaping international relations that would be adequate to the realities of the nuclear and space age.

In short, comrades, we will be discussing key problems of the five-year plan, taking into account both domestic needs and external conditions. The plan is the basis for our work in the immediate years ahead and over a longer period.

At this stage of work since the Congress we must show an ability to reorganize and build, seek new forms and methods, and not allow success to go to our heads even for a moment. Fast economic growth rates, high efficiency and major positive changes in the social field are now becoming the main yardstick for assessing performance. We will be judged not by our intentions alone, but primarily by real changes in society, by practical results.

I. THE FIRST RESULTS OF REORGANIZATION

Comrades, it is from the point of view of practical work and results that we must assess the activities of all Party committees, government and economic agencies, public organizations and work collectives.

This approach will enable us not only to find our bearings in the current situation but to proceed further. We must do this also because, as experience shows, we are dealing not only with positive trends, which, of course, are predominant in society, but also with factors which hinder the reorganization process. Some of these factors are objective, but most of them are due to sluggishness, bad habits and outdated psychology.

People who are exerting themselves today are those who strongly supported the stand of the 27th Congress and became actively involved in the common effort, who do not spare either time or energy and are contributing to the process of reorganization. However, there are quite a few people who, while realizing the political need to work in a new way, simply do not know how to do this in practice. We must help them in every way possible. We must also realize that there are still people who have not grasped the essence of the changes that are under way, who take a wait-and-see position or simply do not believe that the economic and political breakthrough charted by the Party can be successfully carried out.

The Congress's directive on encouraging the creative activity of the masses as the basis of accelerated growth is having a profound influence on our society. It is closely related to the drive for social justice, greater democracy and complete openness, and for ridding society of all manifestations of petty-bourgeois psychology. Soviet people are showing a growing interest in politics and economics, culture and morality, in public life in general. And this is having an important effect on labor and political activity, discipline and order in the country.

Soviet people have also demonstrated extraordinary organizational abilities and patriotism in emergencies, as was the case with the Chernobyl accident. The breakdown at the atomic power station was a severe trial. At that difficult time workers, firemen, engineers, physicians, scientists, and soldiers displayed great fortitude, courage, and selflessness.

The country has risen as one to combat the consequences of the accident. The CPSU Central Committee and local Party and government organizations are flooded with letters from people who want to be sent to Chernobyl. An extensive fund-raising campaign has been launched to help the families affected by the accident. Many work collectives have pledged to work several shifts free of charge in order to help them.

Allow me on behalf of our Plenary Meeting to convey deep condolences to the bereaved families, and cordially thank all those who, risking their lives, did everything they could to contain the accident and who are working selflessly today to eliminate its consequences.

Comrades, we are faced with complex tasks in all sectors of social and economic advancement. Of course, it would be naive to think that it would take us only a few months to overcome the lag and shortcomings that have accumulated over years. However, a trend toward higher rates of economic growth is now apparent. We attribute this mostly to the hard work of the people and the positive processes taking place in society.

In the first five months of this year industrial production rose by 5.7 percent compared to the same period last year. There are also positive changes in sectors which have been lagging behind for many years, i.e., in the mining, iron-and-steel industries, and in railway transport. The timber, wood-working, cellulose, and paper industries are performing better. Workers of the oil industry have not yet overcome their difficulties. However, encouraging trends are evident there too. A number of branches of mechanical engineering are developing rapidly. Intense work is also under way in the agricultural sector.

In many regions and areas of the Russian Federation, the Ukraine, Byelorussia, the Baltic Republics and elsewhere the active work carried out by Party, government and economic organizations and work collectives shows what we can achieve if we encourage initiative and foster creative and businesslike attitudes at workplaces.

The main thing now is to consolidate the rates of growth already achieved and then to increase them. This is feasible, but it would require major efforts since we are at the very start of restructuring, when not everything that needs to be done organizationally has been done, and when the economic levers and incentives crucial for further economic change for the better have not yet swung into full action.

An analysis of economic changes would be far from complete it, along with obvious successes, we fail to note the weak points, the things which impede our advance. I must say that reorganization is still taking place too slowly. Many enterprises still rely on rush work and abide by the old slogan of "fulfilling plans no matter what." The turn to quality, efficiency and new management methods is a difficult and painful process. However, it should be absolutely clear that the Central Committee will firmly support all that is sound and is in keeping with the decisions of the Congress, all that promotes reorganization and the movement forward. We will be just as firm in combating all that stands in the way of this process.

That which is new that was initiated by the April Plenary Meeting and further elaborated in the decisions of the 27th Congress, calls for a profound restructuring not only of the economic sphere, but of society as a whole. This is no simple process. It requires efforts and serious changes in the mentality of our cadres, of all working people. We have succeeded in overcoming passive attitudes to some extent, increasing responsibility, improving organization and giving more room to initiative. At the same time, the restructuring process is not yet smooth enough at enterprises, in the field of management, in research institutions, artistic collectives, and in the work of Party and government bodies. Old ways of doing things and inertia are slowing down progress.

Sometimes words are substituted for deeds, no practical action is taken following criticisms, and self-criticism resembles self-flagellation. Some managers are lavish in issuing appeals for openness and publicity, they quite correctly speak about the important role of the work collective, and about promoting democratic principles. Regrettably, it all stops at that. Restructuring becomes a mere illusion: everything is all right in words, but there is no real change—and the restructuring process marks time.

The post-Congress period has shown that the complicated structure and inefficient performance of our management bodies considerably hamper our progress and the introduction of new management methods. The redistribution of rights and responsibilities between the central economic bodies and ministries, on the one hand, and enterprises, production associations and work collectives, on the other, has proved to be a painful process.

Even though the functions of management bodies have

changed, some officials try to hold on to their leadership position at all cost. Still, no ministry, no central office, however efficient, can successfully solve every problem, given today's large-scale economy, and replace the creative search of work collectives. That simple truth has to be brought home to everybody.

A blind faith in the omnipotence of management bodies is reflected in the fact that the central bodies still receive requests to set up more and more management bodies and appoint more and more staff members. Some republics try, quite unjustifiably, to copy the central management structures and have asked the USSR Council of Ministers for permission to set up new ministries and other central departments, though they have already 50 or more ministries, central departments and other management bodies.

The past few months have clearly shown that it is impossible to carry out social restructuring without changing the style and methods of Party work at every level. Those matters should be discussed in detail, and I shall return to them later.

Now, I should like to stress the tremendously important role of the leaders of Party bodies in asserting the new style. The consistent and vigorous reorganization of Party work depends on the position they take, on their behavior and work.

In this connection I have to call special attention to the part played by the first secretaries of the Central Committees of the Communist Parties of the Union Republics, of territorial and regional Party committees, and, last but not least, of city and district Party committees. They must set the tone at work, show political insight and a profound understanding of the tasks at hand, have organizational abilities and a sense of responsibility, and be able to assess their own and others' work critically—in a word, they must display the Party spirit in the loftiest sense. Only then can a district, city, region or republic hope to achieve good results in their work and create an atmosphere of constructive search and endeavor.

Comrades, what are the main conclusions to be drawn from our work in the first months after the Congress?

The main thing is that the Party and the people actively support the Congress's political line. The Party reorganizes itself as it organizes and rallies the working people. The past few months have once again demonstrated that restructuring is everybody's concern, from a rank-and-file Communist to a Central Committee secretary, from a shop-floor worker to a minister, from an engineer to an academician. We can accomplish this task only if it truly becomes a national concern. We have to overcome every obstacle in its way.

Another important conclusion. There is no replacing people's creative initiative with instructions, even the best of them. Restructuring presupposes the all-round encouragement of independence and initiative by work collectives and by every worker. Today it is inadmissible—and practically impossible—to solve all questions at the center. Everybody has to realize that. Work collectives at enterprises and associations have to shoulder most of the responsibility for day-to-day decision-making. As to creating the necessary economic, legal and social conditions for fruitful work, for progress in science and technology, that is strictly the obligation of central management bodies.

And lastly, the time that has elapsed after the Congress, and the latest developments, have clearly confirmed the vital importance of the lesson of truth of which the Congress participants spoke. In all situations, we should remember Lenin's warning: "Illusions and self-deceptions are terrible, the fear of truth is pernicious." The Party and the people need the whole truth, in big things and small. Only the truth instills in people an acute sense of civic duty. Lies and half-truths produce warped mentality, deform the personality and prevent one from making realistic conclusions and evaluations without which an active Party policy is inconceivable.

II. DECISIVE STAGE IN THE IMPLEMENTATION OF THE PARTY'S ECONOMIC STRATEGY

Comrades, we will now discuss the new five-year plan and the tasks which the Party and all working people must carry out in order to fulfill that plan.

The 12th Five-Year Plan has a special role to play. The rates of socioeconomic development and the level of people's well-being will depend on the foundation which we will lay over the coming years for the implementation of radical reforms in the national economy, and on the acceleration of scientific and technological progress.

As you know, the drafting of the new five-year plan has not been easy. As calculations show, the old methods of management and dead-stop planning were only leading our economy into a dead end. For a whole year we had persistently sought new approaches which would create the conditions for deepening the process of production intensification and ensure more rapid introduction of the latest achievements of science and technology in production. The Guidelines for the Economic and Social Development of the USSR, meeting the requirements of the present-day economic and social policy of the Party, were submitted to the 27th CPSU Congress for consideration and approval.

In drafting the new five-year plan we were able to reach the highest level, in terms of most of the quantitative and, more importantly, qualitative indicators, as regards the targets outlined in the Guidelines for the country's economic and social development. The draft plan has been thoroughly discussed in the Politburo of the CPSU Central Committee, has been approved by it and is being now submitted for discussion by this Plenary Meeting.

Which particular aspects of the plan should be given special attention?

First of all, I would like to say that on the whole the plan corresponds to the directives of the 27th Party Congress. It provides for the concentration of efforts and resources in the key areas of economic development and for changes in the structural and investment policies in the interests of the intensification of social production. The plan is aimed at raising the efficiency of the economy, saving resources, increasing the effect of economic levers and incentives and using stable work standards and new methods of economic management.

One can get a clear picture of the changes in the economy by looking at the absolute increment figures envisaged in the plan. The principal ones among them are 50 percent higher than in the previous five-year period. For example, the national income will grow by 124,000 million rubles compared to 79,000 million in the 11th Five-Year-Plan period. Industrial output growth will add up to 200,000 million rubles compared to 133,000 million and the average annual increment in the gross agricultural output to 29,000 million rubles compared to 10,000 million in the preceding five-year period. It should be noted here that the planned growth rates are to be achieved from the very start of the new five-year-plan period.

The high targets envisaged in the plan call for a new approach to defining the sources of economic growth. The decisive factor here is a radical improvement of the production efficiency indicators through more rapid scientific and technological progress. This is the basis, comrades, on which the whole plan is built.

In the new five-year-plan period the share of the accumulation fund in the national income is to be increased to 27.6 percent. This will create real conditions for boosting the absolute growth figures in capital investments. In the terms of the national economy as a whole, the rates of their growth will rise from 15.4 percent in 1981-1985 to 23.6 percent. The plan envisages an extensive program of technical modernization and retooling of many enterprises now in operation. The appropriations for these purposes will go up by 70 percent, while their share in the overall capital investments will exceed 50 percent by the end of the current five-year-plan period.

The new five-year period will see large-scale mechanization and automation of production and the introduction of new technologies. All this will lay the groundwork for improving working conditions and relieving more than five million people of manual jobs by 1990, or more than twice as many as over the previous five years. Large-scale measures have been taken to save material and energy resources.

On the whole, comrades, the series of measures aimed at introducing new achievements of science and technology in production and at improving economic management methods, envisaged by the plan, will make it possible to increase the average annual rates of national income growth to 4.1 percent, or nearly by a third compared to the previous five-year period.

There are also plans for carrying out a broad social program on the basis of accelerated development of the economy. The real incomes of the population will grow; the supply of foodstuffs and consumer goods will be improved; services industry will be extended and new measures will be taken to upgrade the health service and public education.

Special attention is being given to the housing construction program. The housing stock will be increased by 595 million square meters; the new houses will be of better quality and have more amenities. The rates of housing construction will be particularly high in the countryside. All these are important measures, but they should not make us complacent. The search for new ways of improving the Soviet people's living conditions must be continued with the use of all available means and possibilities. Cooperative and individual house-building should be actively promoted.

About four-fifths of the national income are to be spent on improving the people's well-being. The defense capability of the country will be maintained at a proper level, too.

In a word, the 12th Five-Year Plan is an important step in carrying out the economic and social policy worked out by the 27th Congress of the CPSU. Essentially, it is a program of action for each branch, each republic, the entire national-economic complex and the society as a whole. The Politburo believes that there is every ground for the Plenary Meeting of the Central Committee to endorse this plan and instruct the Council of Ministers to submit it for consideration by a session of the Supreme Soviet of the USSR. Nikolai Ryzhkov will report to the deputies on this plan.

A. Past Mistakes Must Not Be Repeated

Objectively assessing the plan submitted, it must be openly stated that strenuous work will be required for its fulfilment. It is essential that we attain the goals set, carry through the reconstruction of the economy so as to create conditions for the further growth of its efficiency. Comrades, all this must be accomplished in the next five years.

Performance has improved somewhat in the recent period. However, this has been achieved primarily by drawing on the reserves that are readily available in order to ensure long-term and stable success. It is necessary to look for more cardinal measures. Our experience in building socialism has taught us that at turning points in the society's development we must boldly make drastic changes and not be afraid of decisive reforms.

We all know what the Russian economy was like before the Great October Revolution. Its industrial production was only 12.5 percent that of the United States. For Lenin and the Bolshevik Party it was absolutely clear that socialism would be able to win only by embarking on a basic reconstruction of the economy and by achieving the highest possible labor productivity. From the first years of Soviet government the Party worked for a major renovation of the national economy, using all available resources to this end.

With Lenin's plan for the building of socialism our people soon created a material-technical base for industry, with factories equipped with machinery advanced for that time serving as the core. Industries guaranteeing rapid technical progress were set up, and the reequipping of large-scale production proceeded apace. The economy focused primarily on advancement in science, the promotion of education, and the training of qualified research and engineering personnel.

It was precisely in this way that the rapid pace of economic and social development was achieved. In a historically short time, the formerly backward peasant country became one of the world's leading industrial states. By the fifties, despite enormous losses in the war, the volume of our industrial production had reached 30 percent, and by 1970, 75 percent of the U. S. level; the USSR's national income was two-thirds that of the United States.

But in the seventies and the eighties we lost to a certain extent our previous dynamism. The economy did not succeed in switching over from extensive to intensive development in time. By inertia the previously achieved level guided economic planning. Departmental interests hindered the transfusion of capital investments and resources into more promising industries. The volume approach to assessments of the economy distorted the real state of affairs and gave false indications of its condition.

The structure of our production remained unchanged and did not meet the requirements of scientific and technological progress. The Soviet Union produces considerably more iron ore and steel than the U. S. A. though it manufactures significantly fewer engineering products; it produces as much timber, but fewer timber products. Under these circumstances, each unit of increment in the national income or in industrial and agricultural output requires of us more resources.

In order to rectify the situation, it is necessary to see clearly the causes of the lag. They boil down primarily to serious errors in the policy of capital investments. The reductions in investment increases from one five-year period to the next were entirely unjustified. As a result, such basic industries of machine-building as machine-tool construction, instrument-making, computer technology and the manufacture of modern structural materials were not properly developed. Furthermore, capital construction was conducted ineffectively, and the building time of projects increased, and the stores of uninstalled equipment grew.

We perceive the rapid growth and accumulation of fixed production assets in the country as a great achievement and, by and large, this is correct. But at the same time, comrades, we cannot fail to see that negative trends in the reproduction of these assets accumulated in the course of a number of years. Unjustified enthusiasm over the construction of new enterprises and neglect of the requirements of existing ones became typical of the planning agencies and many ministries. The bulk of machinery and equipment went to the new facilities, whereas a timely replacement of the obsolete equipment in existing factories and plants was not effected. The process of asset renewal was too slow and their age structure deteriorated.

Among the negative effects of the extensive reproduction of fixed assets is excessive swelling in the repairs sphere. In industry alone equipment repairs cost 10,000 million rubles, and of this sum over 3,000 million goes to the repair of equipment which is being operated beyond the standard maintenance time limits.

It should also be mentioned that such an approach slows the turnover of the country's metal stock. Rather than sending the obsolete machinery for remelting at the appropriate time, the metal is tied up, so to speak, in low-efficiency equipment repeatedly subjected to expensive repairs. In order to produce new machinery, the production of pig iron, steel and rolled metal, as well as the output of iron ore, coal and other mineral resources must be increased.

And finally, the extensive forms of the buildup of fixed production assets have led to an artificial shortage of labor. Some people still cling to this life-buoy when explaining the causes of low growth rates, or failure to make contract deliveries or fulfil the plan. Naturally, we are aware of the demographic situation in the country. But we may ask: if there is a labor shortage, then why continue to build ever new enterprises, and on the basis of obsolete equipment at that, and not infrequently turn out outdated products?

This is precisely the way things stand. At present, in industry alone there are about 700,000 job vacancies. And this is when equipment operates practically for only one work shift. If the shift ratio is raised to 1.7, the number of job vacancies in industry will exceed 4 million. Thousands of millions of rubles have been spent on creating these vacancies. So it works out that old machines function in the existing enterprises, and the new ones have no workers to operate them. The money has been spent, but there are no proper returns.

Comrades, today at the Plenary Meeting I consider it necessary to draw special attention to the fact that the shortcomings in investment policy have had the most adverse effect on the development and the technical level of the engineering industries.

The share of machine-building capital in the total volume of investments was unjustifiably down-rated. Both the planning bodies and the ministries had a hand in this. The prestige of creativity in engineering was undermined, and the once world-famous national schools of technology designers withered away. A pernicious philosophy of imitation and mediocrity has taken shape. As a result, some products are not up to the present-day level of science and technology.

So what is the trouble, comrades? What is the fundamental cause of the situation with the technological standards of our machines? It lies first of all in the fact that until now we have not made a systems analysis of the latest world achievements. Attainment of top quality and reliability was, in effect, not envisaged in the designing of new technology. True, we have recently begun to evaluate technology on the basis of analogues. However, it is not the latest foreign models that are used as standards. This is a sad example of the outmoded thinking and eyewash on the part of those who are responsible for the creation of essential technology. Whom are they deceiving? As it turns out, they are deceiving their own people.

The existing orientation on an average or even low technological level of products was to a certain extent permitted by the standards which were in effect. The system of standards did not encourage designers to search for new ideas, nor did it raise a barrier in the way of producing outdated machines and equipment. Apparently, a kind of inferiority complex that emerged at some research institutes and design offices has also played its part. They tried to justify the poor results of their work by claiming that it was impossible to work better. Nor was there complete success in stimulating effective work among scientists, designers, and engineers.

For many years proper attention was not given to the development of scientific research and experiment, and necessary investments and resources were not channeled in this direction. Naturally all this could not but tell on the technological level of machine-building and on the rates of scientific and technological progress.

Such was the situation prior to the April Plenary Meeting. It was comprehensively analyzed by the Central Committee. Measures worked out were unanimously approved by the Plenary Meeting and the Party Congress. I want to repeat to those who are trying to pull us backwards: we cannot and will not put up with this attitude and must stem all attempts to perpetuate the former approaches and errors, first and foremost in the sphere of scientific and technological progress.

I am sure that the Plenary Meeting of the Central Committee will adopt a principled line in this fundamental question of our home policy and will support all the necessary measures of the Politburo and the government designed to revolutionize the development of our economy and lead it to the vanguard positions of scientific and technological progress. I have already spoken about the responsibility in this connection which lies on the members of the Central Committee elected by the 27th Congress of the CPSU. Comrades, we must not shun this historic responsibility.

What should be done first of all in order to optimally fulfill the rigorous 12th Five-Year Plan and create the necessary prerequisites for the further acceleration of scientific and technological progress?

B. To Accelerate Modernization and Energetically Develop Machine-Building

In our efforts to realize the Party's economic strategy we will rely heavily on the reorientation of the investment and structural policy: we will increase the share of capital investments in the modernization and retooling of industrial enterprises now in operation, accelerate the development of machine-building, and shorten the investment cycle.

We have recently taken some far-reaching measures with respect to the cardinal issues of economic growth. I am referring to the resolutions calling for a fundamental reorganization of metal production, broader and more effective application of chemicals, modernization of engineering, faster advance in computerization, installation of flexible production systems, rotor lines, automated design systems, industrialization of capital construction, and improvement of design-and-estimate work. Guidelines have been laid for resource saving. Work of tremendous importance is under way to upgrade the quality of output in every sector of the national economy. Finally, solid groundwork has been laid for a transfer to new methods of economic management and administration.

The decisions taken are oriented toward intensive economic growth through more timely application of advances in science and technology. The whole of this work must be carried out, comrades, with all determination in every respect. Naturally, we must act now within the framework of the five-year plan. Within this framework, we have vast opportunities for the further intensification of the national economy and enhancement of its efficiency.

Speaking of reserves, I would like to begin with the problem of better utilization of fixed production assets and optimization of their renewal. For this, comrades, is the key component of the wealth of a socialist society, the material base of our economic potential. We must set things right as far as the use of fixed production assets is concerned, and ensure a genuinely proprietary, rational attitude toward them and their effective renewal.

We can bring about a substantial qualitative improvement in our economic performance, above all, higher productivity and increased returns on capital, if we accelerate the renewal of fixed production assets, discard their outdated part as soon as possible, and use technically modern machinery and equipment more intensively in various ways, including by raising the equipment shift ratio. By cardinally renewing fixed production assets and reducing the scale of new construction, we can make substantial capital investments available for speedier social development, above all, the development of housing construction.

These, comrades, are potentialities of vast proportions which fall in the mainstream of the Party's present economic policy. They are not a figment of imagination divorced from life but an actual reality confirmed, notably, by the initiative of the Leningrad Party organization.

While working out means for continued intensification of industrial production, the Leningrad regional Party committee has analyzed the draft economic development plans of industrial enterprises for the 12th Five-Year Plan period. It turned out that the overwhelming majority of the ministries are still committed to extensive development in the enterprises under their jurisdiction in this region. Close to 40 percent of the capital investments are earmarked for new construction and for the expansion of operating capacities. At the same time, the scope of the technological updating of production is clearly insufficient.

Following a thorough investigation of the state of affairs, the regional Party committee has arrived at the correct conclusion: new and advanced components of the fixed production assets must be used in two or three shifts, and the assignments of the 12th Five-Year Plan must be carried out on that basis. In the meantime outdated equipment must be phased out and the space thus released used for the installation of modern productive capacities. This means, as our Leningrad comrades have calculated, about three million square meters of space. The proportion of advanced types of machinery in the total machine-tool inventories of the city and the region will double by the end of the five-year-plan period as machinery and equipment are renewed. There will be a rise in quality standards in industry.

Decisive cuts in new building will allow the Leningraders to decrease capital investments for the purpose. Some of the resources thus saved will be directed toward the technical modernization of the enterprises concerned, but the bulk of it will be used to expand housing construction and provide more amenities in towns and villages. In this way, major technological, economic and social problems are being tackled integrally.

As you know, the Politburo of the Central Committee has considered and approved the proposals of the Leningrad regional Party committee and found that they open up quite a promising area of accelerated development of social production. The initiative thus taken is one of national importance. This is an effective means which should be followed by the industries of other regions.

We see the changeover to a two-shift work regime as an important initiative today. This type of work schedule has long been standing practice in many countries. There enterprises crucial to scientific and technological progress work in two or even three shifts. This reflects a determination to make the best possible use of advanced equipment and replace it with even more effective equipment as soon as possible. Workers on afternoon and night shifts are encouraged by additional incentives. Our central offices must address themselves to this matter without delay and advance proposals for improved moral and material incentives for workers on afternoon and night shifts. We expect the All-Union Central Council of Trade Unions to make an active and constructive contribution to this matter of great national importance.

Even in the early stages, as the initiative of the Leningraders was being discussed, someone suggested that it would not be so simple to get engineering factories to operate in two or three shifts. This, indeed, is not a simple thing. But we have the right to say: why is it that people can work three shifts at continuous production plants, such as metallurgy or chemistry, as well as in the food or textile industries, where, incidentally, female labor predominates? Why then is there only one-shift work, as a rule, in the engineering and metal-working industries where working conditions are certainly no worse?

The Politburo believes that all ministries and departments in conjunction with local Party, government, trade union, and Komsomol bodies must immediately get down to the actual job of intensifying production, taking into account the Leningraders' initiative. In this context, it is important to remodel the operation of transport services, institutions of learning, day-care centers and all the social services in order to create proper conditions for effective work.

In switching over to a multishift work schedule, it is obviously worthwhile to allow the regions, territories and republics to retain the overall capital investments they are entitled to under the five-year plan, leaving them free to use the resources they save by reducing the amount of new industrial construction for updating their productive capacities and advancing their social and cultural development. And they, in their turn, must guarantee the achievement of their five-year-plan targets. Such proposals have, incidentally, already come from some Party and local government officials. I think they must be supported.

One of the most urgent issues of the new five-year plan is to speed up the technological updating of operating production capacities. The plan envisages a substantial increase in capital investments for these purposes. But there are many additional opportunities and possibilities here as well.

The Central Committee of the CPSU set great store by the initiative of the Volzhsky motor works and the Sumy research and production association, which resolved to reach new frontiers of technological progress, improve the quality of products and ensure fast economic growth rates through the use of internal reserves and the upgrading of the organization and methods of managing production. Many other enterprises are emulating their practices. More than 200 other large industrial enterprises are to adopt the principles of self-financing and self-sufficiency next year.

The work collectives of the ZIL motor works, the Leningrad metal works, the Voronezh synthetic rubber factory, the Rosa

Luxemburg knitwear factory in Kiev, the Ekranas plant in Panevezys, Lithuania, and hundreds of other enterprises are successfully utilizing internal reserves to enhance efficiency at each workplace.

Many enterprises in the machine-tool manufacturing industry are being reorganized for the production of advanced machine-tools and equipment capable of increasing productivity many times over and ensuring high quality of products. These include the machine-tool-making associations and plants of Leningrad, Ivanovo, Gomel, Odessa and Ulyanovsk.

The instrument-making and electronics industries are doing their best to speed up the development of computers and microprocessors. They have now created realistic opportunities for quickly solving the problem of organizing the production of high-performance computers and ensuring large-scale production of technological means for electronizing engineering and other sectors of the economy. The 12th Five-Year Plan envisages a 140 percent increase in the production of computers, as compared with the previous five-year-plan period, and manufacture of 1.1 million personal computers.

The practices of Byelorussian railway workers are gaining ever wider recognition. Ten railways have already adopted new methods of organizing and stimulating work. The implementation of this project of national importance will ensure the more efficient functioning of transport and, at the same time, make it possible to increase labor productivity and release nearly 100,000 workers. Such creative attitudes toward work deserve high praise and active support. Generally speaking, a creative search is taking place in all sectors of the economy and in all regions of the country.

Comrades, retooling and modernization of production call for new attitudes. You are aware of how many plants were retooled in the past. Thousands of millions of rubles were spent on replacing obsolete equipment. Nevertheless, the efforts often failed to produce the desired result. One of the chief reasons for this was poor quality of detail design, often based on low-efficiency technology and antiquated methods of labor organization. New equipment often differed from the old only by the date of manufacture.

How are ministries dealing with the problem of modernization now, in this time of change? What projects are to be tackled in the new five-year-plan period?

A sample analysis of plant modernization projects of some industrial ministries has been made at the request of the Central Committee. What are its results? By no means could all projects be accepted as matching modern standards. Many of them require thorough revision. Moreover, some of them had become outdated, and it was thus recommended that they no longer be implemented.

Here are a few examples. The plan for the reconstruction of the Voznesensk hydraulic press plant was drawn up by the Kharkov Ukrgipromash Institute of the Ministry of Machine Building. Note the figures programmed into this plan: the number of workers is to be increased more than five-fold, while labor productivity is to be raised by a mere 70 percent. Moreover, only one-third of this growth is to be achieved through technical solutions, and the remaining two-thirds through a rise in prices on the products.

The situation in other places is much the same. The state institute for the design of textile industry enterprises drafted a plan for the reconstruction of the Moscow printed-calico factory of the Ministry of Light Industry of the USSR: half of its machine fleet is to be made up of equipment that has been manufactured without modernization for more than 15 years. It is impossible to produce high-quality fabric of the required assortment, or to achieve high productivity of labor with this machinery.

The question is where are they sending the country, those wretched planners and ministerial officials who endorsed these plans? It is clear that such plans can discredit the idea of accelerating scientific and technological progress, and burden the economy with enormous expenditures.

So, comrades, we must learn important lessons from all this. We must review promptly, and in the shortest possible time, all plans for technical retooling and reconstruction which are slated for implementation in the 12th Five-Year-Plan period. Those which do not correspond to the tasks of speeding up scientific and technological progress should be discarded without hesitation, their implementation prohibited, while the funds thus saved should be channeled into the development of high-technology production.

Responsibility for the level of the plans for technical retooling and reconstruction should lie, above all, with the ministries which are called upon to be true technical headquarters of industries. Above all it is they who should be held accountable. The attention of ministers was drawn to these questions at a conference held in June of last year. They were directly instructed to review the plans for technical retooling and reconstruction.

The approach to business has to be changed dramatically, comrades. We cannot allow thousands of millions to be invested in obsolete projects which are based on technically unsound solutions. In so acting, we will not rise to the modern world standards of production. And we cannot, I would even say we must not, accept this.

Everyone is aware of the urgency of the problem of supplying the people with products of light industry. Some specialists propose building new enterprises for this purpose. Nobody rules out this path of development, particularly as it concerns the output of modern materials and goods. But basically the task of expanding the production of goods can only be solved through the technical retooling and reconstruction of light-industry enterprises. The main thing is to find the correct solutions to this problem.

Calculations reveal the following information. If the most advanced equipment and technologies are used in the reconstruction of enterprises, we will be able to increase their effectiveness by 30 to 40 percent.

Evidently, we must proceed in the following manner: where such equipment exists reconstruction should be conducted vigorously, and where it is absent reconstruction should be put off for two or three years until the production of efficient equipment starts to run smoothly, and then it will be possible to make up for the delay on a new production basis. Generally speaking, ministries and central offices must approach these matters with utmost responsibility, and stop clinging to the old. Otherwise, they will let down their own people.

Comrades, you well realize that plans for updating the national economy on the basis of the latest scientific and technological achievements depend, in the final analysis, on machine-building. It is here that all of today's burning economic questions are focused. We will not be able to cope with the tasks the Congress sets before us unless we quickly modernize machine-building and reorient it to produce new machine systems and sophisticated equipment for all branches of the national economy.

This matter was recently discussed at the conference of machine-building branch leaders at the CPSU Central Committee. We had a serious talk with the ministers. The discussion showed that we cannot afford to limit ourselves to the measures charted by the well-known resolution on developing machine-building. Additional and equally extensive efforts are needed in order to thoroughly update the machine-building complex. Proposals have been elaborated on instruction from the Central Committee for additional measures to accelerate progress in machine-building.

First of all, guidelines have been established for an overall improvement in the technological standards of machines, instruments and other equipment, for an increase in the production of items equipped with automatic control devices, for a dramatic rise in the output of special-purpose technology to be used at the very enterprise which produces it, and for a substantial expansion of the capacities of stock preparation shops. Measures have been worked out to further step up science and production integration, and consolidate the experimental bases of scientific research institutes and design bureaus.

When implemented, these measures will ensure that 80 to 95 percent of the total output of basic nomenclature goods will correspond to world standards by the year 1990, with the figure for newly developed products reaching practically 100 percent. It is planned to switch production entirely to top-quality articles between 1991 and 1993.

The share of microprocessor equipment will grow sharply, as will the automation of research and development work. The demands of the instrument-making industry for the latest electronic equipment will be met in full.

Machine-building enterprises will be reequipped much quicker, with 38 to 40 percent of Soviet-manufactured technology to be assigned for this purpose. In 1990, the production of special technologies for use at enterprises producing them will reach 4,000-4,200 million rubles, as compared with the initially planned 2,500 million.

Capital investments in developing the machine-building complex are fully ensured by contract allocations and equally distributed for each year of the five-year-plan period. In order to concentrate investments on the crucial lines of scientific and technological progress, and observe the specified time limits in construction, it is planned to freeze more than a hundred outdated-design machine-building projects now under construction.

Major steps are envisaged to improve the economic mechanism in machine-building. Beginning next year, the number of confirmed assignments will be drastically cut by means of increasing the role of such general indices as profit, labor-efficiency growth and decrease of relative consumption of basic materials and resources.

The planning of machinery and equipment production in tons is ruled out. Solutions to most of the questions determining the interaction of industries within the machine-building complex have been found, and other reserves for the further enhancement of the technical level of production revealed. The machine-building ministries have been asked to complete in 1986 the formulation of plans for technically reequipping each enterprise and the industries as a whole on the basis of the broad use of scientific and technological achievements. The solution of the problem of providing the machine builders with high-quality progressive materials will require additional development of component suppliers' capacities. This will also have to be accomplished.

The Politburo has examined and expressed its support for all these proposals. Now it is submitting them to the Plenary Meeting of the Central Committee for approval.

As you see, comrades, the realization of such a very crucial and complex program will call for tremendous effort, strenuous and competent work. It must be carried out—we have no other path. Any other road means relinquishing positions, falling behind. This the CPSU Central Committee cannot accept.

We hope that the heads of the machine-building ministries and the work collectives will treat the fulfillment of this important national task with full understanding and due responsibility. Recalling the lessons of the past, we must warn in advance all those who are responsible for fulfilling the program of modernizing the engineering industry: there must be no retreats from what has been outlined, and no excuses citing objective or subjective reasons will be accepted.

Comrades, speaking of our work for a major technical re-equipping and reconstruction of the economy, we cannot bypass the problems of capital construction. Its volume in the new five-year-plan period is enormous. Almost 1,000,000 million rubles is being allocated for this purpose. More than 500,000 million rubles worth of building and assembly work alone will be carried out. This is 20 percent more than in the 11th Five-Year-Plan period.

Yet, the situation in construction remains unsatisfactory and the process of reconstruction has become protracted. Nearly half the construction trusts chronically fail to fulfill their plans and bring capacities and facilities into operation on schedule. Serious defects mark the organizational structure of the management of construction work. The establishment of design and building associations and firms for the mass industrialized "turn-key" construction of multiple-recurring projects still has not gone beyond good intentions.

Generally speaking, comrades, a thorough streamlining of the entire construction industry will have to be undertaken and progressive experience will have to be more widely utilized.

Everyone is aware of the successes of the Byelorussian builders, for example. In the course of the 11th Five-Year-Plan period, they reduced the number of projects under construction at one time by 21 percent and their average building time by 28.6 percent. Considerable savings in labor and materials were achieved, and at the same time the commissioning of all completed projects and facilities was ensured. The overall volume of capital construction rose by 19 percent, and the commissioning of fixed assets increased by 23 percent. And this was accomplished throughout the entire republic. But this very successful experience has not yet been implemented anywhere outside Byelorussia.

There are good examples in other areas of the country as well. In 1979 a building team led by Nikolai Ilyich Travkin was organized in the Moscow region. Cost-accounting principles and elements of self-management revealed great potentials and ensured the achievement of good results. In 1983, on the basis of this collective, a new prime contractor organization, the PMK-96, was established. And later the entire trust Mosoblselstroi No. 18, led by N. I. Travkin, went over to cost accounting. Here are the results. In the past year the trust delivered 1.5 times more commercial building products than in the previous year. Productivity rose by 25 percent, and production costs were reduced by 12 percent. Having earlier operated at a loss, the trust now received almost 1.5 million rubles in profit. The average pay increased by 11 percent.

It is also important to stress that the successes of the Byelorussian and Moscow builders have been achieved on practically the same material base. Therefore, claims that the shortcomings in capital construction are due to a shortage of labor or transport facilities are often groundless. Experience has shown that capital construction can be successfully conducted with existing potentials. It is essential only to ably utilize everything the builders have right now, and show creativity and economic initiative in work.

We obviously face the need for a cardinal restructuring of capital construction. The time has come to demand prompt action from all those who are responsible for utilizing progressive experience in this industry. It is necessary to change the planning and organization of construction and, of course, to update its material base.

C. Thrifty Management and Skillful Administration

Comrades, there are many other reserves within the framework of the five-year plan which can provide additional momentum to our advance. When we speak of the need for a fundamental restructuring of the economy, we view a substantial improvement in the quality of products as one of its most important results. The Party Congress presented the problem of quality as a nationwide task. The CPSU Central Committee addressed a special letter to all working people.

We can now definitely say that the majority of Soviet people realize the need for an urgent solution to this most important problem.

Many work collectives have taken a much more serious approach to their work. Without particular expenditures, but rather, largely due to a conscientious attitude toward work, stronger labor and technological discipline, the adoption of a series of urgent organizational and technical measures, such enterprises as the Alma-Ata machine-tool manufacturing plant, the Tallinn machine-building works, the Fergana-based Azot amalgamation, the Elektroizolit amalgamation in the Moscow region, the Bakelektrobytpribor production amalgamation and a number of others have sharply reduced the number of unsatisfactory equipment reports and ensured the output of products in strict compliance with the standard requirements. I would like particularly to emphasize the fact that they have achieved a breakthrough in raising the quality of output using practically only the existing equipment.

Thus, decisive steps to improve the quality of machines, equipment and consumer goods can and should be taken today, without waiting for the appearance of new technology. As you know, the Politburo of the CPSU Central Committee and the Council of Ministers of the USSR passed a special resolution. Measures of a technical and economic nature, standardization and certification of products, price-setting, a system of moral and material encouragement are directed at improving the quality of output. A system of state-controlled independent approval of products is being introduced at enterprises.

It is important that the Party committees actively support the work of production collectives and state control and approval bodies in order to right the situation in the near future. The fact that this is realistically possible is evidenced by the experience of those enterprises where the system of independent approval was introduced as an experiment last year.

Radical changes are to be achieved in the utilization of material resources as well. Not long ago the CPSU Central Committee and the Council of Ministers of the USSR passed a resolution that presents challenging tasks as regards the saving of energy and resources. The saving of resources is a decisive means of meeting the growing requirements for materials, fuel and electric power. We hope to receive over one-quarter of the increment of the national income in the current five-year-plan period as a result of this factor.

This is an important task, though not all managers fully realize it and remain locked into the narrow sphere of their outmoded conceptions. The Ministry of the Automobile Industry, the Ministry of Heavy Machine-Building, the Ministry of the Coal Industry, the Ministry of Electric Power Development and Electrification, and the Ministry of Light Industry systematically fail to fulfill the tasks relating to a number of types of resource saving. No small number of enterprises continue to permit direct losses of the most valuable raw materials and products. Thirteen thousand million cubic meters of casing head gas is burnt needlessly in flares every year. Millions of tons of coal are lost in transport by rail. The loss of agricultural produce is high, reaching nearly 20 percent on the whole. And how much electric power, heat and water is still being wasted needlessly? The utilization of secondary resources is still poorly organized.

Let us be frank—we have reached a point beyond which such mismanagement is intolerable, and what's more, we simply cannot afford it. Our scientific and technological policy, planning, and economic and administrative levers should be used to eliminate these ills that have struck root.

We must launch an all-out war on wasteful practices and exercise the strictest economy. Steps should be taken to make the fulfilment of tasks as regards the saving of resources and the level of their utilization one of the main criteria for assessing the performance of every enterprise and collective.

The saving of feedstock and materials should be further encouraged. Can we consider such a practice as normal whereby the payment for the saving of resources amounts to mere kopecks? This simply won't do. Thriftiness should also become a habit; every worker should learn to be thrifty. Thriftiness should be constantly fostered in the rising generation, both in the family and at school.

Comrades, special attention in the five-year plan is devoted to the development of the agroindustrial complex. The planned targets are in line with the policy formulated by the May 1982 Plenary Meeting of the CPSU Central Committee. On the whole, the volume of capital investment, the output of farm produce and the amount of material and technical facilities for the agroindustrial complex have been planned in keeping with the targets of the Food Program. Enterprises that process and store farm produce, and plants making agricultural machinery will be developing at priority rates.

In general, favorable conditions are being created for a buildup of the potential of the farming sector. This is undoubtedly justified. At the same time we must realize that the immense resources being channeled into that sector are not yielding sufficient returns. On the whole, the 11th Five-Year-Plan period was completed with low indicators. This affected the supply of foodstuffs to the population and the rates of the country's economic development.

For the sake of objectivity it should be said that positive changes have been carried out in the farming sector of late.

However, they are not taking place in all branches of the agroindustrial complex, and not in all regions, territories, and republics. We are now faced with the urgent task of ensuring stable output of crops, primarily grain and fodder crops. This is the main problem on whose successful solution the stable development of livestock farming, the incomes of collective and state farms and the economic performance of the processing enterprises largely depend.

Work in the farming sector must be intensified in order to change the situation decisively for the better. We have vast reserves, comrades, for that. They are found above all in the huge potential that has already been created. We now have experience in running an efficient agriculture in practically all zones. Thanks to the measures taken to improve administration and the system of management, the economic and organizational prerequisites have been created for heightening the labor activity of agricultural workers.

Without going into details, I would like to emphasize the main thing once again—to achieve higher productivity in crop farming and livestock breeding intensive technologies should be used on a wide scale. This is both the most realistic and the most efficient way of achieving better results in crop growing and in livestock production.

We should continue our policy of concentrating efforts and means on the decisive branches of the agroindustrial complex. This is a reliable way of getting tangible returns on investments in the countryside. The experience of our country and of other states shows that one should concentrate resources on those farms and in those regions where they promise the best results in terms of the volume of production and of economic efficiency. In this connection, there is every reason to consider once again the question of redistributing resources and allocating them for the specific volumes of production.

Also worth considering is the question of setting up research-and-production amalgamations on a regional scale, and in some cases perhaps also on a district scale, so that they would become catalysts for the accelerated development of the collective and state farms in their zone and help them in applying advanced technologies and advanced methods of husbandry. This approach guarantees a rational use of the economic potential and the achievement of good end results.

Moldavia, the Ukraine and other republics already have experience in this. Amalgamations have been formed there on the basis of zonal institutes, research and experimental farms. Similar work has been carried out in a number of fraternal socialist countries. I believe it would be expedient to study it thoroughly and make active use of it in practice.

If we are to make great achievements in our agroindustrial complex, we must not merely follow traditional paths. It is only by concentrating resources, providing for the priority development of key sectors, and skillfully using the advantages inherent in the new economic mechanism and structure of management that we will be able to work efficiently, increase output quickly and successfully carry out the tasks set by the Food Program of the USSR.

Finally, comrades, our success in the 12th Five-Year-Plan period will depend on how we will further conduct the work to perfect management and the entire economic mechanism. The principles of this work have been defined. On the one hand, we must continue to improve centralized management of the national economy, enhance the role of the State Planning Committee and other economic agencies and specify the functions of ministries, and on the other hand, increase in every way the rights and economic independence of enterprises and amalgamations and also their responsibility for the results of their activity.

I believe everybody agrees with this now. But the practical work to implement democratic centralism in management is not proceeding in a way that is required in the present situation. We have carried out experiments and obtained promising results, but we often shrink back when it comes to disseminating them on a large scale. Much in the system of the economic mechanism has already been tested and it is necessary to introduce what is new more boldly in practice. To operate, so to say, along the entire front. To this end the central economic bodies should, on the basis of the Guidelines laid down by the 27th Congress, draft and adopt more quickly documents necessary for the transition to the new principles of management.

The numerous instructions, regulations and methodological guidelines that we have been accumulating for decades should be reviewed in accordance with the decisions of the Congress and the resolutions adopted after the Congress, and those which contradict the transformation should be resolutely discarded. We will not be able to advance without this, comrades. Genuine centralism in management has nothing to do with a bureaucratic regulation of the multifaceted life of production, research, and design collectives. The system that has formed over many years in which these collectives have been burdened with far-fetched instructions and methods deprives managers and development engineers of the possibility to promptly solve the economic and technical problems that arise.

This results in the loss of profits amounting to many billions of rubles on a nationwide scale. We encounter such phenomena at every step. The Director General of the Kriogenmash research-and-production amalgamation, V. P. Belyakov; the Director General of the Electrosila amalgamation, B. I. Fomin; the Chief Designer of the Zavod Imeni Vladimira Ilyicha amalgamation, V. I. Radin; and many other experienced managers, scientists, and development engineers have written about them.

Order must be installed here and concern shown for a real expansion of the rights of work collectives. This requires that the draft law on the socialist enterprise (production amalgamation) be completed as quickly as possible. This document should be based on the concept of the new conditions of economic management, sum up the recent experience, and consolidate all the best trends in implementing the course toward greater economic independence, in increasing the role and responsibility of enterprises and production amalgamations.

Thereby we will lay the foundation for the optimal distribution of rights and duties among ministries and enterprises, and for legislatively protecting work collectives from petty tutelage and arbitrary administration, from unjustified interference in their day-to-day economic activity. This, comrades, will mean a serious step forward in democratizing the management of our economy and developing the initiative of working people.

As you know, the 27th Congress set the task of really mastering economic methods of managing the national economy. In this connection we will have to ensure first of all the formulation of advanced standards and quotas. The State Planning Committee should head this crucial work and draw ministries and agencies, scientists, specialists of amalgamations and enterprises into it on a broad scale. Moreover, this work should not be dragged out. Without creating substantiated economic standards we will not rid ourselves of the yoke of all sorts of instructions fettering the performance of enterprises, and it will be difficult to move from administrative methods of management to economic ones. This will slow down the application of the principles of self-financing and work without state subsidies, which we intend to use ever more widely.

Finally, mention should be made of the key importance of price-forming in developing economic methods of management. Many unanswered questions have accumulated here. Prices of machinery and equipment, and estimates of construction costs are raised under the pretext of modernization. Changes in the range of products and pursuit of "gross" indicators often bring about an unjustified increase in prices of consumer goods as well.

Regrettably, state and economic bodies often look the other way, so to speak, and quite often themselves turn out to be interested in increasing volumes of production by "playing" with prices. Following last year's audits alone more than 100 million rubles received by enterprises in unlawful profits through violations of price-setting regulations were confiscated and directed into the budget.

I would like to warn you, comrades, that this is an extremely dangerous trend. Artificial price-raising does not cure economic ailments but only corrupts officials and puts a brake on technical progress. Exaggerated prices based on the input approach conceal shortcomings in technology and the organization of production, and generate a disdainful attitude to the search for economic methods of management.

Price increases are justified only if they are due to substantial improvement in the consumer quality of commodities and higher effectiveness of products. We must introduce order in price-forming. The State Committee for Prices must take a more clear-cut and principled stand here. Questions of perfecting crediting and banking in general are also rife. As we switch to new methods of management we must enhance the role of the bank as a key organ of economic management.

I would particularly like to single out a problem, which, if not solved, will make the task of introducing resource-saving technologies and overcoming the input-oriented nature of the economy impossible to successfully attain. I am referring to the notorious "gross" indicators. Various forms of assignments in terms of such indicators play a major role in assessing the performance of industries, regions and enterprises. Since this is so, costly materials are often used for the sake of increasing this "gross," the weight of machines is built up, ton-kilometers are chalked up, intraenterprise turnover is inflated, etc. We are struggling for efficiency, but look at the really ridiculous situation in which economic managers find themselves: they manufacture a cheap product and get a dressing down for failing to meet the target of production in terms of rubles; they introduce a novelty, save resources, and again it turns out that they have put their enterprises and sometimes even the whole industry at a disadvantage.

I will give you the following example. An economic experiment at motor transport enterprises of a number of ministries was started two and a half years ago. The participants in the experiment began planning their work in such a way as to interest people not in ton-kilometers but in the timely delivery of all ordered freight with the least outlay. The causes prompting managers to pad their accounts with nonexistent tons and kilometers were removed.

And here are the results: the fulfillment of orders, that key indicator of work, rose to 100 percent. At the same time demand for motor vehicles and drivers declined and fuel expenditure dropped by 18 percent. The introduction of such conditions of work nationwide would free thousands of motor vehicles and drivers and save more than five million tons of motor fuel.

It would seem that planning bodies should embrace this new method of work. But far from it. Certain high-ranking officials of the State Planning Committees of the USSR and the Russian Federation began to defend the outmoded planning systems with might and main, as the saying goes. The fact is that the earlier planned "gross output" and the volumes of transportation turned out to be exaggerated. Planners did not want to admit that these estimates were no good. This is a fine example of nonacceptance of the new, of reluctance to deal with the restructuring of the economic mechanism and to renounce outdated methods of work.

Gross output indicators still dominate in many sectors. Moreover, efforts are being made again to revive "gross output" as the main evaluating indicator in, for example, construction, and not without approval from the USSR State Planning Committee and the Ministry of Finance of the USSR. This is happening despite the fact that the experience of the leading building organizations testifies otherwise; namely, that their work should be evaluated and encouraged on the basis of finished products, the commissioning of projects, and not on the basis of the volume of construction and assembly work. I believe, comrades, that the time has come to unravel this "gross output tangle," otherwise we will not be able to move ahead and successfully tackle the input mechanism.

Considering questions of management, it is impossible not to mention the responsibility of the USSR State Planning Committee for the solution of national economic problems advanced by life itself. Conceived at its founding as the think tank for managing the economy, the State Planning Committee continues to perform traffic controller's functions in many respects. Not infrequently, it has to deal with matters which top industry executives, and perhaps even directors of enterprises, could sort out. At the same time it does not perform the main function of the strategic planning body of the country.

Routine business hinders planners seeking ways of resolving the main socioeconomic tasks, choosing proportions and priorities in the development of the national economy, defining structural policy, locating productive forces and balancing the economy. This is why we have overlooked many things. Generally speaking, a serious restructuring is required in planning work.

Comrades, discussing questions relating to the long-term development of the country and drawing up measures for the future, we must not lose sight of the tasks of the current moment. The successful fulfillment of the plans for this year, and hence for the entire five-year period, depends on whether these tasks are tackled correctly. Workers in the countryside have some special responsibilities today. The results of the current year in the farming sector are of exceptional importance for us. As you know, fairly good results have been achieved in livestock production in the past five months. It is important that they be consolidated.

However, the main task is to grow and gather in without loss grain, fruits and vegetables, fodder and industrial crops. This is a task of nationwide importance, and should be approached as such in everyday work. And what is especially important in those many regions where present conditions are not easy is to take in and preserve everything that will have been grown, to prevent losses.

A crucial period is beginning in the operation of industry, capital construction and transport. There must be no slackening in the results of work: efforts should be made to try and increase the pace of production growth and to fulfil all the plans without fail. It is important to get ready in time for work in winter. We must learn lessons from the past. With this in mind the CPSU Central Committee and the Council of Ministers of the USSR passed a resolution a few days ago charting specific measures to prepare the national economy for the forthcoming autumn and winter seasons.

The attention of the Party, state, and economic bodies should be directed toward fulfilling it even now. The entire life-sustaining sphere of cities and villages should be put in proper order—the reliable operation of electric power and heat supply systems, the repairs to energy-generating units and the planned commissioning of new capacities, the timely buildup of stocks of fuel at enterprises and in the utilities should be ensured. In short, matters should be dealt with in such a fashion as to ensure that the population does not experience any discomfort in everyday life under any circumstances, that the work collectives operate in the normal production regime, and the economy develops at a stable pace, gaining momentum.

These, comrades, are considerations on the principled and current questions relating to the economic policy—questions the solution of which will determine to a decisive extent the fulfilment of the wide-scale program for transforming the national economy in the 12th Five-Year-Plan period. The fulfillment of the assignments of the five-year plan will provide new evidence of the dynamism and vitality of the socialist system, and will become a major step forward in the realization of the policy course charted by the 27th Congress of the CPSU.

III. ACTIVE EFFORTS TO RESTRUCTURE PARTY WORK

Comrades, when the country's destiny was at stake, or when it was a matter of solving questions of vital importance for its present and future, Lenin emphasized: "The Party is responsible."

Ours is the ruling Party. It has in its hands powerful levers for influencing social processes. The theory and the policy, the ideas and the strength of organization, millions of Communists in production and management, in science, technology and culture are the mighty potential of the Party.

The activity of the millions of working people, and the scope and depth of the people's creative endeavor, which is the decisive factor of acceleration, in many respects depend on how Party organizations operate. Only by placing the human being at the center of Party work will we be able to carry out the tasks set by the Congress. The essence of the radical restructuring of Party work lies precisely in turning to people, to real work.

What has been shown by the months that have passed since the Congress? The ideas of restructuring have been appreciated by the majority of Party cadres and are beginning to manifest themselves in practical activities. New relationships between local and central Party, government and economic bodies have developed. Many practical matters are dealt with faster and with a greater understanding. We have mounted another step where frankness and urgency in the way problems are put and in the level of criticism and self-criticism are concerned.

The Moscow, Leningrad, Kiev, Minsk, Donetsk, Chelyabinsk, Sumy, and Tatar Party organizations are profoundly engaged in the large-scale intensification of production. Questions of developing the economy and the social sphere are being tackled energetically and purposefully by the Communists of Brest, Volgograd, Ulyanovsk, Kharkov, Irkutsk, Lipetsk, Rostov, and of many other regions, territories and republics.

Important steps are being made by all Party organizations. The quest for new forms and methods of work that will accord with the present time is itself proceeding with difficulties. One encounters the idea that the guidelines laid down at the Congress apply to the sphere of big-time politics and that practical work should proceed along its own course, keeping to the beaten track. It can be said that such sentiments still exist within Party circles.

Take, for example, the Kursk regional Party organization. The spirit of imaginative attitude to work, of criticism and self-criticism has by no means penetrated all of the districts there. A domineering style of work has proved exceptionally tenacious. For example, Comrade V. A. Anpilogov, first secretary of the Oktyabrsky Party district committee, and some other Party workers, used to hold a negative view of criticism, cover up for "yes-men" and try to conceal failures. In order to color the real state of affairs, they quite often induced economic managers to resort to report-padding. They showed little concern for the development of the initiative of the Party organization, or for the labor and social activity of people.

Comrade M. S. Shevelev, secretary of the Party organization of the Krasnoye Znamya collective farm, wrote about all this to a central newspaper.

The fallacious methods of work could not have been unknown to the regional Party committee. But, obviously, the bureau and the first secretary of the regional committee, Comrade A. F. Gudkov, failed to rise to the occasion. The regional committee was lavish in giving Comrade Anpilogov the most flattering character references, virtually holding him up as an example to others. When the Central Committee instructed its staff to look into the state of affairs there, it turned out that what Comrade Shevelev had written was the truth pure and simple, and the opinion of the leaders of the Party's regional committee proved to be untenable.

Eventually, the story was brought to an end by the members of the district committee, who gave Comrade Anpilogov a vote of no-confidence and decided to relieve him of the secretaryship. Why did the regional committee fail to notice in time and duly assess the unbecoming style of the work of the secretary of the district committee, and the situation which had developed in the district Party organization? Apparently, the secretaries of the Party's regional committee themselves and the committee's bureau are in no hurry to reorganize their work, and still cling to the obsolete style under which the initiative of working people does not get due support.

Since the Congress, Soviet people have shown a growing interest in the Party's affairs and in the processes taking place in society. They want to find their place in the countrywide work to realize the ideas advanced at the Congress and make their contribution to the restructuring effort. This is borne out by the numerous letters that have been received by the Central Committee and the editorial offices of newspapers. Some of these letters you are holding in your hands. It would seem that the task of the Party committees is utterly clear: it is essential to support the social and labor activity of people in every way. But in many places everything remains as it used to be: initiative runs into a wall of indifference and, at times, overt resistance.

At the Irbit chemical and pharmaceutical plant of the

Sverdlovsk region, the Party bureau and the management, with the backing of the city's Party committee, took to task a shop superintendent who advocated the introduction of advanced forms of organization and remuneration of labor. The initiative of a Communist, a resourceful person, ran into out-and-out red tape. We deemed it necessary to discuss this fact, in view of its exceptional importance, at the CPSU Central Committee. You know what decision the Secretariat of the Central Committee took on this matter. I think there are lessons to be learned from this and not just for the people in Sverdlovsk.

The Congress oriented the Party committees to mastering political methods of leadership. However, the striving of Party bodies to assume managerial functions continues unabated. Just listen to what some Party leaders say. They readily and with expertise speak of the current economic campaign, of milk yields and weight gains, tons, etc. But when the conversation turns to a political analysis of social phenomena, socioeconomic tasks, scientific and engineering problems, and of the resources inherent in the human factor, they are quite often at a loss.

Frankly speaking, we should reorganize and get rid of the elements of arbitrary administration at all levels—from primary organizations to the Central Committee. Only all-round political, organizational and ideological activities at all levels of Party leadership will ensure the accomplishment of the tasks set by the Congress.

An increase in the capacity for action of primary Party organizations is acquiring a particular importance in this context. We have more than once become convinced of their inexhaustible resources. I would say that we should begin restructuring work precisely with developing the independence and vigor of primary organizations, the initiative and activity of Communists. This is the main element, and it should be tackled in real earnest.

This must be done by the Party's district and city committees, which are the closest to work collectives and know the potentials and resources of primary Party organizations. We have quite a number of Party committees at district and city level that in the new situation are giving greater scope to the initiative of the cadres and shift the center of gravity to control of their work by the grass roots, by the public and the press.

At the same time, there is still gravitation to traditional methods of leadership, or rather management. All this, comrades, was practiced at one time out of necessity, as if in compensation for flaws in the economic machinery. At present, such practice is not only unnecessary but harmful, too. One should more boldly renounce a controller's functions. The work collectives and people are the main sphere of the activities of a secretary and of members of a Party district committee.

Recently I have had many meetings and conversations with directors of enterprises, workers, engineers and secretaries of Party committees, and they all agree that opportunities for resourceful work are broadening slowly. Red tape, that twin brother of arbitrary administration and arch opponent of the broad participation of the masses in managerial affairs, makes itself felt.

Take managerial bodies, for example. When one gets directly acquainted with their activities, one can see that some ministers and heads of departments and enterprises have altogether lost the habit of speaking to one another and of establishing direct business contacts, and that everything is done by correspondence. Does this mean that comrades are unable to speak to one another over the telephone, to get together and settle problems or is this an attempt to shield oneself from responsibility by means of documents?

This applies, to a certain extent, to Party bodies. For example, the Tashkent city Party committee and the city's district committees within four months have sent 50–100 percent more of their resolutions to primary Party organizations than in the corresponding period last year. One can come across such excessive reliance on correspondence in other places as well.

Unnecessary paper work, far from being a technical question, is a political one. Just see what any inspection boils down to: a study of information, tables, minutes and plans of activities, and to finding out whether the matter was discussed and whether an appropriate decision was taken. In short, there is a habit of working with paper, and not with people, and of looking at people through paper work. As for how people work, live, what they think, what their problems are and their attitude of mind—all that is remote. Yet Party work is all about precisely these things.

There will be no restructuring if an atmosphere of intolerance to drawbacks, to stagnancy in work, to ostentation and idle talk is not established within the Party and its organizations. This is why, in the spirit of the Congress, we must enhance criticism. What we need is principled criticism, which is directed to an exact address, and which reveals the causes of shortcomings and omissions, and ways of removing them, the criticism that upholds the spirit of concern, and of healthy dissatisfaction with what has been achieved.

Comrades, the concept of acceleration is inseparable from a vigorous personnel policy. The plans for the five-year period envision fundamental measures in personnel training and development of a system of continuous education. All of them are directed at providing professionally competent workers for every area of material production and cultural and intellectual life.

This task is being tackled not only in educational establishments where we have initiated serious reforms. Our time demands that everyone continuously update their knowledge, improve their skills and broaden their ideological, political, scientific, technological and economic horizons. Otherwise one cannot efficiently use the latest technology or be a knowledgeable manager and a skillful administrator.

Special importance is attached today to work with senior managers and officials, called upon to organize the restructuring effort in the areas entrusted to them. By the April 1985 Plenary Meeting, as you know, we have quite a few unresolved personnel issues.

That situation drew criticism from both Communists and non-Party people. The Central Committee made the proper conclusions. Many well-trained and mature Communists, who have proved themselves in practical grass-roots work and who understood the current situation well, were advanced in the course of the review-and-election campaign. There should be continued improvement in the placement of cadres.

While speaking in Togliatti, I noted that now that work is getting under way to accelerate scientific and technological progress, people with an innovative spirit should be particularly valued. All the more so since we are urging everyone to act rather than to sit back and wait. One cannot help seeing that a man with initiative often comes into conflict with outdated regulations that do not meet the new tasks. Everything possible should be done to ensure that questing, creative people do not find themselves in a tight spot and suffer defeat. This is not an abstract discourse.

I would like to illustrate what I have just said with one outrageous example. In Cherkassy there is a plant under the Ministry of the Electrical Engineering Industry and a research institute working in the same field. The institute, which was headed by Comrade A. I. Chabanov, has developed machine tools of a new type and control systems for them. The machine tools won recognition at international exhibitions and orders began to come in for them from our plants and from abroad.

Meanwhile, the plant, which should have been the first to utilize those achievements, stubbornly ignored the new technology. And when last July Comrade Chabanov was appointed acting manager of the plant on a temporary basis, he decided to go ahead with production without waiting for approval of specifications for new products. So, the advanced technology was brought to life and the plant's finances were improved. But then some people began to complain that the new manager had departed from the regulations and padded his reports. And what was the response of the ministry and the regional Party committee?

One cannot say they acted in the spirit of innovation. The manager was relieved of his duties and the case was turned over to the investigating bodies. The CPSU Central Committee and the Procurator General had to interfere to sort things out. No violations, let alone crimes, were found. The matter seemed to be clear. But even after the truth was restored, the Party bureau expelled Comrade Chabanov from the Party. Moreover, a letter sent to the Congress by Communists who had taken his side, was intercepted at the post office by the local authorities and never reached Moscow.

These, comrades, are the sort of facts that one comes across. We turned the case over to the Party Control Committee, and justice has now triumphed, it seems. But the question is: where was the regional Party committee? Could it not have promptly grasped the essence of that case and prevented a breach of Soviet laws and the victimization of a Communist?

At our Plenary Meeting we should state in the most principled manner that the Party committees are called upon to protect the honor of the Party, and not the honor of rank. Everything is important in Party work, not least the way a person is met at the Party committee, the way he is talked to, the way the questions that trouble him are settled and, finally, the role the Party committee plays in his fate.

What continues to happen is this. A Communist shares his doubts or expresses his personal opinion in a city or district Party committee. But instead of giving him a substantive answer, they tell him: "Don't forget the place you are in." And what is that place? It is his home. Where else should he take his problems and concerns if not to his Party committee? And because Party comradeship means a Bolshevik standard of relationships among Communists regardless of rank or title, he has every right to expect to be treated with sensitivity and attention rather than receiving a high-handed reception.

The spirit of comradeship should pervade our entire Party life. Making stricter demands on the performance of one's duties, it is necessary to always draw a clear distinction between Party principle and a dressing-down that denigrates human dignity. Deviations from this rule—and we know of such cases—crush the human soul, sow uncertainty in the work collective and depress public interest and activity. We cannot reconcile ourselves to such things.

We should continue to work perseveringly to ensure that a healthy atmosphere in our society gains ground and becomes firmly established. I would say that, in this context, the war on drunkenness and alcoholism remains among the most urgent tasks. We should be guided in this war by the opinion of our people rather than those who are addicted to alcohol. We have assumed a commitment to our entire people to wage a resolute battle on drunkenness, and it is our Party duty to fulfill this mandate.

We should also fulfill the mandate to step up the war on unearned incomes. The recent major resolutions on this matter were welcomed by society with satisfaction. They should be put into practice in such a way that, while rooting out this phenomenon, which is alien to socialism, they contribute to improving the living conditions of the working people.

To sum it all up, comrades, we should strictly respect our main socialist principle: supporting and encouraging honest and conscientious work in every way and waging an uncompromising struggle against all parasitic elements, against those who would like to live at the expense of others, at the expense of society.

We should proceed from the fact that as the tasks in the social, economic, cultural and intellectual fields grow more complex, the demands on ideological work will also grow. I would like to note today the great contribution that is being made by the press, television, radio and the other mass media to the process of restructuring. They are doing a great deal to broaden publicity, to translate the democratism of our society into practice, and to raise serious, socially meaningful problems. Today it is especially important for our press to sensitively detect the emergence of everything new and advanced that is generated by the restructuring in all areas of life, and to help put it within the reach of the entire society. The objectivity, high exactingness and responsibility of the mass media are inviolable principles of the Party press, that guarantee them their authority.

The newspaper is the face of the Party committee. It reflects the style and methods of its work, its standards of leadership and its attitude to every outstanding problem. If the Party committee restructures itself, the press follows suit. I would like to draw your attention to the fact that the degree of publicity and effectiveness in many local newspapers is still far below that of the centrally published press. As an analysis of this matter shows, this is directly dependent on the position of the Party committees. Hence the need, both in the Party committees and in the editorial offices, to draw the correct conclusions in a self-critical manner. I am certain that they will be made.

In short, we count on stepping up efforts in the ideological sphere and on the rallying power of truthful ideas which bring together millions for a common cause.

IV. ON THE RESULTS OF THE BUDAPEST MEETING OF THE POLITICAL CONSULTATIVE COMMITTEE

Comrades, I shall now move on to the second item on the Plenary Meeting's agenda.

The documents of the recent regular meeting of the Political Consultative Committee (PCC) of the Warsaw Treaty member countries have been published. What could one say about the importance of the PCC meeting? First of all, it should be pointed out that the meeting took place immediately after several fraternal parties had held their congresses. So, it is only natural that the foreign-policy principles endorsed at the highest Party forums should be in the focus of collective discussion. Because of that, the meeting acquired a greater dimension, and the emphasis in the discussion was on matters of a strategic, global nature.

It was particularly stressed that the course of accelerated socioeconomic development adopted by our Party and by other fraternal parties had evoked a broad international response and, as it was implemented, would have an increasing effect on the entire course of world social development. It was pointed out that this was exactly what worried our class adversary most of all.

There was an exchange of views on the course of events in Europe and in the international arena over the period of time that had elapsed since the Sofia PCC meeting and the Soviet-U.S. summit meeting in Geneva. All participants in the meeting agreed that the situation remained complex and that there were no grounds so far for speaking of a relaxation of tension.

You know about the steps we have taken to make sure that the positive trend that originated in Geneva will not fade away or be lost to view in the whirlpool of international life. They include a concrete plan for the elimination of nuclear weapons by the end of this century, a moratorium on nuclear explosions, and proposals on the destruction of chemical weapons. Our initiatives have helped to improve and will continue to help improve the international climate.

But it is precisely the prospect for a relaxation of tension that is being regarded in the West and, first of all, by the reactionary ruling upper crust in the United States, as a threat to their interests. Recent months and weeks have seen a series of rejections of Soviet proposals on cardinal questions of present-day development: the refusal to end nuclear tests; the renunciation of existing agreements on strategic arms; and the refusal to keep outer space weapon-free. In addition, there is an unwillingness to conduct negotiations in good faith in Geneva and Vienna.

Washington's actions in Berne showed a haughty disregard for the interests of all countries of Europe, and not only of Europe, and as a result no important accords on human rights were achieved. A total nonacceptance of present-day realities alone can explain why the U.S. leaders are counting on brute force, on the nuclear fist, on terroristic piratical acts closely combined with ideological intolerance and hatred. They continue to assess the present world situation in terms of Star Wars and nuclear warheads, the arms race and militarist blackmail, thus more and more undermining the security of the entire world and of their own country.

It is becoming increasingly clear that the real threat to U.S. security does not come from outside. The threat, and a substantial one at that, is being posed by that country's military-political elite, its adventuristic behavior in the world arena.

The 27th CPSU Congress proposed sensible ways of resolving the problems facing humanity. Our objectives are absolutely clear. They are: acceleration of the country's social and economic development, broad international cooperation that benefits all, disarmament and the elimination of nuclear weapons, and peace for humanity. Hence our political course both inside the country and in the international arena. As more and more people on earth come to know the truth about the Soviet Union's policy, there will be more and more supporters of this course.

This in fact is what is worrying the ruling circles of imperialism. They regard the Soviet initiatives as a formidable obstacle in the way of the implementation of their imperial designs aimed at world domination and social revenge. Unable to offer the peoples a peaceful historical alternative, one that would meet the interests of all, they are whipping up militarist psychosis which they think can put a brake on historical progress and help them preserve economic and political power. Moreover, they are pinning their hopes on the possibility, however illusory, to hinder the implementation of our plans, impede the development of the socialist countries, push us off from the course of the 27th CPSU Congress and keep us in the fetters of the arms race.

It stands to reason, comrades, that the main aim of our foreign policy should be the frustration of these dangerous plans. The Soviet Union will continue persistently to try and bring about the implementation of its initiatives which accord with the cherished hopes of our people, of all peoples in the world. But we will never allow the United States to achieve superiority in nuclear missiles. And here our Leninist foreign-policy course and the might of our defense rest on the reliable basis of the strategy of accelerating socioeconomic development worked out by the Party and clearly reflected in the draft 12th Five-Year Plan which we are discussing.

The destiny of peace must not be put into the hands of imperialism; imperialist reaction must not be allowed to succeed in imposing a deepening of the military-political confrontation on humanity. This would mean only one thing—sliding toward nuclear war. This was the conclusion expressed in the speeches of all the participants in the Political Consultative Committee conference.

We have discussed with our friends the existing situation in our talks with the United States at Geneva. The following question has now arisen: should we continue marking time at the Geneva talks squabbling with the Americans, something that fully suits them, or search for new approaches that will make it possible to clear the road to a reduction of nuclear arms? Having decided to firmly adhere to the course of searching in practice for a mutually acceptable agreement at Geneva we offered the Americans the following interim variant:

a) that agreement be reached on nonwithdrawal from the ABM Treaty for at least 15 years and that work in the field of SDI be limited to the level of laboratory research, i.e., the threshold the United States has already actually approached;

b) that the strategic offensive arms (ICBMs, SLBMs, and heavy bombers) be limited by equal ceilings. In this case the question of medium-range weapons, including long-range land-based cruise missiles, capable of reaching the territory of the other side, should be solved separately.

This variant once again demonstrates the Soviet Union's desire for a mutually acceptable accord. Although, of course, we would prefer to agree at once on a drastic 50 percent reduction in strategic offensive arms capable of reaching each other's territory.

We have also submitted a draft agreement on medium-range missiles in Europe. We agreed that in the event of a zero ratio between the Soviet Union and the United States in this type of arms, there should remain as many British and French nuclear missiles in the European zone as there are now. We have also stated that we will not increase the number of medium-range missiles in Asia.

In other words, the Soviet Union has made new steps facilitating the search for mutually acceptable accords at the Geneva talks. Time will show the attitude of the United States to this. In any case, it should be clear: if the American side ignores our initiatives this time once again, it will become obvious that the present U.S. Administration is engaged in an unseemly game in a most serious matter on which the future of humanity depends.

The problem of ending nuclear tests has now acquired a special acuteness. To a certain extent this is also a result of the accident at the Chernobyl nuclear power plant. This accident showed that even a small emission of radioactive substances brings misfortune and alarm to thousands of people.

As they expressed their sincere sympathy and offered disinterested help to us, all honest people saw in this accident a far more serious danger. They ask themselves and others: what will happen if the military uses of atomic energy get out of control, accidentally or through evil design? The explosion of even one nuclear bomb would become a far more terrible tragedy for the peoples of many countries. This is what the earth's people have been increasingly pondering.

The United States of America is assuming the gravest responsibility before humanity in refusing to end nuclear testing and join the Soviet moratorium. The world is alarmed by the American behavior. But the seriousness of the situation also calls for doubling and trebling the efforts for ending all nuclear tests and eliminating nuclear weapons.

The misfortune of Chernobyl is our misfortune. We will be able to overcome it. We sincerely and profoundly thank everyone for the sympathy and assistance expressed in connection with the accident. But let Chernobyl, as well as other cases in which atomic energy stopped obeying man, serve as a stern warning to those who have yet to fully realize the nuclear menace that is looming over the world, and who still regard nuclear weapons as a political instrument.

I would like to comment particularly on the new Soviet-American summit meeting. We are in favor of dialogue with Washington. We are not slamming the doors shut: a new meeting with the U.S. President is possible, but, clearly, it requires an atmosphere that would open up prospects for reaching real agreements. We have said this to President Reagan and to the entire world. This position has met with understanding among friends.

But how is the U.S. Administration acting? It is sabotaging the disarmament talks and has declared its intention not to comply with the SALT-II Treaty, saying it was "dead"! Actions that further aggravate the international situation are being taken throughout the world.

A legitimate question arises: Does Washington really want a new meeting, or is all the talk around it merely an attempt to delude world public opinion?

The significance of the Political Consultative Committee meetings is known to be largely determined by the new initiatives they advance. Central to the Budapest meeting was the jointly elaborated, detailed proposal for reducing conventional armaments and armed forces throughout Europe, from the Atlantic to the Urals. Its content is known to you. We are talking about a 25 percent reduction in the armed forces of both sides in the upcoming years. Thus the speculations that nuclear disarmament in Europe, in the event of the preservation of conventional armed forces at their current level, would be to the disadvantage of the West European states are refuted. The fact that the West has not found it possible to simply dismiss this proposal is quite revealing.

Several other important initiatives were agreed upon in Budapest. The idea of pooling the efforts of all countries in peaceful uses of outer space and of creating a special international organization for this purpose was approved. This idea, which was put forward shortly before the meeting, in the speech in Csepel, has already found expression in the proposal sent to the UN Secretary-General. Questions pertaining to the continued advancement of the concept of establishing a comprehensive system of international security were discussed.

Special mention should be made of the lively, constructive atmosphere of the Budapest meeting.

All comrades—and this is a telltale sign of the times—viewed concrete issues in the light of the common foreign-policy strategy of the allied socialist states. In short, Budapest revealed the unity, the creative cooperation which enriches socialism's international policy and lends even greater weight to its actions in the world arena.

All participants in the conference noted with satisfaction that the work of the supreme body of the Warsaw Treaty Organization has shown greater dynamism and efficiency of late. The decisions adopted at Budapest are a major contribution of the socialist countries to the struggle for improving the international situation.

To sum it up, comrades, we have always made maximum efforts to preserve and consolidate peace, and we will continue to do so. In this noble undertaking, we feel active support for our position from our friends, from all peace-loving forces on earth.

Comrades! Such are the main lessons and conclusions of our post-Congress development, which we must study and use in full measure to advance with success. Such are the domestic and international conditions in which we have started implementing the decisions of the 27th CPSU Congress.

The political task of the five-year plan is to restructure our economy, create a modern material and technical base to ensure faster development of Soviet society, solve major social tasks and maintain a reliable defense of the country. There is not a moment to lose. Everything that we have planned must be done in time, for at issue are the might and prosperity of our country, the positions of socialism in the international arena and the consolidation of peace throughout the world.

A memorable date is approaching—the 70th anniversary of

the Great October Socialist Revolution. Our common patriotic and internationalist duty is to meet that remarkable holiday with rapid economic and sociopolitical advances, with achievements and successes worthy of the land of the October Revolution.

I think that it is necessary, on behalf of the Plenary Meeting, to call on all working people to develop nationwide socialist emulation in order to successfully attain the targets set by the 12th Five-Year Plan, and to appeal to them to transform bold plans into the energy of practical actions. The Central Committee is calling on every Soviet worker to take part in the emulation campaign, to rank among the best during the five-year-plan period, and to make a tangible personal contribution to the common cause at his or her workplace.

The attention of the Party committees and of all Party organizations should be focused on how to tackle the tasks set by the Congress and how to conduct political, economic, organizational and educational work to attain and exceed the targets of the five-year plan. Herein is the highlight of the moment. Therefore, there must be more analysis, more action, greater efficiency, less vague talk and fewer references to objective circumstances.

From every leader and from every Communist the Party expects concrete deeds to lead us forward along the projected road, not vows and assurances. The Central Committee will support the initiative and innovative quest of Party organizations, work collectives, ministries and departments, aimed at achieving the best results. To act persistently and energetically, with initiative, and with a high sense of responsibility is what life today requires of each and every one of us. I am confident that the appeal of the Plenary Meeting will find understanding and response in the working class, among farm workers and the intelligentsia, and will be embodied in the heroism of the everyday, routine work of millions of people. On this, comrades, everything depends!

33

MEETING

With Representatives of the International Forum of Scientists for a Nuclear Test Ban

Moscow, July 14, 1986

Professor G. B. Marini Bettolo presented Mikhail Gorbachev a declaration to the leaders of all nuclear powers, and especially the Soviet Union and the United States. The declaration was approved unanimously at the forum.

Handing over the document, the professor said:

Dear Mr. General Secretary, it is a great honor and pleasure for me to convey to you, on behalf of all the participants in the International Forum of Scientists for a Nuclear Test Ban, the text of a declaration which we have been drafting for three days. This document is the result of open, constructive and mutually beneficial discussions. Our declaration was approved unanimously.

This was made possible due to the atmosphere created by the Soviet Union's unilateral moratorium on nuclear testing and to the cooperation between scientists in the use of seismic monitoring to verify that nuclear tests are not being conducted.

Mr. General Secretary, allow me to express our hope that all the heads of state will appreciate and accept our actions and efforts in the interests of all mankind.

Mikhail Gorbachev: You are guests and I am here at your request, therefore if anyone would like to say something, please go ahead.

Professor Frank von Hippel: I have been asked to say a few words in addition to what my colleague has said. The Soviet Union's unilateral moratorium on nuclear explosions is of exceptional importance. It has exerted a tremendous influence on world public opinion and has demonstrated the Soviet Union's growing confidence in a new way of thinking. It demonstrates once again the realization in the Soviet Union that the introduction of new nuclear weapons cannot change the fact that both the Soviet Union and the United States have the ability to destroy each other many times.

This new way of thinking is also gaining ground in the United States. The majority of physicists at leading U.S. universities have signed an open letter, in which they state that they consider the SDI program dangerous and express their refusal to work for this project.

The Soviet moratorium on nuclear explosions has also strengthened the position of this new outlook in U.S. public opinion. According to the public opinion polls, the majority of Americans want the United States to join the Soviet moratorium. The latest studies show that 56 percent of all Americans support this idea.

Such matters are the prerogative of the President, and therefore the U.S. Congress usually does not interfere in deciding such questions. Nevertheless, a considerable minority of Congressmen believe that the allocations for nuclear testing must be cut back.

The first such proposal submitted to Congress will most likely be defeated, but if it is supported by a considerable number of Congressmen and if it is defeated by a narrow margin, the positions of opponents of nuclear testing will grow much stronger. In that case, we could expect some positive developments this year. However, this will happen only if the Soviet Union's unilateral moratorium continues.

The forces for peace in the United States have been reinforced considerably due to cooperation between the Academy of Sciences of the USSR and the U.S. Natural Resources Defense Council. The American public fears that the Soviet Union is concealing secrets and this fear is being exploited by the advocates of new nuclear weapons. Your consent to the installation of American seismic equipment in the area of Semipalatinsk, near the Soviet nuclear test range, shows that the Soviet Union has indeed taken a new attitude. This fact is revealed clearly by your willingness to allow others to observe your activities.

To judge by an article in *The New York Times*, the American public is showing interest in our joint venture and this interest can be expected to grow as our joint activity expands. Apart from the fact that seismologists are anxious to dispel fears of Soviet secrecy, they are likewise actually confirming that with specialized instruments it is possible to prevent even the smallest nuclear explosion from being concealed.

I have a seismographic chart which clearly shows how several years ago an earthquake in Kamchatka was monitored in Norway. It also shows a monitored small nuclear explosion—500 tons—which occurred at the same time roughly 2,000 kilometers away from the monitoring device. Thus this kind of equipment can monitor even the most insignificant nuclear explosions.

Yevgeni Velikhov: I would like to mention very briefly the fact that scientists from thirty-two nations have attended our forum and that over seventy people have taken the floor. Among these people are seismologists and physicists who at one time worked on nuclear weapon development. The consequences of using nuclear weaponry were also discussed.

This has been a broad forum, and the major conclusions are the following. It has been convincingly demonstrated that today the problem of control practically does not exist as a technical problem and that the methods of verification worked out by geophysicists are absolutely reliable. Of course, there are various possibilities of concealing nuclear explosions. But it is clear that the improvements made in seismic technology have practically eliminated such possibilities. This is the objective of the joint research activities by the Academy of Sciences of the USSR and the U.S. Natural Resources Defense Council. The question of the importance of a total nuclear test ban was also discussed at the forum. In particular the speakers noted that underground nuclear tests have been and will continue to be used to develop new means of nuclear warfare and thus destabilize the world situation. Therefore, a total ban on tests is essential to close all channels for the qualitative development of nuclear weapons.

[Another speaker at the forum was Professor Cochran. Working with Soviet scientists, he has already installed seismic equipment near Semipalatinsk and obtained his first oscillogram.]

O. Nathan: The speech made by Dr. Theodore Taylor, one of the creators of atomic weapons in the U.S.A., made a great impression on us. He explained that the development of new nuclear weapons by testing requires a lot of time. He claimed, therefore, that the Soviet Union need not be concerned that the United States still has not reached a rational decision concerning nuclear tests. Furthermore, Dr. Taylor contends that the Soviet Union should continue its moratorium without fearing that the Americans might develop new weapons within a short period of time.

Mikhail Gorbachev: Is this the Teller who advocates escalation of the arms race?

Voices: No, they simply have similar names.

Mikhail Gorbachev: Otherwise I would have expressed doubts in the advisability of heeding the views you have just related because Teller's opinion is well known to us.

Joseph Rotblat: I would like to say a few words about the public opinion polls on the Soviet initiative which were taken in Great Britain. The following question was asked: "Should Great Britain reciprocate the Soviet Union's unilateral nuclear moratorium?" Eighty-four percent of the answers were "Yes." What was most interesting, was that this question was answered in the affirmative by 60 percent of the Conservatives, that is, Margaret Thatcher's supporters.

Mikhail Gorbachev: This is interesting in itself and also interesting from a political viewpoint: presidents and prime ministers secure their posts by receiving a majority of votes in elections . . .

Joseph Rotblat: . . . A few remarks about the role of scientists who participated in this forum.

Although we are scientists, we are discussing an issue which is mostly political. But scientists have played a very important and sometimes negative role in this issue. At times we have been forced into this role. I'm speaking as one of those who began the work of developing the atomic bomb in Great Britain at the beginning of the Second World War. Later, however, many scientists voluntarily and even enthusiastically participated in the nuclear arms race. This race is continually fueled by new scientific discoveries, which not only provide an impulse to the nuclear race but at times determine its rate.

Almost any scientific achievement can be used for destructive purposes very quickly. But this is absolutely wrong, for the situation must be the reverse: science must serve the welfare of mankind.

The opportunities for international cooperation among scientists are vast. The Chernobyl disaster can serve as an example. A program which would benefit entire generations could be developed in connection with this disaster.

In the course of the discussion on the problems of banning nuclear tests, we, as scientists, gave our recommendations to you, a political leader. These recommendations can help you in your continuing work to stop the nuclear arms race.

And we hope that the efforts we have undertaken here will help restore the tarnished image of science as a creative force working for the good and welfare of mankind.

Thomas Cochran: I am proud of having been granted the honor of meeting you.

As you know, only one month ago our U.S. Natural Resources Defense Council signed an agreement with the USSR Academy of Sciences. As was noted by previous speakers, the principal goal of our cooperation is to refute the opinion popular among American politicians and the American people that it is impossible to guarantee the infallible detection of all nuclear explosions in the Soviet Union. We are thereby trying to prove that the United States must also stop its tests immediately and work for an agreement banning all nuclear tests.

We have selected our best seismologists from the Universities of California and Colorado for this cooperation effort. We arrived in your country only six days ago. Owing to the assistance of Soviet experts from the Institute of Earth Physics, we have already installed our equipment at one of the three chosen sites. The first seismograms have already been obtained from Karkaralinsk, which lies about 200 kilometers west of the testing ground.

Mikhail Gorbachev: The White House does not believe that the Soviet Union will agree to any, even the most radical, forms of control, both national and international, including on-site inspection and installation of monitoring equipment.

And actually such work has already been accomplished and without any red tape, and moreover without the political leadership; well, not entirely without it, for the political leadership cannot be excluded altogether. Your only concern should be to verify whether tests are being conducted or not, rather than to exercise control over continued testing and improvement of nuclear weapons.

Thomas Cochran: I believe we have fully disproved the arguments advanced by the White House that a comprehensive treaty on banning nuclear tests is impossible and does not lend itself to complete verification.

Mikhail Gorbachev: We are of the same opinion. I believe no one, neither the Soviet Union nor the United States, can count on deceiving the other. The search for new ways to damage the security of the other side must cease. Such an approach is inadmissible. I believe that this is also a sign that a new way of thinking has recently developed. Security must be equal. Otherwise, suspicion and uncertainty appear, and stability is upset as a result of the suspicion and mistrust. Hence the arms race accelerates as each side seeks to increase its own security, just in case. This is the psychological result of such a situation. And this is why a new way of thinking is essential.

Thomas Cochran: The cooperation between Soviet and American scientists can be described as quite exceptional. The assistance offered by Academician Velikhov and the other members of our joint experiment is worthy of all praise. We will find it very difficult to reciprocate when Soviet scientists come to the United States.

The joint Soviet-American research program, which is the topic of discussion, has already met with favorable reaction in the United States. Our research program must be enlarged if the new method, the new approach is to be consolidated. The program proves that scientists not only can make important political statements but can also conduct very valuable scientific tests on a joint basis.

Angel Balevski: I would like to say a few words in connection with the statement made by my colleague from Denmark. I do not know who will outstrip whom; that is unknown. But I do know that the continuation of American nuclear experiments evokes constant fear among mankind. This psychological aspect is very important and I spoke about it at the forum. It is terrifying. All the more so when people fail to perceive the deterioration of the human spirit. It is terrible to live in constant fear, and I think we must allow people to rest from this fear and live a human life. No one has the right to hold humanity in the grips of continuous tension. No matter what the intention may be, this is a crime.

Sune Bergström: I was chairman of the International Committee of Experts in Medical Sciences and Public Health to consider the effects of nuclear war, a committee established by the World Health Organization. Two years ago we submitted a report on the results of our work. The unique cooperation between Soviet and American scientists made a great positive impact on world public opinion.

Mikhail Gorbachev: I welcome the substantial contribution made by medical scientists. I am referring, first of all, to Academician Chazov and Professor Lown. It was of great importance that the whole world heard the competent statement of the outstanding representatives of medical science on the possible consequences of a nuclear conflict and also on the ability of medical science to perform its functions if some madman unleashed a nuclear war.

Sune Bergström: As many have stressed at the forum, the cooperation in verifying nuclear explosions has already improved the international climate. We now consider it important to extend our activites beyond the bounds of this sphere and include other major problems, especially those concerning the developing countries.

If your scientists and your academicians came forward with such an initiative, it could play a tremendous role and make possible the formulation of a long-term program for improving international relations in general.

O. F. Lenci: First of all, I would like to say that the unilateral Soviet moratorium on nuclear explosions has helped in many ways to create a new atmosphere. This fact is recorded in the declaration passed by our forum. The moratorium is, in effect, the first real step toward a comprehensive treaty on the prohibition of nuclear weapon tests, which, in turn, can lead one day to the complete elimination of nuclear weapons.

I also believe that the preservation and extension of the Soviet moratorium on nuclear explosions will be influential in other countries, and especially in my country, Italy. It does not possess nuclear weapons but holds membership in certain organizations. I think that countries such as Italy can play a role in the solution of this problem, different from the one which they are playing today. For instance, such countries could be induced to take more vigorous actions for the conclusion of an agreement on the complete ban on nuclear weapons.

Pyotr Fedoseyev: A distinctive feature of the forum was that there was not just a feeling of concern for the current international situation, but also a desire to act continuously and to show initiative for a ban on tests and against nuclear weapons in general.

The agenda for the round-table discussion concluding the conference included a program of follow-up action as one of its items.

It was proposed both at the forum and in the lobby that the action group continue its activities; the group should not only continue to circulate the adopted documents world-wide and to popularize the results of the forum, but should also serve as a liaison and source of information for the scientific community. The group has pledged to continue its work.

Anatoli Alexandrov: I have attended many international forums, but I would like to point out that this is the first time I have seen such a community of views. We, all of us, representatives of various countries, may have had differing opinions on certain questions, but we were unanimous in our belief that a nuclear war must be prevented, that such a war would be tantamount to the destruction or degradation of mankind.

Mikhail Gorbachev: It would be degradation at the very least, but the most likely result would be destruction.

Anatoli Alexandrov: All agreed that the Soviet Union's unilateral moratorium on nuclear tests was an extremely important move which received response throughout the world. Each called it in his own way—the first step, or the most important step—but these were basically different shades of the same meaning.

All were also unanimous in the belief that all other nuclear countries, beginning with the United States, and nonnuclear states, too, must join the Soviet Union in this endeavor. This would be of paramount importance now, and would serve to relax the colossal tension present today in international relations.

Koji Fushimi: I highly appreciate the bold decision of the Soviet leader to stop underground nuclear testing. This is not only my opinion but, I believe, that of a great many Japanese citizens. I have with me several things which testify to this sentiment among the Japanese people. Here is one of them, a message from the religious leaders of Hiroshima. [He presents the message to Mikhail Gorbachev.]

Derek Paul: Five years ago my colleagues and I founded the organization called Science for Peace. Since then I have attended many different conferences on disarmament, the campaign for peace, etc., in the Soviet Union, and I would say that this forum which I have just attended has made a greater impression on me, for reasons already mentioned. All of us—in any case, the forum participants from the West—will return home more optimistic and resolved in our hope to accomplish something, however small, in the name of peace.

Mikhail Gorbachev: First of all, I would like, through you, to greet all the participants of the Moscow forum of scientists. This forum has discussed the most burning problem of today—the problem of preserving human civilization.

The initiative which was realized at this forum of scientists from more than 30 countries is extremely important, as is everything which is being done today in the effort to stop the arms race and begin a real disarmament process.

I have already had occasion to say, and I will take advantage of this meeting to repeat, that we still hear people ask why we are in such a hurry, and whether it might not be better to draw out the drive against the arms race for many years and even decades. This type of thinking is erroneous. We have reached a stage in the scientific and technological revolution when new discoveries can spur on the arms race and create a situation in which it will be far more difficult to even start talks.

Let us presume that the arms race spreads to outer space. Who can say for certain what will happen then? There are just a few dozen satellites and spaceships in space right now, but emergencies of all kinds happen to them time and again. So what if echelons of military systems are moved there? They would be controlled by computers, which would issue data, but would not analyze the reasons for whatever was happening up there. As a result, the "decisions" upon which the fate and lives of millions of people depend would be made at the technical rather than political level. The whole of civilization would become technology's hostage.

Or take conventional arms. In this sphere, too, scientific discoveries serve as the basis for the appearance of weapons which, in terms of destructive capacity, are not at all inferior to nuclear weapons. In addition, there are chemical and biological weapons. The consequences of their use would be no less disastrous.

Thus we have all reached the point beyond which unpredictable processes can begin. Everyone must act today—politicians, scientists, and people everywhere.

This morning I received the Russian-language text of your forum's declaration. I want to state my attitude toward this document straight away: it is a responsible document and one which meets the interests of all countries regardless of their political systems, and of all people regardless of what political organizations they identify themselves with. This document has special significance because it was drawn up and approved by people competent in their field, and approved unanimously at that, which gives it even more weight.

The results of your forum show that the preconditions now exist in the world for the formation of new approaches to, and a new way of thinking about, the solution of the main questions of the day—halting the nuclear arms race and beginning disarmament. And this process should start, as you have correctly pointed out, with an end to nuclear tests.

You have informed the entire world public in your declaration that we are all now faced with the simple and harsh reality that human civilization will not survive a nuclear war. This warning is timely and convincing, and it demands a great sense of responsibility.

You raise the question of reducing the risk of nuclear war and of the need for energetic measures. The Soviet leadership will support this call, and it agrees with your view that the ending of nuclear tests should be the first step in this direction.

Convincing arguments have been voiced both in the declaration and at our meeting here to the effect that it is possible to verify that nuclear tests have been terminated. This is of immense importance, as it reflects the opinion of people who know what they are talking about.

We are assisting and will continue to assist Soviet and American scientists in carrying out their initiative designed to use special equipment to make sure that no nuclear explosions are taking place. I have no objection to a single line in your document.

You have asked the Soviet Government to reexamine the possibility of extending the moratorium. Well, in the first place, it is still in effect. And that is the most important thing, so there is still time and it must not be wasted. Naturally, your request will be considered most carefully. The Soviet Government will make a decision, which will then be conveyed to you. But, frankly speaking, this decision will depend largely on whether or not the United States of America is going to begin disarmament after all.

Following the meeting with the U.S. President in Geneva, where we agreed to move in the direction of making the contents of our accord meaningful and concrete, we began acting in precisely such a manner. We extended the moratorium—extended it twice. We put forward a program for the complete elimination of nuclear weapons within 15 years. We came up with new, far reaching proposals on the abolition of chemical weapons, including measures to verify that the industries producing them are being dismantled. We put forward an enormous program for the reduction of conventional arms so as to allay the fears of the peoples of the Western countries. Finally, we recently put on the table compromise proposals at the Geneva talks. I spelled them out in a letter to President Reagan—they concern both medium-range missiles and reductions in strategic nuclear weapons.

Naturally, we expect adequate response from the American side and from the West in general. So far we are not satisfied with the position of either the American Administration or the other Western governments. That Administration has taken a negative stand regarding an end to nuclear tests. At one time the issue of verification was used as an argument. Now that this problem, as we see, is being conclusively resolved by virtue of the well-known position of the Soviet Union and of your arguments, that is, the arguments of scientists, we are waiting to see what new reasonings will turn up to support the continuation of testing. We have already begun to hear talk to the effect that the Soviet leadership's idea to eliminate nuclear weapons is utopian, for in a world like ours one can hardly do without these weapons.

Nor have we yet received satisfactory replies to our proposals on medium-range missiles and on strategic arms. We have received only the declaration that SALT-II is dead. Thus, not only are no efforts being made to find and work out new international mechanisms to halt the arms race and subsequently begin disarmament; the only remaining brakes on that race are being dismantled. SDI, so they say, is necessary, among other things, because many countries today are capable of developing a nuclear bomb of their own and, allegedly, a countermeasure is needed in case some madman launches a nuclear attack or makes an attempt at nuclear blackmail.

Totally paradoxical arguments are used to defend SDI. This, alas, draws a certain response from scientists and politicians. It is said that SDI is the way to the development of science, to new heights in scientific and technological progress. But I will tell you that this type of thinking is warped—everything is turned upside down. Can we not make advances in science and technology, every part of scientific knowledge, including the development of new materials, radio electronics, computer technology, mathematics, etc., through civilian projects? The Vega program is a recent and convincing example of this. I heard the reports of Academician Sagdeyev and other Soviet scientists who carried out this most interesting project with the participation of their foreign colleagues. They needed new solutions and new materials. These were found. They needed new solutions to the problem of controlling the maneuvers of a sophisticated craft over great distances. These were developed. They needed a stable radio and TV communication link. This was established. They needed new mathematical discoveries and computations to accomplish such a complex task. These were made. They needed accurate information about the situation on Venus and near Halley's Comet. This was obtained.

Many countries, Western included, participated in the project. Especially fruitful cooperation in that field was achieved with scientists from France.

Now we have come to grips with the problem of developing a dependable source of energy. The problems of energy, like those of food and ecology, are the central, global problems of the future. If there were no projects in the military field, efforts in this peaceful sphere would be making progress at a much faster rate. Recently the Chairman of the Council of Ministers of the USSR, Nikolai Ryzhkov, submitted to the United Nations the Soviet Government's proposals on the development of international scientific cooperation in peaceful uses of outer space.

Thus, advances can be made in science on the basis of civilian projects. The argument that science and technology can be developed only through an arms race is simply absurd. The question to ask then is this: what is the problem? Who, God perhaps, has taken away the ability to grasp the realities of today's world, of the nuclear-missile space age? These two men [pointing to portraits of Marx and Lenin] taught us that in order to get to the heart of the matter, we must clear the surface of all sorts of rubbish and lay bare the motives and interests behind one position or another.

Whose interests are met by the proposals of political forces, scientists and the public, who are insisting on scaling down the arms race, on starting disarmament and on the eventual elimination of nuclear weapons? I believe these proposals meet the interests of all nations and there are no higher interests.

We realize that a group of countries which would like to use their superior arms arsenals for political pressure might have interests of their own. And there are other interests, I would say, of a lower order. There are the interests of the military-industrial complex, which are also very real. But, first of all, these are not the interests of any nation, let alone human civilization. And, second, neither civilian research, nor research into energy problems, nor anything else would suffer if military research and war production were stopped. The forces which are involved in the development of weapons today could work fruitfully in civilian areas. Neither science nor the industries currently involved in war production would be left idle. Everyone would only stand to gain.

So, we need a new way of thinking. It is impossible to solve the burning problems of today, let alone of the coming century, if one is to be guided by views characteristic of past centuries, past decades, or, in any case, of times prior to the emergence of nuclear weapons and the recent upsurge in the scientific and technological revolution.

I do not wish to impose my views on anyone. I do not expect you to accept them without careful thought. Our views were spelled out at the Congress. Their essence, in brief, is that we all live in the nuclear-space era, in a complex, interrelated and controversial world. And we must learn to live together, no matter how different we may be. Other countries have their own type of democracy; let them enjoy it. But do not let them encroach on our right to our democratic values. But then, these are matters of secondary importance.

The most important thing now is this: either we survive, cooperating and preserving the earth, the ocean, the skies, the whole environment, or we lead civilization to disastrous consequences. We must get rid of the outdated notion that the world is someone's domain. The world of today means coexistence of nations and states. It is a multitude of countries, each with a history of its own and each at its own stage of development. But everyone must recognize that each country has the sovereign right to choose its own type of state structure, to conduct its domestic affairs independently.

We recognize this right and will act accordingly. But we demand that others respect this right as well. International relations will become chaotic unless the sovereign right of every nationality and every country is recognized. Philosophical recognition is not enough; we must act according to this recognition. You can rest assured that the Soviet Union will uphold this conviction firmly. At the same time, we have absolutely no intention of placing the fate of the world, our country, and other nations at the mercy of those who expect to dictate their will to the entire world.

We are in constant debate with America, and at times this debate is heated. Nevertheless, we do not paint America all black, or even in just two colors, black and white. We see the real America, America as it is. And we realize that there are many people in American society who share a realistic approach to the problems of today.

We must work and create relations of a new type in international and interstate affairs. Neither the Soviet Union nor the United States will be able to be in command of the world. The world has changed. And unless this is recognized, gross blunders may be made in politics. We proceed from precisely this view, as you will witness for yourselves. I think the Soviet

Union has already advanced serious arguments confirming this viewpoint.

Returning to the subject of the forum, I would like to conclude by saying that I fully agree with your opinion that an end to nuclear testing would be a major step in the right direction, a step toward ending the arms race and the process of technically improving nuclear weapons, and toward their eventual elimination altogether.

The opinion was expressed that this forum should not become an isolated event, that the action group should continue its work. The initiative of the Soviet and American physicians has set a useful example. Their work began with what seemed a one-time meeting. This first meeting, however, laid the foundation at what has become a very influential movement of people competent in their field. I think that if the efforts started in Moscow were continued by scientists in yet another field, that of technology, their work would only be welcomed. But this, of course, must be your own decision.

I am most pleased with this meeting and, most importantly, with its spirit and content. Today it is more important than ever before that politics and science cooperate. Today it is essential that every field of science analyze the political consequences of its discoveries and achievements. And likewise, politics must be based on scientific achievements, on the strict analysis, objective evaluations and predictions offered by science.

I favor the unification of politics and science. Every country stands to gain from such a unification in regard both to domestic affairs and to the solution of the problems which we are discussing today.

Thank you. I hope that the work you have started will continue and will be supported by all those who are concerned about the present-day situation in the world.

34

TELEVISED SPEECH

On Foreign Policy

Moscow, August 18, 1986

Good evening, dear comrades!

At our meeting tonight I would like to make a statement on one of the key issues of international politics.

The Soviet unilateral moratorium on nuclear tests, which the Soviet Union, as is known, had strictly observed for one year, expired several days ago, on August 6.

What was this not so simple, extremely responsible and, I would say, difficult decision based on? What prompted it?

In brief, it was based on the realities of the nuclear-space age.

What are these realities? How do we regard them?

First, mountains of nuclear and various other types of weapons have been stockpiled, but nonetheless the arms race continues unabated, is even escalating; the danger has emerged of its extension to outer space; the militarization of the United States and the entire NATO bloc is being carried out at full speed. It is important to stress that the pace of the development of military technology is so high that it leaves less and less time for people, states and politicians to become aware of the real danger, and limits humanity's possibilities for stopping the slide toward the nuclear abyss. No delay can be allowed, or else such sophisticated weapon systems will emerge that agreement on their control will become altogether impossible.

The situation is becoming increasingly intolerable. It is not enough today to preserve the existing treaties; major practical steps are needed which are capable of curbing militarism and reversing the course of developments for the better. The "balance of fear" is ceasing to be a factor of restraint, and not only because fear in general is no advisor to reason and may prompt actions that are unpredictable in their consequences. This fear is actually a direct participant in the arms race: by increasing mistrust and suspicion, it forms a vicious circle of heightening tension. There are many examples.

It has become crystal clear to all that the old notions of war as a means of attaining political objectives are outdated. In the nuclear age, these obsolete tenets are feeding a policy that may result in an all-out conflagration.

Second, our decision on the moratorium was based on the adherence of socialism as a social system to the cause of peace, and on the profound understanding of its responsibility for the destinies of civilization. The Soviet Union, as a socialist state and as a nuclear power, considers it its supreme duty to do everything possible to ensure a peaceful future for the planet.

Our striving to steer international development toward detente is dictated by our philosophy, our socialist morality. In the nuclear age, saving the earth from atomic annihilation is a universal human task, the cause of all peoples.

Third, the present-day world is complicated, diverse and controversial. At the same time, it is objectively becoming more interdependent and integral. This distinct feature of the human community today, at the end of the 20th century, cannot be disregarded in foreign policy if it is based on reality. Otherwise, there will be no normal international relations: they will be frenzied and will ultimately lead to catastrophic confrontation.

Prenuclear thinking essentially lost its significance on August 6, 1945. Today it is no longer possible to ensure one's own security without taking into account the security of other states and peoples. There can be no genuine security unless it is equal all around and all-encompassing. To think otherwise means to live in a world of illusions, in a world of self-deception.

The new way of thinking needed by the modern world is incompatible with the notion of the world as someone's domain, or with the attempts to "do others good" through patronage and instructions on how to conduct oneself and what path to choose—socialist, capitalist, or some other.

The Soviet Union believes that each nation, each country, has the right to be master of its own destiny and resources, to determine its social development autonomously, uphold its own security, and participate in the establishment of a comprehensive system of international security.

The aggravation of global problems is also characteristic of today's world. They cannot be resolved without pooling the efforts of all states and peoples. The exploration of outer space and the ocean depths, ecology and epidemics, poverty and backwardness are the realities of the age, and they demand international attention, international responsibility, and international cooperation. Many new world processes have thus become very tightly interwoven. Disarmament could play an immense role here by releasing considerable funds and the intellectual and technical potential for constructive purposes.

Our foreign policy draws inspiration from the fact that throughout the world, the conviction is becoming increasingly rooted in the consciousness of the peoples and of political and public forces of various orientations and world outlooks that the very existence of the human race is at stake, that the time for resolute and responsible steps has come. It calls for a complete mobilization of reason and common sense.

Two tragedies involving nuclear-space age technology occurred recently: the death of the Challenger crew and the accident at the Chernobyl nuclear power plant. These events heightened the feeling of alarm, and served as brutal reminders of the fact that people are just beginning to master the fantastically potent forces they themselves created, are only learning to make them serve progress. They showed what would happen if nuclear weapons were used.

Everyone, above all statesmen, should draw specific and obvious lessons from that. The most important lesson, perhaps, is that weapons devised by man should never be used and that today it is downright suicidal to build interstate relations on the illusion that superiority in horrible means of annihilation can be attained.

The only way toward genuine peace is to eliminate these weapons altogether. To embark on this path means to pass a historic maturity test. This applies to all political leaders who have been entrusted with this lofty humane mission.

One must learn to face the facts with courage: experts have

estimated that the explosion of the smallest nuclear warhead would be equal in level of radioactivity to three Chernobyls. This is most likely true. If this is the case, the explosion of even a small part of the existing nuclear arsenal will become a catastrophe, an irreversible catastrophe. And if someone still dares to deal a first nuclear strike, he will doom himself to an agonizing death—not even from a retaliatory strike, but from the consequences of the explosion of his own warheads.

This is not propaganda, political improvisation, or the heightening of "fear." This is a reality which it is simply irresponsible to reject and criminal to ignore.

An objective and honest analysis of all these realities prompts different approaches to world politics. They underlie the principled conclusions we have drawn recently, particularly at the 27th CPSU Congress.

Soviet foreign policy, including issues of disarmament, is based on the comprehension of the profound changes in the world.

We believe that the Soviet proposals of January 15 of this year for eliminating nuclear weapons worldwide by the year 2000 fully meet the demands of the time.

We have demonstrated our readiness to search for compromise solutions to the problems that are the cause of debate and suspicion.

The Soviet Union has placed a package of constructive proposals on the table of Soviet-American talks on nuclear and space armaments.

Together with our Warsaw Treaty allies, we have submitted a set of measures for reducing the armed forces and conventional armaments in Europe from the Atlantic to the Urals. In this sphere, too, we would like to see advancement—mutual and consistent—toward lower and less dangerous levels of military confrontation.

New proposals relating to chemical weapons have been advanced, making it possible, in our view, to sign a convention on banning chemical weapons and eliminating their stockpiles, as well as the industrial base for their production, before the end of this year or in the next year.

At the Stockholm Conference, the socialist countries, constructively cooperating with other participants, did a great deal to find solutions to such key issues as nonuse of force, notification about military exercises and troop movements, exchange of annual plans of military activity, invitation of observers, and inspection.

We have advanced a broad platform of ensuring security and cooperation in the Asian-Pacific region, and we invite all to participate in this process.

We have showed initiative for cooperation with all interested states in establishing international conditions for the safe development of nuclear power engineering.

We have recently submitted to the United Nations a program for building Star Peace, for establishing a world space organization, as an alternative to the Star Wars program.

The 27th CPSU Congress formulated the foundations of a comprehensive system of international security. This system is a generalization of our new approaches in foreign policy. The other day, the group of socialist countries submitted the issue of establishing such a system to the regular session of the UN General Assembly for consideration.

At the same time, I would like to stress that we understand that no matter how important and significant our proposals might be and how committed we are to them, we will not be able to do everything by ourselves. The problem of international security is a common problem and, therefore, a common concern and common responsibility.

When working out our proposals, we study and take into account points of view and initiatives of other governments and of public and political movements. We make every effort to provide equal security to all at each stage of the proposals' implementation. And nevertheless we do not at all consider these proposals final or not open to further discussion. Confrontational deadlocks can be overcome through dialogues and contacts, discussions and talks. This is the only way the ice of mutual mistrust will thaw and real results can be achieved.

This is what we base our position on in the issue of control in the solution of all the disarmament problems. For example, when we put forward our proposal to discontinue all nuclear explosions, we offered no objections to international verification. We agreed to the installation of American monitoring devices in the area of Semipalatinsk and this serves as convincing proof of our openness to international verification. It would seem that the issue of verification has ceased to be an obstacle in reaching agreements. However, this issue continues to be used in a persistent fashion in order to conceal the true position—an unwillingness to disarm.

People of good will welcomed our decision concerning the moratorium on nuclear explosions. People from all over the world approved and supported this decision. Politicians and parliamentarians, public figures and public organizations regarded this step as an example of the correct approach to the problems facing the world today. They saw in this step the hope that the world might rid itself of the fear of nuclear catastrophe. The Soviet moratorium was approved by the UN General Assembly, which is the most representative assembly of states in the world.

We were supported by outstanding scientists—physicists and doctors—who understand better than anyone else the dangers inherent in the atom. I saw for myself at a recent meeting with scientists in Moscow that our moratorium had inspired scientific workers from various countries to take concrete action on the nuclear issue.

However, all these definite and encouraging manifestations of a new way of thinking are in confrontation with the militarization of political thought, and in the United States in particular. The politics of the Western ruling circles is dangerously lagging behind the profound transformations taking place in international relations, while scientific and technological progress is rapidly overtaking social and moral progress.

The right-wing militaristic group in the U.S.A. representing the powerful military-industrial complex seems to have gone mad with the arms race. Their interests seem to have three purposes: to continue to profit from the manufacture of arms, to secure U.S. military superiority, to exhaust the Soviet Union's economic potential and to weaken its political position. Finally, the long-term goal is to ensure U.S. world domination, to realize the long-sought imperial ambitions, and to continue to pursue the policy of plunder in regard to developing countries.

This all leads to the formation of a foreign policy which with all its intricacies and verbal camouflage continues to be based on the following dangerous delusions: the underestimation of the Soviet Union, other socialist countries and newly free states, and the overestimation of its own potential, which nourishes technological self-confidence and political permissiveness.

Some American politicians contend that our participation in the talks is the result of the growing military might of the U.S.A. and its program of Strategic Defense Initiative. Basing its policy on such erroneous premises, the U.S. Administration cannot begin to enter into honest agreements or to improve international relations. And nevertheless the realities have to be considered, for they cannot be avoided.

As to our proposals, I repeat that they stem from the realities of the modern world; their source is not one of weakness but rather an awareness of our lofty responsibility for humanity's destiny.

This is the situation at the present moment.

On the one hand, our moratorium is in operation. Our compromise and extensive proposals have been announced and presented at the negotiating table of various forums. The forces for peace have gained considerable strength. Political leaders, including those in official positions, are giving greater attention to the issues of international security out of concern for the seriousness of the situation.

On the other hand, we are faced with the refusal to stop nuclear testing, with a stubborn resistance to peace initiatives and ostentatious disregard of public demands and the opinions of many authoritative parties and organizations. The concerns of the people and allies from other countries are even being ignored.

This is the state of affairs that we, the Soviet Union's leaders, are faced with as our moratorium has expired.

What is to be done? What choice is to be made? What decision will be the most correct and most appropriate in consideration of the situation? What decision will be most apt to promote positive processes and lessen the threat of military confrontation?

Our people resolutely support the foreign policy of the CPSU, of the Soviet state, and insistently demand that the foreign policy course taken at the 27th Party Congress be continued. At the same time, the Soviet people are justifiably expressing in both written and spoken form a deep concern: is it expedient to continue the moratorium when nuclear explosions reverberate one after another through the Nevada desert? Is not the risk too great? Is not the security of our country lessening with time?

Indeed, the United States has been the champion in regard to the number of explosions over the period of 40 years. Throughout the year during which the Soviet Union adhered to the moratorium, another 18 nuclear devices were exploded in the United States. I repeat: 18, three of which were unannounced. Furthermore, these explosions as a rule were used as a demonstration, timed to correspond either with a Soviet announcement of the extension of the moratorium, or with some other new Soviet initiative. And we were even invited to Nevada to watch the proceedings. It should be added that the present U.S. Administration is implementing the broadest of military programs.

In a word, the Soviet Union has sufficient reasons for resuming its nuclear testing. And yet we are still convinced that the ending of nuclear testing by both the Soviet Union and the United States would be a real breakthrough in stopping the nuclear arms race and would accelerate the process of entirely eliminating nuclear arms. The logic in this is simple: without nuclear testing the nuclear weapons, which both sides have stockpiled in abundance, cannot be upgraded.

The appeals made by a significant and authoritative sector of the world community to the United States and to the Soviet Union support the simplicity of this logic. Those who have made such appeals include the Delhi Six, a permament forum of leaders representing countries of the four continents—Argentina, Greece, India, Mexico, Tanzania, Sweden. A few days ago in Ixtapa the Mexican Declaration was adopted calling once again for an end to all nuclear explosions. This is also the demand of the majority of the countries participating in the nonaligned movement.

We have received messages from politicians and public figures, from individuals and organizations of many countries, including the United States and other NATO countries. They are also asking us not to resume nuclear testing and to give those who adhere firmly to nuclear testing one more chance to come to reason.

We are certainly aware, and I have spoken about that already, that the forces refusing to disarm are taking strenuous actions in the U.S.A. Moreover, they are making every effort possible to draw the Soviet Union into ever new spirals of the arms race and to provoke us into abandoning negotiations.

But we would like to hope that realism and the awareness that mutual efforts are required to find ways to improve the international situation, to end the senseless arms race and to eliminate nuclear weapons will prevail as the United States makes assessments and takes action.

At the same time, we know with whom we are dealing. The security of our country is therefore sacred to us. A matter of principle, this must be clear to all.

We proceed from this position as we respond to any challenge presented by the United States, including the notorious SDI. In this, too, it would be wrong to hope to intimidate us or to induce us into making needless expenditures. If need be, we shall promptly come up with a response, but it will not be the one the United States expects. It will, however, be a response which will devalue the Star Wars program. I say this with one aim: let those in the U.S. Administration weigh again and again the real value of the new military programs and of the arms race as a whole from the point of view of the United States' interests and its security. After all, SDI is most damaging in that it undermines the prospects of the talks and leads to increased mistrust. This is the entire problem. It is no less a political problem than it is a military one. That is why we once again are calling for measures to change the world armed to the limits into a world free of weapons.

Thus, comrades, the Politburo of the CPSU Central Committee and the Government of the Soviet Union have comprehensively and scrupulously weighed all the pros and cons and, guided by their responsibility for the world's destiny, have decided to *extend the unilateral moratorium on nuclear explosions until January 1, 1987*.

In taking this step, we believe that the people of all countries in the world, the political circles and the international public will correctly evaluate the long-reigning silence of the Soviet nuclear test ranges.

On behalf of the Soviet people, I am appealing to the

wisdom and dignity of the American people not to miss another historical chance which could lead to an end to the arms race.

I am asking the U.S. President, Ronald Reagan, to evaluate the present situation once again without bias, to discard everything extraneous and to overcome delusions about the Soviet Union and its foreign policy.

The Soviet Union is confident that an agreement on ending nuclear tests can be reached soon and signed even *this year at the Soviet-American summit meeting*. That event would, undoubtedly, be the *main real outcome of this meeting*, a considerable step toward ending the arms race. The signing of such an agreement would serve as a prologue to future progress at the talks on nuclear weapons and on their elimination and to a radical improvement of the entire world situation.

With its moratorium on nuclear explosions the Soviet Union hasn't simply made a proposal, but has taken definite action. It has proved the seriousness and sincerity of our nuclear disarmament program and of our calls for a new policy—one of realism, peace and cooperation.

More than a half of 1986, which the United Nations organization declared as the Year of Peace, has passed. By extending its unilateral moratorium, the Soviet Union is making another weighty contribution to the common striving to ensure that this year go down in history worthy of its name.

This is the essence of the Soviet Union's new political initiative.

This is the message which our country is sending to the governments and peoples of all countries, and in particular to the government of the United States of America and to the American people.

Thank you. Good night.

35

INTERVIEW

Answers to Joseph Kingsbury-Smith

December, 1986

Following is the full text of Mikhail Gorbachev's interview with U.S. journalist Joseph Kingsbury-Smith.

Q: What would you like to tell the American people on the occasion of the new year 1987?

A: I would like, first of all, to say that Soviet people want to live in peace with the Americans and do not feel any hostility toward them. On behalf of the leadership of the USSR, I could add that when working out our policy in matters of war and peace we are as honest with the American people as with our own people.

Our age—that of nuclear weapons and high speeds, and of growing economic and political interdependence—rules out the security of one to the detriment or at the expense of the security of another. I shall repeat once again: Only together can we perish or survive. Security nowadays is conceivable only as a mutual thing or, to be more exact, as a universal thing.

So, whether we like one another or not, it is essential to learn to coexist, to live in peace on this tiny and very fragile planet.

Q: Are you in favor of continuing the Geneva talks between Soviet and U.S. representatives in 1987 with a view to achieving progress in matters pertaining to limiting and reducing arms?

A: Yes, we are. We are for talks which would get out of the state of being fruitless and inert and would acquire real dynamism or, in a word, become real talks on reducing nuclear arms and on preventing an arms race in outer space.

We pressed for this in Reykjavik, and we shall press for it

still more vigorously in 1987. I am convinced that a radical turn in the talks would meet the vital interests of the American people as well.

At the same time the U.S. Administration's stand on this issue disappoints us deeply. Following the Reykjavik summit, the American delegation in Geneva even moved backwards.

Although the USSR has not conducted nuclear explosions for a year and a half, the United States has continued tests and declined to negotiate a comprehensive ban on them, and this despite the fact that the United States undertook to conduct such negotiations under two treaties, those dated 1963 and 1974. The defiant act of abandoning the important Strategic Arms Limitation Treaty (SALT-II) by the White House was added to that in November. Deliberately and pointedly wrecking old treaties does not help the conduct of successful talks on new agreements. This is a serious problem which deserves the closest attention.

I reaffirm once again: We are for agreements on the most radical reductions in arms, both nuclear and conventional. Now the ball is in Washington's court.

Q: Should the two sides show mutual flexibility, do you envision the possibility of reaching a compromise agreement during the next two years on antimissile defense matters if there is an accord on nondeployment of a space-based strategic defense system within a mutually agreed-upon period of time?

A: Under all conditions, nothing should be done which would erode or undermine the ABM Treaty. That would deprive us of any hopes for a reduction in nuclear arsenals and would upset strategic stability.

We are for the ABM Treaty of unlimited duration signed in 1972 to be maintained and maintained indefinitely. Article XV of the treaty envisages only one cause for denouncing it: extraordinary events jeopardizing the supreme interests of a party to the treaty. It depends only on the two of us, the Soviet Union and the United States, for such extraordinary events never to occur.

We regret that the U.S. Administration adheres to a different line which allows for the possibility of the U.S. abandoning the ABM Treaty if it deems that advantageous to itself during the implementation of the SDI program.

The Soviet Union is not just for the preservation of the ABM Treaty but is for consolidating it. This is precisely what would be promoted by an accord with the U.S.A. on defining the limits on allowed laboratory research in the ABM field, as is being suggested by the Soviet side.

This treaty is important in itself, but it is doubly important because without this treaty it is impossible to come to terms on cuts in strategic nuclear arms.

So, in this issue, too, things depend not on us but on Washington. People in Washington should finally decide very clearly what they want: a runaway arms race or reduction and elimination of weapons? No one will do that for the American Government or instead of it. A good deal depends on this choice, including the peace and well-being of the American people. We wish them peace and happiness, just as, of course, we do to all the other peoples.